SIKHIM AND BHUTAN

SIKHIM AND BHUTAN

TWENTY-ONE YEARS ON THE NORTH-EAST FRONTIER

1887-1908

J. CLAUDE WHITE

WITH ILLUSTRATIONS AND MAP

GYAN

Published by

GYAN

Gyan Publishing House
5, Ansari Road
Daryaganj, New Delhi-110002
Phone: 011-47034999, 9811692060
E-mail: books@gyanbooks.com

Distribution Network
gyanbooks.com
India, USA, Canada, UK, Australia, France

ISBN : 978-81-212-4015-4 (PB)
First Published, London, 1909

2nd Impression 2020

Printed at: Gyan Press, Delhi.

Sikhim and Bhutan
Author: J. Claude White

John C White

TO

A. W. PAUL, ESQ., C.I.E.

TO WHOM I OWE MUCH FOR THE
ASSISTANCE HE HAS ALWAYS
GIVEN ME IN MY WORK

PREFACE

My Indian career has extended to nearly thirty-two years of active service, and of that more than twenty years were spent on the North-East Frontier in the administration, as well as the political charge, of the little-known State of Sikhim, and latterly in political charge of the even less-known State of Bhutan and certain portions, including Chumbi and Gyantse, of South-East Tibet; and as I had in addition spent over a year in Khatmandu, the capital of Nepal, I may lay claim to an intimate knowledge of this Frontier, which is my excuse for putting my experiences in print.

When I first visited Darjeeling in 1881 I used to look across the valleys of the Rungeet and the Teesta rivers and long to penetrate into those stupendous mountains and valleys, with their magnificent forests and rivers, to explore the everlasting snows and glaciers, and to come in contact with their interesting people. An added fascination for me was the fact that beyond these mountains lay the mysterious, unknown land of Tibet, about which all manner of things were conjured up in my imagination, and which I fondly hoped I might some day reach.

The Fates were propitious, beyond my most sanguine expectations, for on the outbreak of the Sikhim-Tibet War in 1888 I was sent as Assistant Political Officer with the expeditionary force, and on the conclusion of peace the following year, I was offered the post of Political Officer in administrative charge of the State of Sikhim. Naturally I gladly accepted an appointment which would give me an opportunity of living in a country I was so anxious to see more of, and I have never regretted my decision; although, in consequence of the view taken by the Government of India of my special employment on the Frontier, and the fact that I left the Public Works Department to take up this appointment, I have been a loser from a pecuniary point of view to a very large extent.

In 1903, when it was decided to send a Mission to Lhasa, I was appointed one of the Commissioners, and on the conclusion of the Mission I was placed in charge of our political relations with Bhutan, as well as that portion of Tibet which came under the sphere of influence of the Government of India, in addition to my political and administrative work in Sikhim.

Owing to the friendly relations which had been established by Mr. A. W. Paul, and which I had kept up with Bhutan ever since I came to this part of the country, I found the Tongsa Penlop and the Bhutanese officials who accompanied us to Lhasa most anxious to make friends with me, and I was able to become on very intimate terms with them, a circumstance of great advantage to me later on.

My new appointment afforded many opportunities of visiting Bhutan and of becoming acquainted with the country and its officials and people, and through my friendship with the Tongsa I was given many facilities never before extended to any European.

During those twenty-one years my duties took me to almost every corner of the beautiful mountain countries of Sikhim and Bhutan, with their heterogeneous population of Lepchas, Bhuteas, Tibetans, Bhutanese, and Paharias, about the greater number of whom very little was known.

In climate every variation was to be found, from arctic to subtropical, with scenery unparalleled anywhere in the world for magnificence and grandeur and the brightness and softness of its colouring, the bold, snow-clad and desolate expanses contrasting sharply with the rich and luxuriant vegetation of the deep-cut valleys close at hand.

I was brought into close contact with the people and their rulers, whom the more you know the more you like, in spite of all their faults. During my long sojourn amongst them I had an unique experience not often met with in India in these days, when officials are moved from place to place so constantly that they learn nothing of the districts they govern and still less of the people, who think an attempt to know their officials is not worth while, as they are sure to be changed in a few months, and the task would have to be begun again. It is a grave mistake in the present system of government, and one which is responsible for much of the unrest and anarchy in India.

I have often been urged by my friends to write an account of my experiences, but as long as I remained in Government service I refused, and I now, with some reluctance, have tried in this book to give a short account of these countries both geographical and historical, as well as of my personal experiences during my various tours, and to bring before my readers some pictures of these two most delightful countries; but writing does not come easily to me, and I must crave my readers' indulgence.

Of Bhutan I have given the more detailed historical account, as nothing of the kind exists, and information on the subject can only be gained by research into many books, Government records, and old Tibetan manuscripts. I have also given very full accounts of my missions and explorations in this beautiful and interesting country, in the hope of removing the stigma under which it has for so long lain—a country about which so little is known, and of which as recently as 1894 Risley wrote in his introduction to the "Sikhim Gazetteer": "No one wishes to explore that tangle of jungle-clad and fever-stricken hills, infested with leeches and the *pipsa* fly, and offering no compensating advantage to the most enterprising pioneer. Adventure looks beyond Bhutan. Science passes it by as a region not sufficiently characteristic to merit special exploration."

J. C. W.

September, 1909

CONTENTS

CONTENTS

CONTENTS

CONTENTS

CONTENTS

APPENDICES

ILLUSTRATIONS

ILLUSTRATIONS

The illustrations facing pages 60, 64, 66, and 68 by the kind permission of Mr. Hoffmann.

AUTHORITIES CONSULTED

Tibetan Manuscript
The Lho-cho-jung
History of the Sindhu Raja
Bogle's Mission, 1774
Turner's Mission, 1783
Reports of Kishen Kant, 1815
Pemberton's Mission, 1837
Griffiths' Journal, 1837
Eden's Mission, 1864
Rennie's History of the Bhutan War
Macgregor's Military Report on Bhutan, 1866
Aitcheson's Treaties
Government Records
Sikhim Gazetteer

SIKHIM AND BHUTAN

CHAPTER I

THE GEOGRAPHICAL POSITION AND GENERAL FEATURES OF THE STATES OF SIKHIM AND BHUTAN

SIKHIM and Bhutan are two adjoining countries covering between them an area of about 22,000 square miles, lying to the north and east of Darjeeling, and to the north of the British districts of Jalpaiguri, Goalpara, and Kamrup. Their northern boundary is that portion of the Himalayas which forms the watershed between the Tibetan province of U and India; on the east boundary is the State of Tawang, subject to Tibet, and on the west that of Nepal. Both countries lie entirely in the heart of the Himalayas between 26° 30′ and 28° 30′ north latitude and 88° 0′ and 92° 15′ east longitude.

The northern boundary of Bhutan has hitherto been defined by an imaginary line drawn eastward from Chomolhari to Kulu-Kangri, but my explorations prove that Bhutan extends much further to the north; as far as the snow ranges east of Kala-tsho and south of the Nelung Valley with the Wagya-la situated on the frontier, and in my map I have shown the correct boundary.

The Chumbi Valley, formerly a part of Sikhim, but now belonging to Tibet, forms a wedge which divides the northern portion of Sikhim from Bhutan, while Sikhim itself lies within the watershed of the river Teesta.

Western and Central Bhutan may conveniently be divided into three zones:

(1) The outer or foot hills, adjoining the plains of India.

(2) The central belt lying between these hills, and—

(3) The uplands immediately under the high snow ranges on the Tibetan frontier.

The first zone includes the whole of the outer ranges for a depth of twenty to thirty miles. They rise sharply and abruptly out of the plains and are cut into deep valleys or gorges by rivers liable to sudden floods, sometimes rising 40 feet to 50 feet. The annual rainfall is excessive, from 200 inches to 250 inches, and the hill-sides are densely clothed with vegetation, forests as well as undergrowth. In this zone the valleys are unhealthy and very feverish in the rainy season, hot and steamy, while the higher hills rising in places to an altitude of 12,000 feet are cold, wet and misty.

The second, or central zone, consists mainly of valleys of an elevation varying from 3500 feet to 10,000 feet which, with their dividing ridges, extend northward behind the first zone for about forty miles. These valleys are healthy, comparatively broad and flat, with a moderate rainfall and fairly well populated and cultivated. They have not yet been worn into the narrow gorges so noticeable in the outer hills, and still bear evidence of their glacial origin ; the rise of the rivers is moderate, according to the marks on the banks not more than four feet to six feet, and the slopes of the mountains are much more gradual and to a certain extent, cultivated.

The third zone comprises the high valleys, of an elevation of 12,000 feet to 18,000 feet, running down from the great northern barrier of snow, with snow ranges between them, the peaks of which attain occasionally a height of 24,000 feet. These valleys are only used for grazing in the summer months, when the hardy Bhutan cattle are taken up to 12,000 and 14,000 feet and yaks and sheep even higher.

This division is particularly noticeable in the tract

where the outer hills, rising to high elevations near the plains, intercept the south-east monsoon, and is markedly exemplified in the valleys of Hah, Paro, Tashi-cho-jong and Bya-gha (otherwise known as Pumthang) in Bhutan and in Chumbi.

But in the deep-cut valleys of the River Teesta in Sikhim, and the Lobrak or Kuru River in Bhutan, the above division does not apply. The outer hills are lower, the monsoon current penetrates much further north, through deep valleys which run nearly to the foot of the highest mountains, and consequently the wet zone extends as far as the snows. In the case of the Teesta the elevation of the valley a few miles from Kangchen is not more than 2400 feet above mean sea level, while the Lobrak cuts through the barrier of the Himalayas, at an elevation of only 10,000 feet.

Sikhim, owing to its proximity to Kangchenjunga, to the fact that it lies in the direct path of the monsoon and to the direction of its valleys, is much the wettest portion of the whole area, and has a heavy annual rainfall, about 50 inches even in the dry upper valleys of Lachung and Lachen, increasing to about 140 inches in other districts.

In eastern Bhutan the rainfall is appreciably less as the monsoon current is diverted up the Assam Valley and does not strike the hills directly. Consequently there is a diminished rainfall, and the effect is noticeable in the vegetation which is not nearly so dense.

These hill states are drained:

Sikhim by the Teesta and its tributaries, the chief of which are the Rungeet, the Rungnu-chhu joining at Ringen, and the Lachen and Lachung rivers.

Bhutan by:

(1) The Am-mo-chhu or Torsa draining the Chumbi Valley;

(2) The Wang-chhu or Raydak with its tributaries the Hah-chhu and the Par-chhu draining the valleys of Hah, Paro, and Tashi-cho-jong;

(3) The Mo-chhu or Sankos, which with its numerous tributaries, drains the valley of Poonakha ; one branch taking its rise on the southern slopes of Chomolhari and another in the snows to the east of Kala-tsho ;

(4) The Monass, by far the largest river in this part of the world, with two main branches of which the Lobrak or Kuru-chhu rises in Tibet, its main source being in glaciers on the northern slopes of the Kulu-Kangri and its adjacent snows, while the second, the Dongma-chhu, rises in the snowy range to the east of Tawang. Other tributaries are the Madu-chhu, running past Tongsa and the Pumthang, draining the Bya-gha Valley.

I can best describe the Mountain System as a series of parallel ranges running in a general direction from north to south, springing from the vast snow-range which forms the southern buttress of the great Tibetan Plateau. These parallel ranges are again cut into innumerable smaller ranges forming a vast labyrinth of valleys running in every direction, while the main ranges, running down to the plains, divide the river systems I have already mentioned, and, as they have no distinctive local names, I have called them after certain peaks or passes.

Beginning from the extreme west there is—

(A) The Singli-la range, the crest of which forms the boundary between Sikhim and Nepal. This range runs from Kangchenjunga and on it are the well-known and often visited peaks of Sandukphu and Phallut, as well as the hill stations of Darjeeling and Kurseong. The principal pass between Sikhim and Nepal is the Chiabhanjan-la.

(B) Further to the east is the Chola range descending from Powhunri to the east of the Donkia-la and forming the water parting between the Teesta and the Am-mo-chhu. There are numerous passes on this range, the most generally used being the Jeylap-la and Natu-la, although, before the present roads were made, the Cho-la was much used, and I have crossed it myself as well by four others, the Yak-la, the Sibu-la, the Thanka-la and another.

THE SOURCE OF THE TEESTA RIVER.

(C) Next the Massong-chung-dong range which runs down from Chomolhari, past Hah, to Buxa Duar in the plains forming the watershed between the Am-mo-chhu and the Wang-chhu. The passes on this range over which I have crossed are the Temo-la above Phari, the Hah-la on the main road through Central Bhutan and the Lome-la on the Paro–Dungna-jong road, while to the south there are many others.

(D) The Dokyong-la range, which, as I discovered in 1905, also runs down from Chomolhari, is the water parting between the Wang-chhu and the Mo-chhu. The pass on the main road crossing the range is the Dokyong-la, after which I have called the range. Other passes are the Zadu-la to the north of the Dokyong-la, the Biafu-la to the south, the Taga-la and many others as these lower hills can be easily crossed almost everywhere, and paths are numerous.

(E) The Black Mountain range, which divides the waters of the Mo-chhu from the river system of the Monass, has its rise in the snows near Kulu-Kangri; and practically divides Bhutan into two portions both administratively and ethnographically. The people to the east, who originally came from the hills to the north-east of Assam, are directly under the jurisdiction of the Tongsa Penlop, while on the west they are of almost pure Tibetan origin and under the jurisdiction of the Thimboo Jongpen and Paro Penlop. The main pass is the Pele-la, but there are many others both on the north and south.

(F) The Tawang range, to the east of the Monass river system, which probably has its origin in the snow ranges to the north-east of Tawang and south-east of Dongma-chhu. One of its many ramifications forms the eastern boundary of Bhutan and ends in the hills to the east of Dewangiri.

The minor ranges, or those which terminate before reaching the plains, are too numerous to mention, but the principal ones are the Moinam range between the Teesta and the Rungeet; the Chiu-li-la dividing the Hah-chhu and the Pa-chhu; the Bei-la range between Pa-chhu and the Wang-chhu; the Yoto-la range which springs from the snows to the east of Kulu-Kangri, dividing the Madu-chhu and the Pumthang-chhu; the Radung-la between the Pumthang-chhu and Kuru-chhu; and the Dang-la range springing from the snows near the Kar-chhu Pass and dividing the Kuru-chhu from the Dongma-chhu.

CHAPTER II

THE PEOPLE: THEIR MORALS, RELIGION AND LANGUAGE

SIKHIM

THE aboriginal inhabitants of Sikhim are the Lepchas, and the language they use is Lepcha. Their origin is doubtful, as they did not enter Sikhim from across the Himalayas or from Tibet, but are supposed to have come from the East along the foot hills from the direction of Assam and Upper Burmah. They bear little resemblance to the Tibetans, they are smaller and slighter in build with finer cut features, in many cases almost Jewish, and their language is a distinct one, not a dialect of Tibetan. They only number about 6000. They are people of a mild, quiet and indolent disposition, loving solitude, and their homes are found in the most inaccessible places, in the midst of forests if possible, and seldom above an elevation of 4000 feet. They are also very improvident, living from hand to mouth; with abundance when the crops are good, but once the supply is eaten up going often in the direst straits, picking up what they can in the jungle till the next crop ripens. They are great nature lovers and good entomologists and botanists, and have their own names for every animal, insect and plant, and are, I should think, unequalled anywhere as collectors. They make most excellent and trustworthy servants and are a quite exceptional people, amongst whom it is a pleasure to live. I speak from a very intimate knowledge of their ways and habits after having spent a very happy twenty years amongst them with friends in every degree, from the Maharaja himself to some of the humblest coolies.

They now profess Buddhism and are generally very devotional, although they originally worshipped the spirits of the mountains, rivers and forests, a natural outcome of their surroundings. Leading solitary, isolated lives, everything would tend to foster such beliefs in a country where the mighty snows appear immortal, the raging torrents irresistible, as though impelled by some unseen avenging spirit, combined with the curious shapes taken by everything when veiled in grey mist and the ghostlike and awesome forms to be met in the shadows of the damp dripping forests full of phosphorescent stumps of old trees scattered round in strange contortions, with the accompaniment of the weird sound of the wind, as it moans round some projecting crag or through some giant tree, and where even the melancholy cry of the birds is pitched in a minor key, all must encourage such beliefs and leave a deep impression on the character of the people who live amidst it.

A few Lepcha families are to be found in the lower valleys of Western Bhutan, and also in Eastern Nepal, where they apparently settled at the time they came to Sikhim.

The next race to enter Sikhim, probably long before the time of the accession of the Sikhim Rajas, were the Bhuteas who are of Tibetan origin and who spread at the same time into Bhutan. In Sikhim they number a little over 6000 and are more traders and herdsmen than agriculturists, although they cultivate small areas round their houses. They are for the most part of good physique, big and sturdy with a Mongolian type of features, and are not so reserved or so fond of isolation as the Lepchas. Their houses are substantially built at elevations always above 4000 feet and never in the hot steamy valleys. The whole family, sons and sons' wives, live together under one roof in patriarchal fashion, instead of each man having his own house and establishment. Their religion is Buddhism or Lamaism, and their language is a dialect of Tibetan.

By far the greater number of the inhabitants of Sikhim, however, are the Paharias, who number nearly 50,000. They have migrated from the neighbouring densely populated State of Nepal, and are slowly but surely pushing their way eastward. They are almost all Hindus by religion, with innumerable castes, the few exceptions being the tribes coming from the north-east of Nepal, who still profess Buddhism. They are on the whole a steady, industrious and thrifty people, very pushing, and eager to take up new employments, they make excellent settlers, pay their rent regularly, and give no trouble in that way. But they require a strong hand over them, and some of the castes are most litigious and quarrelsome. Many of their head men are excellent managers, thoroughly to be trusted, and will carry out anything they undertake to do to the best of their ability. In more than one case I have known Nepalese settlers in Sikhim, by dint of hard work and perseverance, rise to important positions which they have successfully filled, in marked contrast to the Lepchas, whose indolent temperament always acts as a deterrent and causes them to be outdistanced by more energetic races.

The only plainsmen from India to be found in Sikhim are a few Marwaris and men of the Bunia or shopkeeper class, who have come for trading purposes and settled under the protection of the British Raj since the expedition of 1888.

BHUTAN

The population of Bhutan, numbering, perhaps, 400,000 may be roughly divided into two, those living on the West and those living on the East of the Pele-la.

The people of the West are for the most part of Tibetan origin who came into the country centuries ago. They are of the same original stock as the Bhuteas in Sikhim, but have developed in Bhutan into a magnificent race of men physically. Why there should be this marked contrast I cannot say, it may be due to the difference in climate, but there is no comparison between the two, although the Sikhim Bhutea is a strong sturdy fellow in his own way. The Bhutanese are fine, tall, well-developed men with an open, honest cast of face, and the women are comely, clean and well-dressed, and excellent housekeepers and managers. Their religion is Buddhism and their language a dialect of Tibetan.

Of their morals, Dr. Griffiths, who accompanied Pemberton in 1838, writes as follows:

"Of the moral qualities of the Booteahs it is not in my power to give a pleasing account. To the lower orders I am disposed to give credit for much cheerfulness, even under their most depressed circumstances, and generally for considerable honesty. The only instances of theft that occurred did so on our approach to the capital. How strange that where all that should be good, and all that is great is encouraged, there is little to be found but sheer vice; and how strange that where good examples alone should be led, bad examples alone are followed.

"To the higher orders I cannot attribute the possession of a single good quality. They are utter strangers to truth; they are greedy beggars, they are wholly familiar with rapacity and craftiness and the will of working evil. This censure applies only to those with whom we had personal intercourse; it would be perhaps unfair to include the Soubahs, whom we saw only once in such a flattering picture, but it certainly would not be unreasonable, and I must make one exception in favour of Bullumboo, the Soubah of Dewangiri, and he was the only man of any rank that we had reason to be friendly towards and to respect. In morale they appeared to me to be inferior to all ordinary hill tribes, on whom a Booteah would look with ineffable contempt, and although their houses are generally better, and although they actually have castles and places called palaces, and although the elders of the land dress in fine cloths and gaudy silks and possess money, ponies, mules, and slaves, I am disposed to consider them as inferior even to the naked Naga.

"They are not even courageous. I am inclined to rank courage among physical rather than moral qualities, yet it could not be so classified in the consideration of a Booteah in whom other qualities are well developed. I therefore consider it among those other qualities which, as I have said, are absent in Bootan. A Booteah is a great boaster but a small performer. All accounts I heard of their reputed courage were ludicrous. . . . Their courage may therefore be written down as entirely imaginary.

"Their ideas of religion appear to be very confused, religion with them consisting, as indeed it may do among other more civilised people, of certain external forms, such as counting beads and muttering sacred sentences. The people throughout are remarkably superstitious, believing in an innumerable host of spirits. . . .

"Of any marriage ceremonies I could not hear, but as chastity would appear to be unknown, no particular forms are probably required. Nor do I think that there is a particular class of prostitutes. We all had opportunities of remarking the gross indelicacy of Booteah women; of this and of their extreme amiableness the custom of polyandry is a very sufficient cause. So far as I could see, there is no distinction of rank among Booteah women, and those only are saved from the performance of menial duties who are incapacitated by sickness or age. . . .

"Of the social habits little favourable could be said in any place where the women are looked on as inferior beings and used as slaves. . . .

"I need scarcely add that both sexes are, in all their habits, inexpressibly filthy. The women, in their extreme indelicacy, form a marked contrast with such other hill tribes as I am acquainted with. The only use either sex make of water is in the preparation of food or of spirits—

no water ever comes into contact with any part of their person; they scarcely ever change their clothes, especially the woollen ones."

Eden formed much the same opinion in 1864, and I cannot help thinking both writers were prejudiced against the Bhutanese by the treatment they received, for it is not possible for a whole race to so completely change in so short a time; and in addition Bogle and Turner's accounts of their experiences coincide exactly with mine.

When I visited Bhutan in 1905, I certainly had more and better opportunities of judging, and I found no signs of such a state of things. My experience of the people was that they were universally polite, civil, and clean, and during the whole time I spent in the country, I only saw one drunken man. I had every opportunity of judging, as I entered numerous houses and temples in all parts of the country, and invariably found them clean and tidy; in many of the houses the floors were washed and polished, and the refreshments they hospitably pressed on me were served in spotlessly clean dishes.

The clothes of the higher officials were always immaculate, their brocades and silks fresh and unstained in any way, and even the coolies were a great contrast to the usual Tibetan or Darjeeling coolie. Therefore I cannot help thinking Messrs. Griffiths and Eden have exaggerated what they saw, and as we know with what discourtesy they were treated, it is perhaps not altogether unreasonable for them to have seen only the worst side of the people.

Neither do I consider the Bhutanese an excessively idle people, the amount of labour expended on their irrigation channels alone dispels that idea, and their houses are all large and substantially built. And as in the case of Dug-gye-jong, in the courtyards we found retainers busily occupied in various trades, while the women of the household spin and weave and make clothes for the men-folk in addition to their ordinary duties. A great part of the country is under cultivation, and they raise sufficient crops to support the whole population, including the lamas, who are a great burden to the State.

We saw no immorality. They follow certain curious customs, such as the right of the head man when girls marry, but after all, the same custom prevailed in Europe not so many years ago in the right of the Seigneur. But even this is being put a stop to by the present Tongsa. The women were open and frank in tneir demeanour, but with no trace of indelicacy. The men were cheery and jovial, always ready for a game at quoits, shooting at a target with arrows, jumping, &c., at the end of a day's march when we had settled into camp. They are fond of their beer, but there is no great harm in that, and small wonder they are thirsty after toiling up the hills with their loads. I have drunk many a choonga (bamboo mug) full of the mild ale myself and been none the worse for it.

Amongst the people of the East who live beyond the Pele-la the bulk of the population is not of Tibetan origin, nor do they speak Tibetan. I give a few words they use, spelt phonetically, which seem to me different to those of Tibetan derivation. *Gami* = fire, *Nut* = barley, *Mai* = house, *Tyu* = milk, *Yak* = hand, *Tsoroshai* = come here. Their origin is not clear, but they are allied to the people of the Assam Valley and to those living in the hills to the east beyond Bhutan. They are of a different type to those in the west, smaller in stature, the complexion is darker and features finer cut, and their dress is different. They also profess Buddhism, but are not so observant of its customs, nor are there so many monasteries and Lamas to be met with as in the other part of Bhutan. Sir Ugyen Wang-chuk estimates there are about 200,000 of them.

The remaining inhabitants are Paharias, the same as those in Sikhim, who are creeping along the foot hills and now form a considerable community extending the whole length of Bhutan where the outer hills join the plains of

India. With the exception of the Hindu Paharias, Buddhism is the religion professed throughout Bhutan.

To my readers who wish to study the subject of Buddhist religion in this part of the world I cannot give better advice than to read Waddell's "Lamaism," as I have no intention of entering deeply into it, and will content myself by saying that in both Sikhim and Bhutan the religion is an offshoot of Buddhism, and was introduced into these countries from Tibet by lamas from different monasteries who travelled south and converted the people. Most of the tenets of Buddha have been set aside, and those retained are lost in a mass of ritual, so nothing remains of the original religion but the name. The form of worship has a curious resemblance in many particulars to that of the Roman Catholic Church. On any of their high holy days the intoning of the Chief Lama conducting the service, the responses chanted by the choir, sometimes voices alone, sometimes to the accompaniment of instruments, where the deep note of the large trumpet strangely resembles the roll of an organ, the ringing of bells, burning of incense, the prostrations before the altar, the telling of beads and burning of candles, the processions of priests in gorgeous vestments, and even the magnificent altars surmounted by images and decorated with gold and silver vessels, with lamps burning before them, even the side chapels with the smaller shrines where lights burn day and night, add to the feeling that one is present at some high festival in a Roman Catholic place of worship. I have been present at the services on feast days in the temples in Sikhim, Bhutan and in Lhasa, and no great stretch of imagination was required to imagine myself in a Catholic Cathedral in France or Spain, especially the latter. There is also some resemblance in the dress and vestments of the priests and lamas, and even in some of their customs. Many of them go entirely into seclusion, and they also have certain periods of time devoted to prayer corresponding to a Retreat, during which they see no one.

Sikhim is not so priest-ridden as Bhutan and Tibet. As a class the lamas are disliked, but also feared by the people, on account of the belief that the lamas have the power to do them harm.

As a rule the lamas are ignorant, idle and useless, living at the expense of the country, which they are surely dragging down.

This is particularly the case in Bhutan, where the lamas are fed, clothed and housed at State expense, and as their numbers have steadily increased, they have become a very heavy burden which cannot long be borne, and an evil which I hope may soon be curtailed by the method proposed by Sir Ugyen Wang-chuk, namely, the gradual reduction by leaving vacancies, occurring through death and other causes, unfilled, and the limitation of the number admitted to each monastery.

There are, of course, exceptions to every rule, and I have met several lamas, notably the Phodong Lama of Sikhim and others like him, men who were thoroughly capable, who acted up to their principles, and whom I thoroughly respected, but I am sorry to say such men were few and far between. The majority generally lead a worldly life and only enter the priesthood as a lucrative profession and one which entails no trouble to themselves.

CHAPTER III

A SHORT HISTORY OF SIKHIM

THE earliest settlers in Sikhim, or Dejong—"the land of rice"—were the Lepchas, who called themselves Rongpa, or dwellers in the valley; they seem to have migrated from the hills of Assam, but when, there is no means of ascertaining. At all events, they were in Sikhim as early as the thirteenth century. The present ruling family are of Tibeto-Chinese origin and came from Kham-Mina-Andong, a small principality taken by the Chinese about 1732 where their ancestor, the great-great-grandson of the Tibetan King of Tibet—Ti-son-desen (A.D. 730) founded a small kingdom. Various scions of the family found their way back to Tibet, where they rose to high positions. Coming to more recent times, one of their descendants, Khye-Bumsu (stronger than 10,000) was so strong that unaided he set up the four immense pillars of the great Sakya Monastery; he migrated to Ha, where he overpowered the Titan robbers of that district and is worshipped for his prowess to this day. His children crossed over to Sikhim and settled at Gangtak.

In 1641 A.D. the Lhasan Lama, with the aid of two other saints, converted the Sikhim people to the Buddhist faith and appointed Penchoo Namgyel to be the first Gyalpo or King. Thotup Namgyel, the present ruler, is the ninth.

In the time of the third Gyalpo—Chador Namgye—Sikhim was overrun by the Bhutanese under Deb Naku Zidar (1700 to 1706). The Tibetans drove them out and

Chador, in gratitude, founded the great monastery of Pemiongtchi, the largest in Sikhim, and wholly Tibetan in character. He also designed an alphabet for the Lepcha language and reduced it to writing.

His successor, Gyurma, was married to a lady from Lhasa, who was so exceedingly ugly that rather than live with her he abandoned his throne and fled disguised as a mendicant: in his reign Limbuana, now the eastern province of Nepal, was lost to Sikhim.

In the time of the sixth Gyalpo—Tenzing Namgyel—(1780 to 1790), the Gurkhas rose and overcame the Newars and Limbus in Nepaul, and in 1788 to 1789 invaded Sikhim and seized Rubdentze: Tenzing and his son Chophey Namgyel fled to Tibet for help. Luckily the Gurkhas in 1791 made war with Tibet and sacked Tashelhunpo, but were in the following year defeated by the Chinese and had to make an ignominious treaty. Sikhim got back a small portion of her State, but was obliged to pay the Gurkhas tribute to Nepal until 1815, when the latter were defeated and driven out by the British, who in 1817 restored West Sikhim and the Terai to the Raja. Several disputes between the Tibetan and Lepcha factions, often ending in bloodshed, broke out from time to time, causing disturbances on the Indian frontier, until in 1826 Government had to interfere, and in 1828 Captain Lloyd was sent to settle matters and reported the excellent prospects Darjeeling held out as a sanatorium. In 1834–35 another internecine strife broke out, and Captain Lloyd interfered and obtained a grant of a strip of territory running from Darjeeling to the plains. In 1849, after Drs. Hooker and Campbell had been maltreated while travelling in Sikhim, the Terai and more territory was seized, and finally, after a military expedition to Tumlong, the capital, the treaty of 1861 was enacted, which confirms our possession of the present district.

Again troubles between the Tibetan and Lepcha parties broke out in 1880, and Mr. A. W. Paul was sent to Tumlong, and in accordance with their own laws, persuaded the rival parties to come to an agreement, which has been kept ever since; from 1880 onwards constant intercourse was kept up and the Lepcha party learnt to rely for justice on the Government at Darjeeling. Unfortunately in 1886, after sanctioning the assembling of the Macaulay Mission to Tibet at Darjeeling, the Home Government prohibited the Mission from moving a yard further, and the Tibetans, misunderstanding the motives of such inaction, advanced into Sikhim and erected a fort at Lingtu within Sikhim land, and actually in sight of Darjeeling: if the Macaulay Mission had been allowed to advance even as far as the Jelep frontier, in all probability more friendly relations would have been opened up and all subsequent troubles avoided. The expedition of 1888, undertaken to punish the Tibetans for their temerity, brings the history up to the date of my appointment, since which time all relations with neighbouring States have continued on a most friendly footing. The Lhasa expedition, although its base was in Sikhim and its line of communications traversed the country, had no quarrel with Sikhim, and received hearty co-operation and assistance from the Maharaja and the Sikhim officials, and unless Tibet and China should again become aggressive, I see no reason why its peaceful security should not continue.

CHAPTER IV

EARLY REMINISCENCES

First visit to Sikhim, 1887. The brothers Khangsa Dewan and Phodong Lama, the Shoe Dewan and Kazis. Return to Gangtak with the Entchi Column, 1888. First meeting with Their Highnesses the Maharaja and Maharani of Sikhim.

In the month of November, 1887, I paid my first visit to Sikhim. I accompanied Mr. Paul, who had been sent from Darjeeling to try and induce the Maharaja to return from Chumbi, whither he had retreated some time before, and to spend more time in his own country. Our first destination was Rhenok, a small village only a couple of miles beyond British territory, but in the hope that we might get into direct communication with His Highness we pushed on another twenty miles to the capital, Gangtak, the place I later spent so many years in. At Rhenok we left the road, and a bad one too, that had brought us so far, and for the remainder of the distance had to follow a track unfit to ride over even on a mule, and had to walk most of the way. Our first halt was at Pakhyong, which, in the expedition the following year, became the headquarters of the Entchi Column, where the 13th Rajputs were encamped for several months. It is a pretty little spot lying just under the saddle where the road commences the last descent before the final climb to Gangtak, and the hillside was covered with woods of chestnut and orchids in profusion.

In this camp I first saw the Kartok Lama, a son of the Khangsa Dewan, and head of the Kartok Monastery, situated a few hundred feet above Pakhyong. He was a headstrong youth, with a not very good record, and had to be admonished for some of his latest escapades, but he took it all in very good part, and although I have since, on several occasions, had to talk very seriously to him, we have always been on good terms.

On reaching Gangtak, we pitched our tents on the ridge, close to the Maharaja's palace, then covered with jungle, now the site of a flourishing bazaar, with post and telegraph offices, dák bungalow or resthouse, charitable hospital and dispensary, and many large and flourishing shops, including that of the State bankers.

Mr. Paul was soon obliged to return to Darjeeling, but I, with a guard of Gurkha police, remained for another fortnight, hoping the Maharaja would either return himself or send some communication, but as he did neither I also went back to Darjeeling. During the time I was there I made the acquaintance of some of the head men and notabilities of Sikhim who came to pay their respects and to receive us on our arrival. First were the two brothers, the Khangsa Dewan and Phodong Lama, men of strong individuality and character, to whose wisdom and good sense Sikhim owes much, as they practically ruled the country for years during the prolonged absences of the Maharaja in Chumbi.

The Phodong Lama, although the younger brother, was the ruling spirit. He personally knew every one, constantly travelled over the country collecting information at first hand, was ever ready to give advice as well as assistance, and though always genial in his manner, was unfailingly strong and just to all, and was consequently universally liked and respected.

His elder brother, the Dewan, was of a more retiring nature and remained more in the background, but his influence was equally felt and the administration during the absence of the Maharaja was carried on in the joint name of the brothers.

Next the Shoe, or Poorbu Dewan, one of the most courtly men I have ever met, a true gentleman in mind and manners and a staunch and loyal friend. In appearance he was tall and spare, with an unusual type of face rarely met with in these hills, with its high cheek bones and rugged outline more nearly resembling that of the Red Indian. Behind a very quiet and retiring demeanour was hidden a fund of information which made him an excellent advisor. Possessed also of an unusual amount of tact and good sense, he did much, probably more than any one else, towards the welfare and advancement of the State, especially when the brothers were growing old and in failing health. He was a man looked up to and respected by all and whose advice was eagerly sought and followed. In my own case I consulted him on all sorts of questions and his opinion and advice were always to be considered and respected. In camp he was an excellent companion and many and many a pleasant hour have I spent sitting by a camp fire talking to him.

All three of these men are now dead, and the deaths of the Phodong Lama and the Shoe Dewan meant an irreparable loss to Sikhim. The younger generation, good fellows enough in their way, are of a different stamp, and there is no one to fill the places of the older men. The Phodong Lama lived to the age of sixty-eight and remained active and at work till within a comparatively short time of his death, but the Shoe Dewan was cut off at the early age of fifty-five.

Here also I first met the old Gangtak, Tassithing, and Entchi Kazis as well as many of the younger generation. Though these Kazis belonged to the leading families who had come into the country in the retinue of the Sikhim Rajas, they were, at the same time, of very little account; belonging to the old school, not caring much for anything that went on and given to getting very drunk; but notwithstanding they were good-natured and ready to do anything that was wanted of them to the best of their ability.

My return to Gangtak in the spring of the following year, 1888, was under very different circumstances. Hostilities had commenced, and on the day the main column of our troops crossed the Jeylap Pass into the Chumbi Valley, the second or Entchi column, to which I was attached, made a night march under Colonel Michell, of the 13th Rajputs, from Pakhyong to Gangtak. A fallen tree across the track caused a little delay, and we arrived on the Gangtak ridge at dawn only to find that the Maharaja and Maharani had again fled to Chumbi over the Yak-la road. I was just in time to stop some of His Highness's ponies, and so lately had they gone their lamps were still burning alongside their beds in the Palace, which, the Maharaja having vacated, was occupied by us, but none of us remained in it very long. It was infested by fleas and they swarmed over us, rendering sleep impossible, and as soon as the sun rose we removed ourselves and our bedding to our tents until we could build huts which would, at any rate, be clean, and would be a better protection from the violent spring hailstorms than the tents.

The Maharaja arrived in Chumbi to find his house there also in the occupation of our troops, and he and the Maharani were sent back to live in Gangtak, and there I met them for the first time.

Thotab Namgyel, Maharaja of Sikhim, was a man of about twenty-eight years of age, of medium height, typically Mongolian in appearance and much disfigured by a bad hare-lip. He was a man of indolent disposition, whose inclination was to live in retirement and aloof from the worries and troubles of the government of his little State, of a very kindly disposition, and although weak and easily led, possessed also a good deal of common sense. He was entirely under the influence of the Maharani, his second wife.

This lady, the daughter of a Tibetan official in Lhasa, is a striking personality. Small and slight, beautifully dressed in brocades, velvets and silks, with much jewellery of rough turquoise, coral and amber, her hair adorned

H.H. The Maharani of Sikhim

with strings of seed pearls, which reached to the hem of her gown, and wearing the curious Tibetan head-dress adopted by the Maharanis of Sikhim, she was a most picturesque object, a harmony of gold and brilliant colours impossible to convey in words and of which the photograph only gives a very inadequate representation.

She is extremely bright and intelligent and has been well educated, although she will not admit that she has knowledge of any language but Tibetan. She talks well on many subjects, which one would hardly have credited her with a knowledge of, and can write well. On the occasion of Queen Victoria's diamond jubilee, she personally composed and engrossed in beautiful Tibetan characters the address presented by the Sikhim Raj, which runs as follows :

> "To the most exalted and beautiful white lotus throne of Empress Victoria—the incarnate—Sri Devi—the glorious Goddess—who has been ruling and conducting the affairs of the great Empire, being Victorious in every quarter of the globe by the dint of her accumulated virtues and merits.
>
> "*The Memorial.*
>
> "Gracious Majesty,
>
> "From the ocean of merits has sprung your glorious self, whose fame has spread all round the world like the rays of the sun. Your Majesty's reign in respect of Government, defence, of light, and in increase of prosperity has been perfect.
>
> "It is our fervent prayer that Your Majesty's glorious reign may with fame encompassing the world, extend to many happy years more.
>
> "This humble vassal being extremely happy, with all his subjects, has been rejoicing at the Jubilee of Your Majesty's reign, and prays that Your Majesty shedding lustre of good, just and benign rule, shall

sit on the throne for a hundred great periods of time.

"With a pure white silk scarf, to represent the sincerity of wishes."

Her disposition is a masterful one and her bearing always dignified. She has a great opinion of her own importance, and is the possessor of a sweet musical voice, into which she can, when angry, introduce a very sharp intonation. She is always interesting, whether to look at or to listen to, and had she been born within the sphere of European politics she would most certainly have made her mark, for there is no doubt she is a born intriguer and diplomat. Her energies were unfortunately, but naturally, owing to her Tibetan origin, misdirected for many years, until, finding out her mistake, she frankly confessed she had been in the wrong, and turned her thoughts and attention to matters which should lead to the welfare of her husband's State. Her common sense and clear-sightedness were on many occasions of the greatest assistance to me in my task of administering and developing Sikhim, and when I laid various schemes before her she was quick to see the material advantages to be obtained and gave her support accordingly.

CHAPTER V

MORE EARLY REMINISCENCES

My appointment to Sikhim. Departure of the Maharaja to Kurseong. Inspection of the country with Phodong Lama and Shoe Dewan. Opening up by means of roads and bridges. Sources of revenue. Mineral wealth. Visit to Yatung, so-called Trade Mart.

At the conclusion of hostilities the Government of India made a proposal that I should remain in Sikhim, with the title of Political Officer, and administer the affairs of the State in conjunction with a Council composed of the chief Dewans, Lamas and Kazis, and of which I was to be President. This proposal I accepted with some diffidence, as it was an absolute change from my own profession (engineering) and practically meant cutting myself adrift from my service and entering an altogether new line with results impossible to foresee. But as years passed I grew to love the work, the country and the people, and I have never regretted my decision to throw my lot in with theirs, though from a worldly standpoint I could easily have done better elsewhere.

Not long after I had taken up my new duties, Government decided that it would be to the advantage of the State to remove the Maharaja from Sikhim for a time, and Kurseong, in the Darjeeling district, was proposed as his residence. It was my unenviable task to have to convey these orders to Their Highnesses, and their reception of the news was most characteristic. The Maharaja remained silent, but the Maharani abused me roundly, called me every name she could think of, and losing her temper entirely, got up, stamped on the floor and finally turned her back on me.

The incident, though amusing, was very pathetic at the same time, and I was heartily sorry for them both. They had come into opposition with the British Government, and from an exaggerated idea of the importance of Tibet and China, and with no conception or understanding of our ways, they had run against a mighty power to their hurt and consequent suffering.

With the departure of the Raja and Rani to their temporary quarters, the task of reorganising the country began in earnest. Chaos reigned everywhere, there was no revenue system, the Maharaja taking what he required as he wanted it from the people, those nearest the capital having to contribute the larger share, while those more remote had toll taken from them by the local officials in the name of the Raja, though little found its way to him ; no courts of justice, no police, no public works, no education for the younger generation. The task before me was a difficult one, but very fascinating ; the country was a new one and everything was in my hands.

The first step was to appoint the Council, a measure which had up to now been delayed by the Maharaja's attitude, and the following men were selected. The two brothers, the Khangsa Dewan and the Phodong Lama, the Shoe Dewan, Lari Pema (a lama from the important monastery of Pemiongtchi), the Gangtak, Tassithing, Entchi and Rhenok Kazis. All were of the utmost help and assistance to me, more especially the first three, and during the whole of my time in Sikhim I have ever experienced the same loyal and whole-hearted support from the Council.

The coffers were empty, and the first thing to be done was to devise some means by which we could raise a revenue. A commencement was made by roughly surveying the different districts and assessing them at so much per acre, taking into account the nature of the soil, &c. This was a most arduous task in a mountainous country, covered with dense undergrowth, which made survey work anything but easy and necessitated cutting lines in every direction. It was, however, accomplished in five years, and thus a basis for taxation and revenue was established. At the same time the forests were placed under control, excise was introduced, and by these means in about ten years the revenue was raised from Rs. 8000, or a little over £500 per annum, to Rs. 2,200,000, or about £150,000. But the country was very sparsely populated, and in order to bring more land under cultivation, it was necessary to encourage immigration, and this was done by giving land on favourable terms to Nepalese, who, as soon as they knew it was to be had, came freely in. Earlier in my service I had spent over a year in Nepal on special duty and had learnt something of the people and their ways which proved now to be of use in dealing with them.

During this period I visited every corner of Sikhim, even the most remote, accompanied by the Shoe Dewan and the Phodong Lama, and became acquainted with every head man and I might almost say with every villager. I never refused an interview to any one, and the people soon realised that they could freely bring before me any grievance they wished to ventilate or case that required settlement. I took up the cases where I was in camp, and unless of a very serious character, decided them then and there, but grave charges, such as murder, fortunately extremely rare, or grievous hurt, had to be brought to Gangtak for trial. This constant intercourse with the people gave me an insight into their character which otherwise I should never have acquired. Their hospitality is proverbial, no Sikhim man or woman ever comes before you without bringing a small offering of rice, eggs, milk or fruit, and on my tours at every village I found a little shelter of branches and green leaves erected, in which such offerings were placed along with chungas or bamboo mugs of marwa, the native beer, and I could show no more severe displeasure with the villagers than by refusing to accept their hospitality, During this time the Phodong Lama and the Shoe Dewan, one of whom always accompanied me, became my best friends, and I found they were men to whom I could turn for advice as well as assistance and for whom I had the most sincere regard. Unlike natives of the plains of India, with ideas on most subjects more nearly approaching our own, these hill men in reply to inquiries told you the truth, and made no attempt to find out first what answer was likely to please you, and consequently it was possible to make friends and companions of them in a way not often feasible in the case of natives.

The monasteries and the lamas were a great power in the land, but in their case also certain settlements and arrangements had to be made with the assistance of the Phodong Lama, Chief Priest in Sikhim, and Lari Pema of the Pemiongtchi Monastery. Many of the head lamas were men to be liked, and although they were not given entirely their own way, their just rights were carefully observed, and I have always been supported by them throughout my time in Sikhim. Years later, when I accompanied the Tibet Mission to Lhasa, the lamas of the important monasteries of Sera and Debung sent me an invitation to visit them, saying they would be glad if I would come as they had always heard from the Sikhim lamas that in my dealings with them I had treated them well, and this I looked upon as a great compliment.

My readers will have seen that when I first came to Sikhim there were no roads, only a few bad and difficult tracks. As the revenue increased and money was available this was one of the first improvements to be taken in hand, and soon the country was opened up by a system of roads, the torrents were bridged, and in a few years time it was possible to ride from one end of Sikhim to the other. Later on, before I left, it was possible to cart goods from Siliguri, the terminus of the Northern Bengal State Railway, 64 miles

THE RESIDENCY, GANGTAK

away, to the door of the Residency at Gangtak, and firewood was being carted into the Bazaar from 5 miles off on two different roads, a very great contrast to the earlier days. This is all easy to relate now that it has been accomplished, but it was uphill work and carried out under many disadvantages, the principal one the want of money. As the country was opened out, more was required in every direction, more roads and bridges, buildings, education, police, the domestic expenses of His Highness and his son, the Kumar, increased, and it was most difficult to make both ends meet. There was also the imperative necessity of creating a reserve fund for unforeseen contingencies, and the question ever present was how was money to be found. In such a mountainous country anything but the smallest land tax is impossible to levy, and even that is difficult; the forests which might be a source of wealth are too remote and the difficulty of carriage of the timber to the markets is unsurmountable. Excise could increase to a certain extent, but that could not continue.

However, by the exercise of constant care and economy, something was accomplished, and each year's budget showed an increase of revenue to meet the increased expenditure; but Sikhim distinctly is, and I fear always will be, a poor country, with the problem ever before her as to how the necessary expenditure is to be met; the upkeep and maintenance of the roads alone being a formidable item in a country averaging 140″ rainfall and in some districts 240″.

Nevertheless, there is another possible source of revenue in which, up to a year ago, I have in vain tried to interest the Government of India. That is the store of mineral wealth buried in the mountains. The difficulties of working this were too great for me to attempt. The State had no funds and Government refused to allow the introduction of foreign capital. I approached them time and again on the subject, always to be met with the same answer, "their reluctance to destroy the simplicity of an arcadian little State," and it was only in 1906, the year before I left, that

I finally persuaded them to allow a beginning to be made, and certain business firms were given permission to send prospectors into the country to take up mining concessions. Had my repeated representations on the subject been listened to in the earlier days, I have no doubt the mineral wealth of the country would by this time have been considerable, and that by their action Government has probably retarded the progress of the country by many years.

Iron, tin, zinc, aluminium, cobalt, arsenic, graphite, lead, gold, and silver, all have been found, while copper is known to exist in large quantities and has been worked by the natives for years past in a primitive fashion. It has been found in places in extremely rich deposits, but these, unfortunately, have proved scattered and small in extent, though there is no doubt that there is an enormous amount, and that if some method can be devised of concentrating and collecting the ore from the outlying seams without undue expense, a very large revenue should be derived from the royalties alone, and now that European capital has been allowed to undertake the task, I see no reason why it should not prove a success and be a means of placing the State on a more easy financial basis, though wealthy it never will and never can be.

Amongst the advantages of this new departure will be an increase of European residents in the country, with a consequent greater circulation of money, a new field for employment of labour, a greater demand for local supplies, with the probability of increased facilities of transport bringing new markets within reach for the produce, and greater still, though I fear not yet to be realised, the utilisation of the latent water-power with all its unforeseen possibilities.

After the signing of the Sikhim Treaty in 1890, the negotiations in respect of trade regulations continued to be carried on for some years, and it was 1894 before I went to Yatung to formally open the Trade Mart there. I crossed the Jey-lap-la in April in deep snow, and was met a little way further on, on the Yatung side of the pass, by about twenty Chinese soldiers sent from the frontier to meet me. They presented a gay appearance in their blue uniforms with large letters in black on both back and front of their coats. A few of them were armed with guns, but the greater number carried tridents, flags, and other unusual things.

About one and a half miles from Yatung a tent was pitched where, to conform to Chinese ideas of etiquette, I had to change into my official uniform, and a little further on I was ceremoniously received by the Chinese and Tibetan officials and conducted to a gorgeous tent in which tea was served. Mr. F. E. Taylor, of the Imperial Chinese Customs Service, was amongst those present in Chinese official dress. The Chinese officials were the Popen or Frontier Officer, Wang-yen-Ling, the officer commanding the troops, Tu-Hsi-hsun, and interpreter, Yee-Shan, and the Tibetan officials, U. Depon, the Tsedun Tenzing Wangpo and Kutzab Lobzang Tenzing. Our conversation in the tent was limited to the exchange of compliments and mere trivialities, and after resting a little, we proceeded down the valley to the house which was to be my residence; a very gay procession with all the umbrellas, flags, pikes, &c., carried by the followers of the Chinese officials.

It was my first experience of the Chinese official, and I have since always found him of the same type, outwardly exceedingly polite and punctilious, but behind one's back deceitful and cunning, intent on the Chinese policy of delay, and most difficult to bring to the point in any negotiation.

The house placed at my disposal was constructed partly on Chinese lines by Tibetan artisans; green wood had been employed, with the consequence that no door would shut, and I could look at the view from my bed through the chinks in the boards of the wall, which, as the temperature registered about 18° of frost, was somewhat chilly.

I shall not enter into a lengthy description of the negotiations, it will suffice to say that I found the so-called

Mart perfectly useless for the purpose, and that the articles agreed to in the Treaty Regulations had not been carried out in any way. The Chinese had built a wall across the valley about one-third of a mile lower down, and posted sentries on the gate and no one was allowed to come to the "Mart" to buy or sell any goods whatever. Extortionate rents were charged for "shops," which were nothing more than hovels, and to crown all the Tibetans refused to acknowledge the Treaty which had been signed on their behalf by the Chinese.

I sent in a report to Government and stayed on in Yatung for about ten weeks, waiting for a reply, and during that time I saw a good deal of both Chinese and Tibetans. The Chinese are well-known sticklers for etiquette and it was a curious commentary on the position that, as their officials lived just beyond Pema in the Chumbi Valley, within Tibet, I was not allowed to return their ceremonial visits. No person, save Tibetans or Chinese, not even Mr. Taylor, himself a Chinese official, was allowed to pass the gateway in the wall. Even the Amban, when he paid his official call on me, waived his right to a return visit. The position of the Chinese in Tibet was certainly a very curious one, or at any rate made to appear so.

I was not sorry when my stay came to an end. There was very little to do ; I was not allowed to go beyond the wall, and in any other direction it meant a climb of thousands of feet. There was a little Monal (pheasant) shooting to be had, but that was all. There was no house for Taylor to live in, so on my departure I arranged he should have the use of the one built for me, and for many years after it remained in the hands of the Chinese Customs Officer.

CHAPTER VI

MORE EARLY REMINISCENCES

Building a house. Lepcha servants. Supplies. A garden party. The Residency garden. Roses and lilies. A wave of colour. Orchids. Visit to Tumlong. Worship of Kangchenjunga. Lama dance. Missionaries. Difficulties of travelling. Crossing the Teesta in flood. Landslips. Leeches.

ONE of the first things to be done on my appointment to Sikhim was to build a house, not an easy task in a wild country where masons and carpenters were conspicuous by their absence, where stone for building had to be quarried from the hill-sides and trees cut down for timber. In my jungle wanderings round Gangtak, I came across a charming site in the midst of primeval forest which seemed suitable in every way, so I determined to build on it, felling only the trees which might possibly endanger the safety of the house, a necessary precaution, as many of them were quite 140 feet high, and in the spring the thunderstorms, accompanied by violent winds, were something terrible and wrought havoc everywhere. By levelling the uneven ground and throwing it out in front, I managed to get sufficient space for the house, with lawn and flower beds round it. Behind rose a high mountain, thickly wooded, which protected us from the storms sweeping down from the snows to the north-east, and in front the ground fell away with a magnificent view across the valley, where, from behind the opposite hills, Kangchenjunga and its surrounding snows towered up against the clear sky, making one of the most beautiful and magnificent sights to be imagined, and one certainly not to be surpassed, if equalled, anywhere in the world. The site selected, my real troubles began; trees had to be felled and sawn into scantlings; stone quarried, lime burnt, and, most difficult of all, carpenters and masons imported. I was fortunate in my carpenters, as I had already in my employment a Punjaubi, Moti Ram by name, the best carpenter and carver I have ever come across, and through him I got other excellent men from his native village, but the masons were distinctly bad. They seemed to find it impossible to build a wall plumb or a corner square—faults that impressed themselves on us later on, to our cost, when the time came for paper-hanging. More than that, too, owing to earthquakes, faulty building and heavy rain, parts of the anxiously watched edifice came down, and I began to think my house would never be finished. But, in spite of all difficulties, at Christmas 1890 we were able to move in, about eighteen months after commencing work.

Next came furnishing and finding a staff of servants. Furniture had either to be made on the spot by our Punjaubi carpenters or imported from England; and the neighbouring hill-man caught and trained to service, as, with the exception of one or two old servants, no plains-man could be induced to penetrate into such wilds, where they declared there was always war and where they would certainly be killed. One little lad, whom my wife found carrying loads in the early building days, Diboo by name, eventually became head bearer and major-domo of the establishment, and only left when we went on board at Bombay on our final departure. He and his comrades, Paling, Irung and others, were a merry lot, full of mischief and mad pranks and impossble to take seriously, for, after all, they were only lads of fourteen or fifteen and seemingly much younger when they came to us to learn. They were to be found in all sorts of strange places, climbing the most impossible trees for the sheer joy of seeing what they could

RESIDENCY GARDEN, GANGTAK

do, dancing war dances on the roof of the house, if by chance a ladder was left within their reach ; and generally on their first appearance on promotion to the dining-room, going off into suppressed giggles, to be summarily dragged out and cuffed by the older servants into a proper sense of decorum. When a little later we took them travelling in India, if their railway carriage doors were locked, they climbed through the windows as a matter of course, or perhaps were found on the engine hobnobbing with the driver and anxious to know what made the fire devil go.

Sikhim was a place where we had to be entirely self-supporting, so cattle had to be bought in order to have our own dairy for milk, butter and cheese, a flock of sheep for the supply of mutton, a poultry-yard, an oven built and baker engaged to bake bread, a blacksmith taught to shoe the ponies, who otherwise would have to take a four days' walk to Darjeeling every time their shoes wanted renewing, and even our own silversmith, who, though he may in one way have been a luxury, was again almost a necessity, as he had to make various other things in metals as well as to mend all the numberless small things which were always getting broken. Stores had to be carried on coolies from Darjeeling or Siliguri, sixty or seventy miles, and this meant large supplies being arranged for beforehand, as transport often broke down, or bad slips occurred on the road, and we had to be prepared for all emergencies and to supplement other folks' commissariat. Some funny episodes occurred in those far-away, early days. On one occasion, Captain and Mrs. P., belonging to the detachment stationed in Gangtak, came to the Residency to beg for some addition to their monotonous fare, and finding no one at home, went round to the open but barred storeroom window and proceeded with great skill to fish out a tin of provisions. They succeeded with much difficulty in getting hold of a Huntley and Palmer's biscuit tin, but imagine their feelings when they found it was an empty box.

Another time, the medical officer with his wife also arrived hungry on the scene, also to find no one at home, and too shy to order tea to be made and brought to the drawing-room where the table was standing ready, sadly went back to their little hut, borrowing from the mess, about as badly off for provisions as themselves, a tin of herrings. The herrings came up for dinner, but were followed by a sweet omelet made by their cook in the same frying pan! This couple lived in a two-roomed hut built of wattle and dab, and most of the furniture was primitive to a degree—four sticks with a packing-case top made a table, and even their bed was the same, with newar or wide tape stretched across. In the rains they said the uprights sprouted and grew green leaves over their heads. Such a primitive state of affairs seems almost impossible nowadays when the Gangtak bazaar possesses its two or three shops for the sale of European provisions, beers and wines, and is looked upon as a shopping centre by the further outposts; but in those early days Gangtak was the furthest outpost itself and end of all things, and we had very happy, merry times and many little adventures and mishaps were the cause of much laughter and many jokes.

My first garden party would have seemed very quaint to European eyes. I had invited the Maharaja and Maharani, with the members of Council, and all the Kazis and headmen with their wives and families. A goodly crowd assembled about four hours before the appointed time and lined the road just outside the Residency grounds, sitting about on the grassy edges until they were told they might come in, determined not to be late. Most of them had never seen, much less tasted European sweets or cakes, and when tea-time came they simply cleaned the tables of everything, and what they could not eat they carried away in the front of their voluminous coats. They emptied the sugar basins, and even took the spoons and liqueur glasses, and it all took place so quietly while my wife and I were with the Maharaja and

Maharani and the more important guests in another tent, I hardly realised what was going on.

The spoons and glasses, which I think they wanted as mementos of the good time they had had, were returned, on the Phodong Lama and Shoe Dewan remonstrating, and they departed very happily, declaring they had highly enjoyed their entertainment, and that all their heads were going round, a polite way of saying I had not stinted the drinks. They were always a very cheerful crowd and very pleasant to deal with, though indolent and improvident.

After my house was finished, nothing pleased them more than to be allowed to wander round the rooms, especially the bedrooms. They never touched anything, but liked to see how we lived and what European furniture was like.

Almost every market day little bands of women dressed in their best clothes would arrive with a few eggs or a pat of butter to make their salaams to my wife and a request that they might be allowed to go over the house, and their progress was marked with exclamations and gurgles of laughter at the strange ways of the Sahib-log.

While the house was building, the Maharani came several times to see how it was getting on, and told me I had built the walls much too thin and it would never stand. In their own houses and monasteries the walls are very thick, from 3 feet to 4 feet 6 inches, and have always a small camber. However, later on I had the best of the argument when, in the earthquake of 1897, the palace, notwithstanding its thick walls, collapsed entirely and had to be rebuilt, while the Residency, though badly cracked, remained standing.

The garden was a great joy and an everlasting source of amusement and employment both to my wife and to myself, although my wife did most of the work in it. The soil was virgin, and with a little expense and care almost anything could be grown. It was a lovely garden, the lawns always a beautiful green even in winter, and perfectly smooth, with masses of flowers, the magnificent forest trees left standing scattered about with clumps of feathery bamboos and groups of tree-ferns adding a charm of their own. In early spring the lawns were fringed with daffodils, primroses, polyanthus, daisies, pansies—almost every spring flower you can name, flowering in a profusion seldom seen in England, where cold winds and frosts nip them and keep them back; while on the house the wisteria was a cloud of delicate mauve, with here and there the tender green of early leaves. By the end of April the roses were in full bloom, a perfectly exquisite sight, excelling anything I have ever seen even in England. The house and all the outbuildings were covered with them—Cloth of Gold, Gloire de Dijon, Reine Marie Henriette, Devoniensis, Noisette and the paper white rose throwing themselves wildly over the roofs and hanging great festoons of lovely blooms from every corner. Over the lawns were scattered great bushes of Marie Van Houtte, Gloire de Dijon, Paul Neron, Souvenir de Malmaison, Madame Lambert, and many more; archways of Cloth of Gold and Devoniensis, and in sheltered corners, protected from the rain, Maréchal Niel and La France. These were all old favourites, but against the terraced slope from the house to the little pond below, I later planted Ramblers and many new varieties I imported from France. A great charm was the rapidity with which things grew in that climate where a rose in its second year became a large bush. They flowered in such profusion, thousands of blooms could be gathered without making the smallest impression, and during the summer, the gardeners had daily to sweep up huge baskets full of fallen petals from the lawns. Perhaps the most beautiful sight was my office, a building a few hundred yards from the house, which was completely covered, roof and chimneys included, with roses, and was a sight worth coming miles to see. Paul Nerons I have gathered 6¼ inches in diameter. Everything grew with the same luxuriance. A stock in front of my study window measured 4 feet 6 inches in height and 3 feet 6 inches in diameter, and was a fragrant mass of

WALLICHIANUM LILIES IN THE RESIDENCY GARDEN

delicate pink bloom. A Lilium Auratum grew to 8 feet with twenty-nine blossoms on a single stalk and the wild Lilium Gigantiums in the tree-fern ravine were often 12 feet high. The other wild lilies, Wallichianum and Nepalensis, made lovely groups, the Wallichianum over 6 feet with four or five flowers on a stem and filling the air with delicious perfume.

As the seasons passed the colouring of the garden changed. With the early spring came the white narcissus and pale yellow daffodils and primroses and lovely shades of browns and yellows of the wallflowers flowering under the eaves, followed by the deeper colouring of polyanthus and pansies and great tufts of arums and the delicate mauve and white of schizanthus. Next, the roses, a flood of pink, white, yellow, and crimson, with deeper shades in the petunias and stocks and blazing masses of brilliant colour from cactus and geraniums in the verandahs to be followed by a wave of blue which spread from the actual lawns away up the hillside, iris, agapanthus, heliotrope, hydrangea so covered with blossom hardly a leaf could be seen. This was the time when the lilies also were in perfection, auratums, tigers, wild ones from the jungle, all scenting the air, as well as English sweet-peas and mignonette.

The blue flowers were followed in their turn by deep yellows, orange, and scarlet, orange lilies, sunflowers, monbretia and cannas, which here again abandoned their ordinary habit of growth and were ten and twelve feet high with huge flower spikes. As the autumn advanced, the colouring became more subdued, though not less lovely, the wild ferns and the foliage taking on exquisite tints and each stump and tree trunk a mass of flowering cymbidiums with their long, handsome racemes of lovely brown and yellow flowers. From one year's end to the other there were always flowers, and in the winter I have seen roses, heliotrope and mignonette flowering under the eaves of the verandah while the lawns were covered with snow.

In the spring the forest trees were white, as though

snow had fallen, with blossoms of the Cœlogeyne Cristata, the earliest orchid to flower, quickly followed by a succession throughout the year, too numerous to give a list of, but which included the Dendrobium Densiflorum, with its heads of brilliant yellow, the mauve sprays of D. Nobile, and later the long hanging wreaths of D. Hookerianum and so on till one again came round to the autumnal cymbidiums. It was a garden in which new treasures and new beauties unfolded themselves from day to day and out of which, when we were in Gangtak, we never wished to move.

My work took me much on tour and away from Gangtak, and I have spent many pleasant days in monasteries and had some unusual experiences. Once, in the early days, at the invitation of the Phodong Lama, accompanied by Mrs. White, I spent a week at Tumlong to see the Lama dance and annual ceremony of the Worship of Kangchenjunga. Neither of us had before witnessed the ceremony, which is carried out in the open air on a terrace in front of the Monastery, with the buildings as a background, and in the centre of a crowd of gaily dressed people and lamas. We had seats in a balcony overlooking the terrace and had an excellent view.

The dance is allegorical, and lasts for three days, the different dances representing the several phases of worship. The story is long and very confusing to the ordinary mind and we could only gather a very general outline of its meaning. The dresses worn, especially at this Monastery, are gorgeous, made of the finest old Chinese brocades, of every imaginable colour, and kinkob, resplendent in gold and silver. The dancing itself is monotonous, as there is one step only which varies in the rapidity of the gyrations made by each dancer, but perfect time is kept to the weird and rather monotonous music of the band of lamas sitting on one side, in their red monastic garb, playing on trumpets, flutes and drums. The dancers frequently change their costumes and reappear in new characters. The masks worn by the performers are curious and sometimes very grotesque. They are carved out of wood and painted to represent animals, birds, demons and gods as well as the spirits of the dead. The whole dance is most picturesque and interesting and a sight well worth seeing, especially when the weather is fine and there is a blue sky and brilliant sunshine to throw up the bright foliage and distant hills and snow peaks in the background, and as the ceremony takes place in October or November, after the rains are over, this is generally the case.

It was at Tumlong a missionary lady from China came to take up her abode soon after I went to Sikhim. The Phodong Lama, who, like most Buddhists, was very broad-minded on religious questions, gave her one of his lama's houses within the monastery grounds, to live in, not thirty yards from the Gompa, or Temple. I am sorry to say she requited these good offices in a very ungrateful manner. She had a small harmonium, and whenever a service was being held in the Gompa she immediately opened it and played and sang hymns as loudly as possible, which, to say the least of it, was in very bad taste. The old lama, however, took it all most good-naturedly and only shrugged his shoulders and said he thought she could not be quite responsible for her actions. Fortunately for her, the people also followed the lama's example in treating her with good-natured tolerance, but such actions may, and often do, lead to serious consequences and give Government officials much annoyance and many anxious moments.

My experience, which extends over many years, leads me more and more to the conclusion that an extreme amount of care should be exercised in the selection of men or women sent to foreign countries as missionaries, not only from their own point of view, for surely their work would produce infinitely better results if they were possessed of special qualifications, but also politically, as incidents such as I have quoted, only one of many others, showing such utter want of tact, could not then occur. History has shown us how dangerous a volcano religious feeling is, and how often terrible and far-spreading disaster is the result of an unconsidered action.

Also I cannot help thinking it would be a very great advantage if different denominations could agree as to their several spheres of influence, instead of, as at present, perhaps half a dozen Roman Catholic, Anglican, Scotch, Scandinavian, Baptist, and other dissenting churches, all having delegates in one small area, to the bewilderment and confusion of the native mind, which cannot grasp the points of divergence. That is a question which, I think, deserves the attention of all interested in Missionary work.

Travelling in those early days was not easy, especially in the rains when the rivers were in flood and the roads were bad, and I remember one occasion when I was travelling to Darjeeling with Mrs. White and we had to cross the Teesta below Temi by a cane bridge. It was towards the end of the rains and we came in for one of the last heavy downpours, the river was in heavy flood and the only means of crossing was by a rickety cane suspension bridge 350 feet in length, and, in consequence of the lateness of the season, very rotten and much sagged in the centre. It was so rotten I was afraid it would give way and forbid any one else crossing while my wife and I were on it ; half the bamboo platform had disappeared and the suspending split bamboos were in many places broken, but we could not stay in the steamy wet valley, a hot-bed of fever, so we were obliged to make the attempt.

I went first, and leaning my weight on the bamboo platform made the bamboo on which I was standing meet the one on which my wife was, she then stepped on to that, and on the pressure being removed the bamboo swung back again, leaving a gap beneath which swirled the flooded Teesta. In this way we eventually got safely across, but it was a hazardous proceeding.

LOWER TEESTA VALLEY

We also had to cross our ponies, about four or five of them, no easy task with the river in such heavy flood, but the villagers and syces managed it successfully. They cut down bamboos, split them and made a rope long enough to reach from one bank to the other. A very strong headstall was put on the horse and the bamboo rope securely fastened to it. The other end was held by a number of men on the opposite side of the stream, the horse was driven into the river and carried in a diagonal course down stream to the opposite bank. It is a marvel how it is done when the rivers are in flood, and the animals have a poor time. More than once I have seen nothing but the legs of my pony in mid stream, but it is wonderful how they go through it and come out none the worse on the other side. I have even crossed an Arab on several occasions, this being one. Of course, if the rope happens to break, you see no more of your horse. The landing is always difficult as it is generally on rough, sharp rocks.

In the rains there was always the danger of bridges being swept away and of land slips. Once travelling from Temi we found a huge landslip had occurred, carried away the bridge on our road and filled the gorge to a depth of several hundred feet with liquid mud. It was nasty stuff to negotiate, but by placing several layers of jungle on it, we managed to cross on a precarious path that trembled under us with each step. On another occasion, on the Lachung road, we had to cross a large slip quite a quarter of a mile broad. The whole hillside was still moving, showers of stones were coming down from above at intervals, but as there was no other road by which we could reach Gangtak, we had to go on and take advantage of a lull in the small avalanches of rocks. It was easier for us than for the mules and ponies, who became frightened by the falling stones, and I nearly lost one—a large rock flying past its ears. But in these hills, with their abnormally heavy rainfall, and owing to the great amount of displacement which has occurred in their upheaval having cracked the rocks, slips are very frequent and one becomes used to them.

Another very great drawback to travelling in the rains at any elevation below 10,000 feet, are the leeches which swarm on every path. Each leaf in the jungle is fringed with them and they look almost like the tentacula of sea anemones as they commence to wave about in the air at the approach of a passer-by in the endeavour to fix on him—indeed in some places they are so bad I believe if a traveller had the misfortune to meet with an accident and be disabled he would soon be bled to death.

CHAPTER VII

THE DELHI DURBAR AND VISIT OF THE CHIEFS TO CALCUTTA TO MEET THEIR ROYAL HIGHNESSES THE PRINCE AND PRINCESS OF WALES

IN 1902 Sikhim was aroused from its quiet sleepy existence by an intimation from Government that His Excellency the Viceroy would send an invitation to the Maharaja to be present at the Imperial Durbar to be held at Delhi on January 1, 1903, to celebrate the accession of His Majesty the King-Emperor.

The Maharaja accepted the invitation, but at the last moment deputed his son and heir, Sidkyong Tulku, the Maharaj-Kumar, to be his representative. I never quite understood his reasons, but I think he was afraid of venturing so far from his own country, and though he has since quite grown out of it, he was at that time still conscious of and very sensitive about his hare-lip, which is a great disfigurement. His lamas also, whom he consults on every important subject, gave it as their opinion that he would probably fall ill and at any rate the result was he declined to go.

For many months we were busily engaged in preparations for the function. Ruling chiefs were allotted camping grounds, but that was all, and only in the case of minor personages was anything more done. Most native States of course possess carriages and horses, elephants, furniture, tents and camp equipage of every kind, and it was merely a case of having these things transported to Delhi. But in addition to being so far away, Sikhim possessed none of them, consequently they all had to be procured, and at the same time, with the small yearly revenue, it was necessary to exercise the greatest care to keep the expenditure down to the lowest possible sum.

Our reception tents were delightfully picturesque and unusual, made after Tibetan fashion with an elaborate design in appliqué cloth of many colours on the roofs, while the sides were decorated with the eight lucky signs: The Wheel of Life; the Conch Shell, or Trumpet of Victory; the Umbrella; the Victorious Banner; the Golden Fish; the Lucky Diagram; the Lotus; and the Vase: so constantly reproduced in Buddhist ornamentation.

The Kumar took this entirely into his own hands, drew out the designs, selected the colouring, and superintended the whole of the details of the manufacture with the best possible results.

The drawing-room was hung with old Chinese and Tibetan embroideries and vestments, including several very fine specimens of Rugen or bone aprons, and filled with a unique collection of quaint altar vessels and specimens of silver gilt, silver, copper, and brass work, sent by H.H. the Maharaja.

The tents were arranged in a semicircle on the edge of a wide drive sweeping from the entrance gates round a grass plot, and the whole of the approach was lined with high poles bearing prayer-flags of different colours printed with the Buddhist mystic formula: "Om Mani padmi hun." We were lucky also in having a background of pretty green trees growing on the banks of the canal instead of a sweep of dusty plain. The camp attracted many visitors, amongst others Their Royal Highnesses the Duke and Duchess of Connaught.

In the absence of the Maharaja, the Maharaj-Kumar was allowed to represent his father and was accorded his salute of fifteen guns, Cavalry escort, and military guard on the camp. He also took his place in all the great State functions, riding an extremely fine elephant lent for the occasion by the Betiah Raj, in the Chiefs' Procession, beside the Maharaja of Cooch Behar, and presenting his address to the King-Emperor through the Viceroy at the great Durbar. The speech was very characteristic and may interest my readers: "May His Majesty King Edward VII., from the time of occupation of this Golden Throne, exercise power over all these worlds; may he live for thousands of cycles and ever sustain all living creatures in joy and happiness."

It was the Kumar's first attempt at playing host to a number of European guests, and he did it very nicely with Mrs. White's help, looking carefully after the comfort of the eight or ten guests staying in the camp and always delighted to welcome people to lunch or dinner. He was most appreciative of any assistance we could give him, and constantly said he would have been quite unable to carry out any of his arrangements alone.

We spent most afternoons on the polo ground, where the polo was magnificent and where all the Delhi world congregated, but so much has already been written about the great Durbar, I only mention it as an episode connected with Sikhim which cannot be passed over in silence.

To me, personally, the most striking features of the Durbar were, not the great State functions, magnificent though they were, but the wonderful kaleidoscopic pictures that presented themselves at every turn. Huge modern camps springing up in a night on the empty plain, fitted with every European luxury, mixed up with gorgeously caparisoned elephants, strings of transport camels, smart carriages, retainers in chain armour carrying antiquated weapons, performing horses, transport carts, ekkas, soldiers, brilliant uniforms native and European, camel carriages, elephant carriages, wild escorts belonging to native princes on prancing horses with drums and fifes, dwarfs, giants, alternating with impressive State functions and military displays all intermingled inextricably, made one think one had been transported back to the days of the Arabian Nights. The whole Durbar was a long succession of wonderful sights resplendent in their vivid colouring, redolent of the East, well worth seeing and which, in all probability, will never again be brought together, even in India : a most splendid pageant, but whether it achieved its purpose only time can show.

It was the first occasion on which a ruler of Sikhim had been present at a State function. The late Maharaja received an invitation to the first Durbar, held by Lord Lytton in January 1877, but he did not accept it. It was much to be regretted that His Highness the present Maharaja did not attend on this occasion, but to the Kumar and the Kazis and headmen in his suite it was a revelation of the extent of British supremacy, and the assemblage of so many chiefs and Rajas from north, south, east, and west come together to pay homage to the King-Emperor, was an object-lesson, brought immediately home to them of the greatness of our Indian Empire.

A couple of years later, in 1904, when Their Royal Highnesses the Prince and Princess of Wales were about to visit India, and preparations were being made for the assembly of chiefs at various points to pay homage to the heir to the throne, it seemed to me both desirable and expedient to include the chiefs from these hill borders amongst those assembling in Calcutta. I accordingly approached the Government of India on the subject of issuing invitations to the Maharaja and Maharani of Sikhim and Sir Ugyen Wang-chuk, the Tongsa Penlop of Bhutan, and at the same time raised the question of inviting the Tashi Lama of Tibet from Shigatsi also to be present. Although in no way directly connected with the British Government, it seemed, for many reasons, particularly expedient that if possible he should be induced to pay

GROUP AT HASTINGS HOUSE, CALCUTTA, 1906

Back Row: BHUTAN SOLDIER, CAPTAIN HYSLOP, RAI UGYEN DORJI BAHADUR, RAI LOBZANG CHÖDEN SAHIB, JERUNG DEWAN, BURMIAK KAZI, BHUTAN SOLDIER, SIKHIM SOLDIER

Front Row: D. E. HOLLAND, SIR UGYEN WANG-CHUK, K.C.I.E., J. CLAUDE WHITE, C.I.E., H.H. THE MAHARAJA OF SIKHIM, H.H. THE MAHARANI OF SIKHIM

a visit to India at this particular juncture. There were many reasons to make such a departure desirable and in addition he, a high dignitary of the Buddhist Church and considered by a certain faction in Tibet the superior even of the Delai Lama, would have an opportunity at the same time of visiting the Buddhist shrines in India which must necessarily be of great interest to him.

Government adopted my views and eventually issued the necessary invitations, which were accepted.

It was quite a new departure, as none of the chiefs on this frontier had ever before left their mountain homes, nor had they, with the exception of one short visit of the Maharaja of Sikhim to Darjeeling, been guests of the Indian Government, neither had any high Tibetan lama before visited India.

The arrangements for their entertainment were somewhat complicated by the fact that as Buddhists and without caste prejudices as to food, everything had to be provided for them, and although an attempt was made to limit the number of followers in their various suites, the total retinue of the three chiefs mounted up to an astounding figure. They were an extraordinary collection of wild, only partly civilised creatures, especially those from Tibet, and most picturesque. The Government Official Guest House, Hastings House, Alipur, was placed at their disposal, as well as a second house in the grounds, and in addition separate camps were pitched in the compound. Water, both for drinking and washing purposes, was laid on to each camp and the tents and grounds were lighted by electricity, lamps were quite out of the question as the camp would certainly have been burnt down had they been used; police arrangements were very necessary, and carriages and means of transport had to be provided for the use of the chiefs and their following. The arrangement of all the details meant a great deal of work and correspondence, and a visit in advance to Calcutta to discuss matters with the Foreign Office, but eventually everything was satisfactorily carried out.

The Tibetan party were placed in charge of my assistant, Captain O'Connor, the trade agent at Gyantsi, and before arriving in Calcutta they made an extensive tour through Upper India, accompanied by the Rajkumar of Sikhim, visiting Buddhist shrines of importance and interest and ending with Buddh Gaya, the most holy of all Buddhist shrines. Unfortunately Buddh Gaya, with all its memories and associations of the great Buddha, is now in the hands of the Hindus, and I am sorry to say, the Tashi Lama while there, owing to want of sound advice, made some grave mistakes and succeeded in alienating the sympathy of the Mohunt and the Hindus, the last thing to be desired, as the Buddhists are very anxious to have the shrine again in their own hands. Of course, allowances have to be made for a man looked upon as sacred in his own country, where his lightest wish is law, and who, in consequence of universal veneration and belief in his own infallibility, has had very little understanding of, or consideration for, any form of religion but his own. However, notwithstanding this, I think the Tashi Lama's visit was productive of good, and he returned with some small idea of the extent and power of our Indian Empire, and, had not the policy of Government, by its subsequent action in Tibet, frustrated these good impressions, I think they might have had memorable results.

The Maharaja and Maharani of Sikhim were in charge of Captain Hyslop, 93rd Highlanders, and thoroughly enjoyed their visit. It opened their minds and did them an immense amount of good, and they much appreciated the honour paid them by the Prince and Princess. His Royal Highness exchanged visits with the Maharaja, as well as with the Tashi Lama and the Tongsa Penlop, while the Princess received the Maharani at Government House.

As can well be imagined, this first visit to a city was full of interest and surprise to them, and during the time they were in Calcutta they saw many things they had hitherto had no conception of. At the conclusion of their visit, they made a pilgrimage to Buddh Gaya and then returned to Sikhim much more contented with their lot than they had formerly been.

But on the whole I think the Tongsa Penlop, Sir Ugyen Wang-chuk, took the most intelligent interest in what he saw and had no hesitation in openly expressing his pleasure in what he liked. He was particularly interested in the various industries, the cotton and paper mills, the iron works, and mint, and the warships were a revelation to him. Major F. W. Rennick, of the Intelligence Branch, was in special charge of him. As a good Buddhist he also visited Buddh Gaya and plainly expressed his opinion that, although no one would be more glad than himself were the shrine restored to the Buddhist community, it was folly to quarrel with the Hindus, who for so many years had cared for and tended it, and that, owing to their own long neglect, the Buddhists had only themselves to thank that it was no longer in their possession and really should be very grateful to the Hindus for their care.

This visit cemented, if that were needed, his friendship towards, and admiration for, the British Government, and instilled more deeply his determination to effect the reforms he had long had at heart in his own country. He was much impressed with his reception by His Royal Highness, and very grateful for all that was done for him during his visit.

It was rather an undertaking to bring this party of unsophisticated chiefs and their wild following to Calcutta, but with the help and co-operation of the three officers deputed as my assistants, Major Rennick, Captain O'Connor and Captain Hyslop, we were able to bring the visit to a conclusion with only one or two unfortunate little incidents. The visit was certainly a success and formed a departure which I hope Government will follow up, of keeping up more friendly and direct relations with their neighbours on this hitherto little-known frontier.

CHAPTER VIII

EXPEDITIONS AND EXPLORATIONS IN SIKHIM

From Gangtak over the Giucha-la to Ringen. Loss of a coolie. Camp amongst glaciers and moraines. A snow leopard. Alpine flowers. Avalanches and ice caves. Crossing a difficult gorge. Lepchas and wild bees. The Rungnu. Sakhyong.

IN 1890 I made one of my first expeditions to the snows, crossing the Giucha-la Pass and from there making my way to Ringen, following a route the latter part of which had certainly never been traversed by a European, and I doubt by any one, except possibly a very occasional Lepcha. As I intended going to considerable elevations, I started in the middle of the rainy season, in July, in order to have less snow to negotiate and also less chance of snow-storms in the high altitudes. From Gangtak I crossed lower Sikhim, travelling *viâ* the Pemiongtchi and Dubdi Monasteries, and so far I had no difficulty, as I slept in either village houses or monasteries, but after that I had to take to my tents, which are certainly not comfortable in pouring rain. It came down steadily in sheets while I was at Dubdi, and when the morning for my departure came it was no better; but it is useless to wait for fine weather in Sikhim, so I started in spite of it. The path led up a narrow and very precipitous valley, with virgin forest on either side and dense undergrowth; smaller streams came down to join the main river at almost every hundred yards, and in crossing one of them, my first mishap occurred.

A torrent, swollen by the heavy rain, came rushing down a perpendicular rock with an almost deafening roar right across the path, which at that point was water-worn rock and very slippery, and then leapt into an abyss below, the bottom of which I could not see. A couple of saplings about four inches in diameter had been placed across, and I had gone over in safety and was resting on an incline on the other side, when one of my coolies came up. For some reason, as he was crossing the poles, he either slipped or lost his balance, I could not see which, but he fell on the up-stream side, was immediately carried under the bridge and swept over the precipice before my eyes. It all happened in a moment, and such was the inaccessibility of the spot and so dense the jungle, it was quite impossible to do anything for the poor fellow. Some more coolies now came up, and we tried to cut a way down through the dense tangle of trees and undergrowth, but this proved quite impossible, though, after an hour's work, one man managed to get down by a circuitous route, only to find that his unfortunate companion had been swept into the main torrent, and that nothing was to be seen of either him or his load. I am thankful to say that in all my wanderings in the Himalayas I have only lost one other coolie.

Nothing more could be done, so we moved on, but the delay caused us to be overtaken by nightfall while we were still in the gorge, with no room to pitch a tent. I was glad to find an overhanging rock under which to sleep, and thought myself lucky to find a comparatively dry spot out of the drip, but it was not a very restful night surrounded by my coolies who, like all natives, talked for hours, and with the air full of acrid smoke from the wood fires which made sleep difficult. It was still raining when I arrived at Jongri, my next halting place, 13,140 feet high, just above tree level, and where our camp was in open country.

The following day I reached the glaciers which come

down from Kabru and Pundeem and had my tents pitched amongst them.

In the morning it was a little finer and I caught occasional glimpses of the snows, but towards afternoon it commenced raining again and became very bleak and cold, and in going round my camp I found one of my coolies, a Paharia or Nepalese, lying huddled up in a wet heap. He was feeling the elevation and the cold and refused to move, so I placed a stalwart Bhutea on either side of him and made them run him up and down until his blood began to circulate. In a little while he went off and cooked his dinner and was none the worse, but had he been left to himself, he would probably have died in the night. I stayed here for a few days exploring the glaciers. The camp was a wild one surrounded by enormous quantities of *débris*, and shut in on three sides by glaciers and snows. The wet, misty weather made it still more gloomy, but on the third day the morning was glorious. Not a sign of a cloud was to be seen, and the snows standing up all round against the pale blue of the sky made the scene a magnificent one.

While I was wandering some little way from camp I saw a snow leopard. He was on the other side of a glacial stream, so I could not get very close to him, and as besides I had only a shot gun with me, I contented myself with watching him, and a very pretty and most unusual sight it was. He was playing with a large raven, which kept swooping down just out of his reach, and to see him get on his hind legs like an enormous cat and jump at the bird was worth watching. Suddenly he saw me and went off up the hill at a pace that made me envious. He was a fine specimen, very large and with a beautiful coat, and I wish I had had the luck to bag him.

The weather now cleared up, and I had one of the glorious breaks which occur at intervals during the rains, and crossed the Giucha-la, 16,420 feet, in clear weather, with not a cloud in the sky. The view from the top is superb. Before one lies an amphitheatre of snow peaks, all over 21,000 feet, save in one gap, which is 19,300 feet. On the right hand Sim-vo-vonchin rises sharply over the 19,000-foot gap, then the splendid shoulder supporting the twin peaks of Kangchenjunga, which towers up to a height of over 28,000 feet, and with something like 11,000 feet of uninterrupted snow and ice falling in a sheer precipice on its south face to the great glacier at its foot, next the ridge connecting Kangchenjunga with Kabru, and on the immediate left a fine unnamed snow peak with hanging glaciers, but Kabru itself is invisible from this pass. On the south side of the Kangchen glacier were some ancient moraines covered with exquisite green turf and masses of Alpine flowers, whose simple beauty and vivid colouring stood out in sharp contrast to the grandeur of the surrounding snows, making a picture long to be remembered. I climbed down and had my tents pitched on this lovely green sward, though it seemed almost desecration to turn such a lovely spot into a noisy camp, with all its ugly and commonplace surroundings.

Next morning I walked up the valley as far as I could go without crossing the glacier, and the scene, if possible, became still wilder and more magnificent. On the right was Kangchenjunga and to the left Kabru with its magnificent glacier, while joining the two mountains in front of me was a wall of snow and ice 21,000 feet high. By and by, as the sun shone on the face of Kangchen, I saw some magnificent snow avalanches. They came thundering down on all sides, making a peculiar hissing noise, and on reaching the glacier, burst into clouds of spray of dazzling whiteness, which here and there was transformed into rainbow colours by the rising sun. A little later, as I was photographing Kangchenjunga, a large piece of snow cracked off, crashed down about 8000 feet, and, reaching the bottom with a noise like thunder, which reverberated through the surrounding heights, filled the head of the valley with a mist of snow. Altogether, it was a day of most beautiful sights never to be forgotten, which amply rewarded me for any hardships or privations I had to undergo to achieve my object.

To show how fickle the climate can be in the proximity of these perpetual snows, I went to bed that night in perfect weather, to be awakened later by the collapse of my tent. A sudden snowstorm had come up, and soon, before any one had noticed it, the weight of the snow became so great every pole of my tent broke and I was buried underneath. Fortunately a little table by my bed saved me from the weight of the canvas and gave me some breathing space, so, as it was very cold, I remained where I was till the morning, when my men could come to clear up the *débris*. By that time the weather was again perfect, and such is the power of the sun at those altitudes, the new snow soon disappeared, but as it had made everything rather uncomfortable, we decided not to move camp that day.

We were now really entering unexplored country, as I wished to go down the Kangchen glacier to the source of the Rungnu-chhu, and thence to follow the stream to Ringen. None of my coolies had ever been over the ground, and as I found to my cost, there was not even a track. The first two marches were very easy, as we kept to the centre of the glacier, which we found quite smooth and very good going, quite unlike most of the other glaciers I have been over, either those on the south of the Giucha-la, which are completely cut up, have enormous holes in them, and over which it would be quite impossible to march; the Zemu glacier, which is much the same, or the glaciers in the extreme north of the Lonak Valley, which again appear more like a rough sea suddenly frozen into enormous hummocks of ice.

This difference in the Kangchen glacier I am unable to account for, unless it may be that the ice, running as it does in a very narrow valley, is of a much greater depth, and also that the valley lying east and west gets less sun and escapes the full force of the south-west monsoon. It is a curious phenomenon and would be well worth investigation, but its solution will, I think, require the study of experts in such matters. This glacier ends at an elevation of 12,100 feet in an ice cliff, from a cavern in which the Rungnu takes its rise, and here my worst difficulties began.

The cliff was topped with *débris* and boulders of every size just on the balance, which at any moment might go down with a crash to the bottom, and it was no easy matter to climb down myself without bringing tons and tons on the top of me, and more difficult to get all my coolies and baggage down. Only one man could come at a time, a long process, but it was eventually carried through without mishap. At the foot of the ice cliff I pitched my camp in the midst of rhododendrons and pines.

Looking directly up the valley was the end of the glacier I had just descended, gloomy and forbidding, and on the right, to the north, was the limit of the glacier from the 19,000-foot gap, adding to the scene of desolate grandeur; for I think there can be no more wild and desolate scene than these moraines, in which the large glaciers end in utter confusion, giving the impression of a battlefield where giants and titan monsters have torn up huge masses of rock to hurl at one another, with the constant fall of stones as the ice melts, and the weird feeling that everything in addition is quietly though imperceptibly on the move.

On close examination, the ice is very beautiful, and the ice caves out of which the river rushes are magnificent. The colouring of the ice was lovely, varying in every shade of green and from pale turquoise blue to almost black in the depths of the caves, with opalescent tints where the sun's rays struck its edges. Immediately surrounding me was a carpet of the Alpine vegetation, so lovely in these hills, and amongst the undergrowth I found oak and silver ferns, anemones, primulas, gentians of every shade of blue, buttercups, violas and innumerable other flowers,

KANGCHENJUNGA

with here and there magnificent rhododendrons and silver pines, though the latter were still stunted at that elevation.

Beautiful as the vegetation is, it makes travelling both arduous and difficult. There was no track of any kind, the bottom of the valley was a mass of rocks strewn in every direction and densely covered with dwarf rhododendron, which necessitated cutting every foot of the way, and progress was in consequence extremely slow, sometimes not three miles in a day. To add to our discomfort the fine weather broke and a constant drizzle set in.

I knew my way out lay down the stream, but whether it was feasible was another matter. We struggled on for several days till we came to a gorge running down from the 17,000 feet gap which lies between the magnificent snow peaks Siniolchu and Simvoo, and which at this point had cut into a water-worn chasm 300 feet to 400 feet deep, and some 40 feet to 50 feet wide, with absolutely perpendicular sides as slippery as glass.

Here we were obliged to wait till we could find a way across. There was no camping ground, not even room to pitch a tent, only some narrow ledges of rock, but here perforce I had to stay, and with luck I managed to throw the outer fly of my tent over some boulders and get my bed inside, and fortunately the night was fine. The next day we spent searching for a means of crossing, and after some hours we came upon a natural bridge formed by two gigantic rocks which had jammed in the gorge and thus formed a somewhat hazardous bridge. We set to work, and with great difficulty succeeded in letting down the baggage with the aid of ropes and jungle creepers, and at last succeeded in getting everything across safely.

From the bridge I had a splendid view into the chasm some hundreds of feet below, where the raging torrent could be heard grinding the boulders together with a noise like thunder, and faintly seen in the dim light, but I was not sorry to have safely accomplished the crossing of my party, especially as, to add to our difficulties, in the centre of the bridge we had to crawl through a hole on hands and knees.

This bridge is called by the Lepchas Tak-nil-vong-do-zah, and is occasionally used by them when they go up the valley collecting wax. The combs of the wild bees are found on overhanging precipices, and the only means by which they can be reached is to descend from above on narrow cane ladders just wide enough for a man's foot, and often 300 feet to 400 feet long. The Lepcha comes down the ladder with an earthen vessel containing fire on his head, and on reaching the combs puts some green leaves on it. This makes a dense smoke and drives the bees away, while he cuts off the combs, which are often 6 feet long and 4 feet thick; he then throws them down to his companions, but it is a hazardous business as, should the smoke not drive off the bees, the man hanging in mid-air has no chance if they attack him. The men waiting below catch the combs, squeeze out the honey and partly clarify the wax on the spot, by placing it in boiling water, skimming it off, and making it into cakes 8 or 9 inches in diameter and 3 or 4 inches thick. The honey is eaten locally, unless it has been made when the magnolia is in flower, in which case it is often poisonous.

A little later we had another equally difficult crossing when we reached the Rungnu. The heavy rain had swollen the river, and the only means of crossing was by placing a tree from the bank we were on, to rest on a small rock in the centre of the stream, from which a notched pole had been placed up the side of a perpendicular rock to a slippery landing on the top. Across this very unsteady and rickety pole I had to go, whether I liked it or not, as there was no other way. It was a very nasty place and I do not mind admitting I would have given a good deal to avoid it.

The river was rushing underneath to dash itself angrily over a precipice some 300 feet high with a deafening roar.

BAMBOO ROADWAY

A false step, and once in the water, that would be the end, with no possible chance of escape. I managed to cross the flat pole safely, but could not face the notched one. One of my Lepcha coolies offered to carry me up on his shoulders if I promised to make no movement, but this seemed even worse than climbing up by myself, as I finally did with the aid of a rope, and heartily glad I was to get to the top and on to the hillside. Unfortunately I had got ahead of my baggage coolies, always a fatal thing to do, and before they arrived, the river had risen to such an extent they could not cross, so I was left on one side with all my baggage on the other, and there was nothing for it but to make the best of a bad business. With me were Purboo, my Lepcha orderly, the coolie with my camera, and one other man, Jerung Denjung, in charge of the coolies.

It was pouring, we were all wet through, and we had only one piece of chocolate between us, and no wood to make a fire with, as everything was sopping. Eventually Purboo took off his Lepcha chudder or shawl and made a shelter by hanging it over some sticks, and under this we all got. They managed somehow to light a fire, but the smoke from the wet wood was perhaps more trying than anything else. Here we sat till morning, when some of the coolies turned up, and we were able to get something to eat and a change of clothes.

We were still not out of the wood, for it had taken me ten days longer than I had expected to come down, and our provisions were running short. Mine were quite finished, but some of the men's rations still remained, and these they shared with me most cheerfully, and we all made the best of things with no sign of grumbling or discontent.

But soon after, the end of our troubles came in view with the sight of some Lepcha cultivation. The men went wild with delight, and I verily believe they had thought that they would never get back to their homes again; they threw down their loads, danced and sang, and then started off with renewed energy to find the owners of the fields in the outlying houses of the village of Sakhyong a few miles further down. Here I was royally entertained by the people, who gave me everything they had, eggs, buckwheat cakes and some other cakes of flour, made by grinding the root of a caladium which grows at high altitudes. These latter were to my taste most unpalatable, but I was only too thankful to get anything after the privations and hardships we had come through.

From Sakhyong everything was comparatively easy, there was a path of sorts, and we were again amongst cultivation and scattered houses, and in a few days more I arrived at Ringen, and from Ringen another five days brought me to my headquarters at Gangtak after a most enjoyable and successful expedition, during which I had thoroughly explored the hitherto unknown valley running down from the big Kangchen glacier.

My prolonged absence had caused some alarm, and even given rise to rumours that I had been captured by the Tibetans, and several parties had been sent out by the Phodong Lama and others to find out what had become of me, and I was greeted with a hearty welcome when I at last arrived.

I do not think this journey could be equalled throughout the world for its beauty and variety of scene, the magnificent gorges, with wonderful waterfalls tumbling down on all sides, the wild desolation of the higher snows, and the richness of colouring and dense vegetation lower down; every few miles bringing new beauties before one.

CHAPTER IX

EXPEDITIONS AND EXPLORATIONS IN SIKHIM—*continued*

From Gangtak to the Zemu glacier, Lonak Valley, Lachen and Lachung. Mr. Hoffmann. Cloud effects. Cane bridges. Hot springs. Talung Monastery and its treasures. Grazing land and Tibetan herdsmen. Yak transport. Locusts. The Sebu Pass. Snow-blindness. Lachung. Goral-shooting.

MY second expedition to the snows was made in June and July 1891, when, accompanied by Mr. Hoffmann, the well-known photographer, my object was to explore the Lonak Valley and to visit Lachen and Lachung on my way back.

It was, however, we found, a little early in the season, as the winter snow had not yet melted on any of the higher passes, and this made travelling difficult as well as uncomfortable. We left Ringen, our starting point, in pouring rain, and the first few marches were very trying. They were through deep gorges all under 5000 feet, which have at this time of year an atmosphere almost supersaturated with moisture, leeches abounded, and fleas were numerous. They swarmed in the houses and monasteries in which we slept, in order to avoid using the tents in the rain, and made it a somewhat doubtful advantage.

Travelling at this time of the year, however, has certain points to recommend it.

The foliage of the trees and the undergrowth is magnificent, most of the flowering shrubs and creepers are at their best, everything looks fresh, and the colouring, when the sun breaks through the clouds, is wonderful. Each leaf and bit of moss sparkles as though set in diamonds, the air is filled with clouds of butterflies of every imaginable colour, the near distance is brilliant, while the middle and far distances shade in blues and purples to deep indigo, and when a glimpse of the snows is obtained at the head of some valley, they stand out, an almost supernatural vision of ethereal beauty, the whole picture made up of the softest of tints not to be equalled, in my opinion, in any other part of the world. The cloud effects are marvellous, the vapour seems to boil up out of the deep valleys as out of some huge caldron, taking the most fantastic shapes and an endless variety of colours as it catches the sun's rays ; then suddenly everything is blotted out into monotonous grey, as though such wonderful sights were too grand for human eyes, until a sudden puff of wind blows aside the veil of mist and discloses again the lovely panorama.

But to return to the journey. We crossed the Teesta, a grand sight in heavy flood, by the cane bridge at Sanklan Sampo. These cane bridges are a feature of Sikhim, and very rarely met with elsewhere. The method of construction is to throw across the stream which is to be bridged sufficient canes to form two side supports. The canes are passed over wooden tressels on each bank of the river, and after stretching, to get them as nearly as possible into the same curve, the ends are fastened to trees, roots or rocks, anything to which they can be made fast. Lengths of split cane or bamboo are then fastened to the cane ropes, thus forming loops, and on these loops two bamboos are placed side by side, making a narrow platform on which an insecure foothold is obtained. This bridge was 220 feet long, but they are often 350 feet. A cane bridge is never easy to cross, and is worse towards the end of the rains, as the cane and bamboo with which it is constructed quickly decay, but my Lepcha coolies thought nothing of it and soon had all the loads across.

From Sanklan Sampo to Be, the road, or rather track, is

SANKLAN SAMPO

one of the worst in Sikhim. It consists principally of a series of ladders up and down precipices or of galleries clinging to the face of cliffs. These ladders are made of bamboo with cross pieces tied to them for steps, generally at an angle, never horizontal, and in wet weather they are abominably slippery. The galleries are also made of bamboos fastened to any projecting root or tree, and often hung by canes from hundreds of feet above; they are never more than two bamboos in width, and only in the very worst places do they ever take the trouble to put up any kind of railing. Progress along such a road was necessarily slow, and our marches were consequently very short, but we eventually reached Be, the last collection of houses of any size, for it cannot be called a village, where a halt was made for a day to make arrangements for the coolies' food before going into the uninhabited regions higher up. As Be was hot and the camping ground cramped, I decided to move on to the Talung Monastery and wait there till the preparations were completed. This turned out to be a wise move, as there was good camping ground and a great deal to be seen both in the monastery and in the surrounding country.

We followed the course of the Rimpi-chhu, a magnificent torrent one mass of foam as it dashed down over the boulders and between precipices without a single quiet pool, in fact it was an uninterrupted cascade which, on nearing Talung, has cut its way into the rocks, forming one of the magnificent gorges, 300 feet or 400 feet deep and some miles in length, which occur on some of these rivers. This gorge is exceedingly narrow, and the branches of the trees at the top meet each other across the chasm, keeping out the light, and only the roar of the river can be heard as the darkness makes it almost impossible to see the bottom.

At one point the trees are bent over from either side and tied together, and so form a good though somewhat precarious bridge. This I crossed, as I wanted to visit some sulphur springs on the other side, and after walking some way through a dense forest, where every branch was hung with moss and long grey lichen, and with a thick carpet of moss under my feet, I found the springs. The water is moderately hot and is used by the Lepchas in cases of rheumatism and skin disease. The bathing arrangements are delightfully primitive ; a hole is dug in the ground or a wall built of stones, the crevices are filled with moss and into this the water is run and the bathers sit, men and women indiscriminately, with no shelter except sometimes a shawl thrown over a bamboo support. The patients sit in these baths for from four to eight hours a day for a period of ten to fourteen days. The Lepchas have the most profound belief in the efficacy of the water and declare the cures are marvellous. I have visited many of these hot springs, which constantly occur in the valleys throughout the Himalayas at a certain elevation, and in some of them the temperature reaches 160°, and one where I stayed for a short time was 120°. I need hardly say that I had my own bath tub in my tent and ran the water into it from the spring by means of a long india-rubber hose. I have no doubt, were better arrangements made, the beneficial qualities of the waters might be made much more useful than at present ; now they are used only by occasional visitors who, to reach them, have to undertake difficult and hazardous journeys, for nearly all the springs are found in more or less inaccessible spots lying far off the ordinary roads.

Talung Monastery is one of the most sacred monasteries in Sikhim, and is full of very beautiful and interesting objects of veneration, nearly all real works of art. During the Nepalese invasion of 1816, many of these objects were removed from other monasteries and brought here for safety, and have remained here ever since. Unlike most monasteries, an inventory is kept and most carefully scrutinised from time to time by the Maharaja, and owing to these precautions, the collection has remained intact.

OLD VESTMENTS, TALUNG MONASTERY

Here is preserved the saddle and saddle-cloth of the Jock-chen Lama, the first lama to enter Sikhim from Tibet, several fine thigh-bone trumpets and some splendid specimens of "Rugen" (apron, breastplate, circlet and armlets), exquisitely carved from human bones, a beautiful set in silver gilt of marvellously fine workmanship of the Tashi Tagye, or eight lucky signs, as well as many other altar vessels and vestments. Here also are all the old dancing dresses and ornaments, beyond comparison finer than any I have ever seen in other monasteries in Sikhim.

All these treasures were produced for my inspection and examination to see that they duly corresponded with the list, and were then most carefully put away and re-sealed, but before this was done some of the lamas put on the old dresses, to enable me to see them to greater advantage.

This monastery had never before been visited by Europeans, and it was Mr. Hoffmann's and my privilege to be the first to see this unique collection of Buddhist ritualistic paraphernalia, which up to the present time still remains intact.

Our preparations finally completed, we made for uninhabited country. The road for some distance was comparatively easy and ran up the valley of the Rimpi, which we twice crossed, through splendid forests of pine, the Abies Dumosa being particularly fine. The rhododendrons were in flower, and together with the new foliage of the birch trees, made bright splashes of colour. Whilst on the first day's march I discovered that a large stream, the Zamtu-chhu, takes its rise on the eastern slopes of Siniolchu and joins the Rimpi on its right bank, thus proving the survey maps to be wrong in showing it, as they have hitherto done, running to the south.

I was much tempted to follow up this stream, as Siniolchu is the most lovely snow peak in Sikhim, and the views at the head of the valley must be magnificent, but it would probably have taken me over a week and I could not spare the time, as I wanted to go north across several snow ranges and so reach a drier climate. These high snow ranges act as a barrier to the south-west monsoon, very little of which penetrates into the higher valleys or into Tibet. We therefore went straight on, and after passing some very fine waterfalls, camped on the edge of the snow, but by afternoon the weather became very misty and wet and we passed an uncomfortable night. From this camp onwards, till we had crossed the Yeumtsho-la (15,800 feet), marching was tedious and difficult through soft melting snow, and we even had to pitch our tents in snow. The Yeumtsho and other lakes were thawing, with water lying on the ice, and with everything in a state of slush it was most disagreeable both for ourselves and our men. The mornings, however, were clear, and we had some fine views of Lama Anden, or Lating as the Lepchas call it, a twin peak which is visible from Darjeeling.

Crossing the pass we found very difficult as the snow was deep on both sides and very soft, but once over we soon left it behind on our way down to the Zemu Valley, where we camped again amidst rhododendrons at 12,800 feet.

Looking down the valley the view was particularly fine, the precipices and rocks on the summit of the hills ending in some very fine screes, while the foot of the valley appeared to be blocked by the snow mass of Tsengui Kang in the range running between Lachen and Lachung.

The Zemu glacier ends, about one-third of a mile up the valley from where our camp was pitched at an elevation of 13,830 feet, in an ice cliff in which are three ice caverns out of which the Zemu river rushes in turbulent, muddy torrents. This glacier is the largest in Sikhim and is fed from the northern slopes of Siniolchu and Simvoo and the eastern slopes of Kangchenjunga, and with it are incorporated some large glaciers from the ridge running to the north of Kangchen. With the exception of the upper part

SINIOLCHU.

the glacier is very rough, with enormous holes and covered with huge masses of *débris*, and in this resembles that to the south of the Giucha-la. By climbing one of the hills to the north I had a very good view and could follow distinctly the moraines brought down by the different side glaciers, which are wonderfully well defined, chiefly by the different colour of the rocks in each, and these lines are continued for miles down the glacier with a very pretty colour effect.

From one of these side hills I had, early one morning, a magnificent view of Siniolchu, the finest snow peak in Sikhim. It was very early, and as the sun rose the clouds lifted for a few minutes, disclosing a lovely picture. The glacier and the hills immediately behind were in deep shadow, but Siniolchu was flooded with rosy light from the rising sun, and no mere photograph can give any idea of the beauty of the scene. It only lasted a few minutes, and then was blotted out by mist, and I never saw it again all the days I remained in the valley.

We marched up the side of the glacier to a height of 17,500 feet, finding excellent camping grounds all the way between the lateral moraines and the hills on the north, and as far as I could judge, being no expert in ice craft, there would have been absolutely no difficulty in walking up to the top of either the 19,000 feet or the 17,500 feet gaps, as the upper ends of these glaciers appear perfectly smooth with apparently no big fissures and very little soft snow. Close to our camp on the north a magnificent glacier ran into the valley. In this the ice falls were magnificent and by far the finest I have seen.

Camping at such elevations in the midst of ice and surrounded by these grand snow peaks, the silence at times is almost oppressive. There is not a sound except an occasional weird noise caused by the fall of stones either on the ice of the glacier or into the water at the bottom of some vast ice pit. But yet there was life in these solitudes, as I saw several herds of burhel in the hills above the camp.

The strata to the north of the glacier are very noticeable and run in thick bands of red and grey, which give the hills a very different appearance to those on the south, while disintegration is going on very rapidly owing to the horizontal strata decaying at different rates.

All this was new country hitherto unvisited, though some of it was traversed later by Mr. Douglas Freshfield and his party in 1899.

The weather continued so bad, I decided to return to the lower end of the glacier, and here I am sorry to say Mr. Hoffmann left me, having no more time at his disposal. My way led me into the mountains to the north, and I made for the Tang-chung-la, 17,100 feet, passing a small lake to the north at 15,200 feet.

The grazing on this and the adjoining hills is very good, the grass from 8 inches to 12 inches deep, but no flocks of sheep or herds of yaks were to be seen. The reason given for not making use of this excellent pasture was its inaccessibility from the south and the unsuitability of its wet climate to animals accustomed to the dryness of Tibet, but it seemed a pity it should be so wasted. Next day I crossed the Thi-la, 17,430 feet, and after a tiring march, camped in the Lonak Valley at an elevation of 15,300 feet. The change in climate after crossing the Thi-la was wonderful. Up the southern slopes it had rained continuously, but I had not gone more than a few hundred feet down the northern side when the rain ceased, the sun came out, and a little further down the ground was dusty, and I camped at the bottom in a perfectly dry climate, the climate of Tibet.

The face of the country too had changed, there were no longer rugged rocks and precipices, the hills were rounded, the result of the disintegration which in this dry climate does not wash away; the bottoms of the valleys were broad and flat, and there were numerous flocks of sheep and herds of yaks grazing in every direction, while everywhere were scattered the black yaks' hair tents of the

YAKS

Tibetan herdsmen who bring their herds and flocks to graze in these Sikhim highlands during three or four months in the year.

The change from Sikhim was in every way complete, there was no longer damp hot atmosphere and deep-cut valleys, the climate was dry and bracing, the hills gently undulating and the sky blue with perpetual sunshine, truly a marvellous change to find oneself at the end of a few miles' march in a country so closely resembling Tibet both in climate and appearance.

Just before crossing the Thi-la I was met by some yaks sent by the Maharaja's orders from his herds in the Lonak Valley, and on to these patient and sure-footed animals I transferred my baggage. This was my first experience of yak transport, and for these altitudes nothing can be better. Provided they are worked in moderation and given not too heavy a load, they will go on for months travelling at an even pace, and will cover from twenty to twenty-four miles a day, which is generally as far as one wishes to go. They are wonderfully sure-footed, will carry their rider up and down and over anything, and only on one occasion have I seen one lose its footing and that was on a comparatively good road. They are not uncomfortable mounts once you become accustomed to the grunting noise they make, which sends a curious vibration through you, and to the alarming appearance of the horns, which look as though, if they put their heads slightly back, it would be the easiest thing in the world to unseat you by putting one on either side below your knees. In appearance yaks are curious animals to look at, with a thick fringe of long hair hanging down under their bellies, huge bushy tails and a thick coat of hair, generally black and white, and holding their heads very low, so low that in riding them there is nothing in front of you. This unusual poise of the head has given rise to a pretty little fable which I think is worth repeating.

Long years ago the yak and the buffalo were on very

good terms and loved each other like brothers, but owing to the malevolence of some evil spirit, they fell out and parted company and the buffalo was banished to the plains. Now they long to meet again—the yak is always looking down to try and see his lost brother, while the buffalo is always casting his eyes upwards to the hills in the hope that he may see his old friend again. Any one who is familiar with the yak and the buffalo will appreciate this little tale.

Before I reached my camping ground I was met by a Tibetan official, the Jongpen from Khamba-jong, who told me very politely that I was in Tibet and must return by the way I had come. It was useless to point out to him that I was some miles within the Sikhim frontier, or even to read him that portion of the Treaty between our Government and the Tibetans which had recently been signed. He declared he knew nothing about that, and that the Thi-la was the proper boundary whatever the Treaty might say. Of course, I refused to return, but finally we came to a compromise, and I consented to turn to the east and to return over the Lungna-la into the Lachen Valley instead of exploring the Lonak Valley. I was obliged to give way to some extent, as my instructions from Government were particularly to avoid any open disagreement with the Tibetans. As soon as I had consented to do this, the Jongpen was much relieved, became most friendly and was always about my tents.

I stayed in the camp some days enjoying the rest, after my recent exertions, and the climate, which was perfect. There was a little shooting to be had and I wandered about with my gun very happily. Amongst other things, I came across a large warren of marmots, *Arctomys himalayanus*, the large Tibetan variety. These little animals are interesting to watch, and for such clumsy-looking brutes marvellously quick in their movements, disappearing into their holes like a flash when alarmed.

The only inhabitants of the valley are Tibetan herds-

UPPER LONAK VALLEY.

men who come during the summer months to graze their yaks and sheep. They were all very friendly and glad to give me shelter from the cold wind in their black yaks' hair tents, but it was a doubtful pleasure entering them, as these people are indescribably filthy. Some of the women were so thickly covered with dirt it was impossible to distinguish their hair under a plaster of grease and dirt, and the only thing apparently ever washed was the mouth, and that only when they drank their buttered tea.

A curious natural phenomenon was the increase in volume of the river soon after the sun rose, caused by the ice melting on the enormous glaciers in which it took its rise, which took place regularly at about the same time every day. The day I moved camp I was late in starting, and found the stream already in flood and consequently had some difficulty in crossing, and lost three of my sheep, which were washed down before aid could reach them.

I was sorry to leave Lonak, partly because I wanted to explore the valley thoroughly, and partly on account of the climate, as I knew that as soon as I crossed the pass I would again find myself in the damp regions of Sikhim, and my anticipations proved correct, as it rained before I reached my camping ground. From the top of the Lungna-la 17,400 feet, I had a fine view of Kangchenjunga and the snow peaks running to the north. To my astonishment, when I reached the top of the pass, the snow was covered with dead locusts strewn everywhere. I later found that India had been infested with flights of these insects and they had been blown up to the heights and perished in the cold. When in my descent I reached the line of vegetation, I found they had stripped the birches, the only leaves they seemed to care to eat, and there also they were in thousands, but dying fast.

From the Lungna-la to Thangu was an easy march, and on reaching Thangu I left all my heavy camp equipage and went down light to the village of Lamteng, the headquarters of the migratory inhabitants of the Lachen Valley, comprising about seventy-five houses. The people are herdsmen as well as traders, and move with their cattle up or down the valley according to the season, and as the summer months are the only ones during which the passes to Tibet are open for their merchandise, they are only to be found in Lamteng during the winter. One of the annual migrations down the valley is a curious sight to witness. In order to insure that no individual shall have the advantage of his neighbour in the matter of grazing, the whole population moves into Lamteng on the same day, bringing with them their entire families, all their yaks, ponies, cattle, goats, fowls, dogs and household goods, and on such a day it is safer to camp some little way off the road, as yaks are no respectors of persons and would soon have all the tents trampled on the ground.

On my way down the valley I had the luck to witness an enormous rock avalanche, the only one of any magnitude I have seen in Sikhim. It was a grand sight; the rocks came thundering down the hillside with tremendous velocity, many of them as large as a house, and dashed into the river at the bottom. I was exactly opposite the slip on the farther side of the valley in an absolutely safe position and could watch this very unusual phenomenon at my ease. My coolies were much alarmed, and I was not surprised, as it was in many ways a most awe-inspiring sight.

From Lamteng I returned to Thangu and went up to Giaogong where I was again met by Tibetan officials with the same story, that I could not be allowed to cross the boundary into Tibet, and that they knew nothing of the late Treaty. Much my easiest way would have been to follow the Lachen river to the Cholamo lakes, and then cross the Donkia-la into the Lachung Valley, but as this necessitated going through the disputed ground, I was obliged to take a more difficult route to the south of Kangchenjhau and then over the Sibu-la between Lachen and Lachung.

Giaogong was visited by Hooker in 1848 and again by Macaulay in 1886. It is a desolate, wind-swept spot lying in the centre of a gorge between Chomiomo, 23,000 feet, on the west and Kangchenjhau, 24,000 feet, on the east, and is a veritable funnel up which the wind is always howling. I managed, however, to find a fairly sheltered spot for my camp and stayed for a few days. On one I climbed the 18,221-feet hill to the west called Tunlo, and from the top I had a magnificent view over the north of Sikhim up to the rounded hills forming the watershed and the true boundary. Looked at from this elevation the scene is a most desolate one, truly typical of, and only to be found in, Tibet; with the exception of the valley immediately below me, nothing was under 18,000 feet, without a shrub, much less a tree, to be seen, and the wonder was how the large flocks of sheep scattered about, numbering perhaps 10,000 or 12,000, found enough grazing to keep them alive.

On leaving Giaogong, some distance to the south-east, where the rainfall is comparatively heavy, my route took me over some ancient moraines, now, after centuries of disintegration, a series of undulating downs called Phalung, covered with thick soft turf and dotted with the yaks and tents of the Lachen herdsmen. I also passed some good flocks of burhel on these moraines, one numbering about eighty. The glaciers running down from this range are comparatively small, although with the splendid backing of the perpendicular cliffs of Kangchenjhau they look imposing.

After crossing these downs, I camped at Sechuglaka and was detained there by bad weather, my coolies declaring the Sebu-la was impassable in soft snow. The pass is 17,600 feet and there is a small glacier which has to be crossed before reaching the summit, but this was negotiated with little difficulty; there were one or two small crevasses, but my men knew where they were and how to avoid them.

The summit of this pass is a knife-edge of rock so narrow that in places 20 feet to 30 feet below the top light can be seen through cracks in the rock, and along this narrow edge the track led for a short distance. The east side was nothing but a mass of rocks everywhere, which made travelling most difficult, and had these been covered with new snow I can quite imagine it being impassable, and I should never have got down without some broken limbs amongst my coolies, while as it was, even without the snow, it was anything but pleasant going.

Some years later, coming from Lachung, I crossed the pass with my wife and daughter. It was quite impossible either to ride up or to be carried in a dandy over such boulders, so they were carried on the backs of two of the strongest Lachung men, splendid specimens, with a chudder (native shawl) tied round them and over the men's shoulders, two other men helping, one on either side. How they managed to get over the rocks was a marvel, but they did it, and very quickly too, and were soon at the top.

After the first descent of half a mile or so the road was an easy one over and between old moraines, while to the left some fine glaciers came down from Kangchenjhau and Tsen-gui-kang.

My camp that night was close to the hot springs at Momay Samdong, mentioned by Hooker in his Himalayan Journals, with the water at a temperature of 160°. They are very unimportant, the flow of water is small, and they are seldom used now for bathing purposes.

From Momay Samdong I ascended the Donkia-la, 18,100 feet, and had a slendid view over the country to the north ; first the Cholamo lakes lying at the foot of the pass, then the rounded hills of the watershed and boundary, and further still the limestone ranges of Tibet. The view though desolate, was very fine, and I naturally longed to explore the unknown country beyond, but this was not to be till many years had passed, so I had reluctantly to turn my back and descend again into the valleys of Sikhim, but before reaching Momay, I explored to the east and discovered an easy pass leading into Tibet which is occasionally used by graziers.

There is some very fine burhel ground on the hills on each side of the valley running from the Donkia to Momay, especially to the east, where I saw some of the biggest herds I have come across, and I think any one really going in for shooting might secure a record head here. It was near this that Dr. Pearse shot one measuring 29¾ inches and I believe the record is 30¼ inches. The shooting, however, along all the Sikhim hills, is very disappointing and most difficult, owing principally to climatic conditions, for in the rains, just as the sportsman is stalking the game, a cloud may and often does, suddenly come along and blot out everything, which, to say the least of it, is most annoying, while in the fine weather at the end of October and November the cold is intense and there is always the danger of being caught by the snow.

On leaving Momay Samdong I did not go straight down the valley, but turned to the east up Temba-chhu and explored up to the glacier, but the weather was bad and I saw very little. I then turned to the south and crossed an unknown pass, 17,700 feet, which led over the range dividing the Lachung and Sebu valleys. It was a grey day when we started and soon commenced to snow and continued to snow the whole day. The snow was very deep and very soft, often up to my armpits, and the going was very difficult, especially for the laden coolies, for although I had sent the greater part of my heavy baggage straight to the Lachung village, I still had a good deal with me. We toiled on for hours and at last reached the summit. The snow was still falling and we floundered down till we came to a flat bit of ground, evidently the bed of an old lake, and here I decided to halt for the night.

Experience teaches, and I certainly had a lesson that day I could well have done without, and which I am not likely to forget. The day was so dull and grey it never struck me there could be any ill effects from the light on the snow, and though I had my snow spectacles in my pocket I did not put them on and felt no ill effects until after my arrival in camp, when my eyes began to smart and I soon could see nothing, and realised that I was in for a bad attack of snow blindness. I passed a wretched night, and when morning came I could not open my eyes and was obliged to lie where I was in bed. I had only a small single fly tent, it was raining hard, very cold, and everything was most uncomfortable. My bearer Diboo brought me my food and practically had to feed me, for I could see nothing. This total blindness lasted for two days, but by the third morning I could see a little, and by carefully shading my eyes, I was able to get down to the forest limit and out of the intense glare. I found that at least one-third of my coolies were in a similar condition, so I was not the only sufferer. The pain in the eyes in snow blindness is very acute indeed, and it was a sharp lesson which I have never forgotten. My men suggested several remedies, none of which were very pleasant, so I contented myself with placing cold wet handkerchiefs on my eyes, which I constantly changed. There was little trouble in doing this, as I had only to hold my handkerchief against the fly of the tent to wet it, and I dare say it was the best thing I could have done. Years later, I learnt a very simple and certain remedy for snow blindness which I have since used on several occasions with excellent effect for coolies who had neglected to cover their eyes when crossing snow. It is to drop a few drops of castor oil into the eyes and the relief is almost instantaneous.

Lepcha and Tibetan coolies when crossing the passes use spectacles made of very finely woven hair, and if by chance they do not have them, they bring their own hair, which is always rather long, over their faces, and this makes a very good veil. I have often seen them do it when suddenly caught in a snowstorm amongst the mountains. It is only quite newly fallen snow that has such a speedy effect on the eyes, and I believe it must be the actinic rays from the extremely white snow that causes it. Old snow will also cause blindness when it has the full force of a tropical sun shining on it, but is not nearly so quick in its action.

From this somewhat dreary camp it did not take us long to descend into the pine forests, and we camped at a place called Sebu in the midst of silver firs. I had been for six or seven weeks high up above all vegetation except grass, and the change to the forest was welcome, especially as the weather was again fine. This continued as I marched down the valley, a lovely one with some of the finest trees there are in Sikhim growing in it. One fallen giant, a spruce, that I measured, was 220 feet from the roots to where it was broken off short, and there it measured 6 feet in girth. What had become of the top I do not know, but it was a magnificent specimen. The road was easy the whole way and delightfully soft to walk on, as it was carpeted with moss and pine needles. This valley, the Sebu, would delight the heart of an artist; there are soft glades with streams wandering quietly through them, splendid forests of pine with beetling crags in every direction and glimpses of snow up every side valley. I often wish I could have painted some of these scenes, for my photographs do not do them justice, as they give no idea of the varied and exquisite colouring.

I joined the main Lachung Valley at Yac-cha, some four miles above the village of Lachung, where I was met by the Phodong Lama, and where we remained some time transacting business with the headmen of the valley.

The two villages of Lamteng in the Lachen and Lachung in the Lachung Valley have an unusual and almost communistic government of their own. On every occasion the whole population meet at a "panchayat," or council, where they sit in a ring in consultation. Nothing, however small, is done without such a meeting, even if it was only to supply me with firewood or to tell off a man to carry water. Everything is settled at these meetings, any business there may be is transacted, and everything from the choosing of their own headman to the smallest detail is arranged in consultation. The consequence is, everything is done very deliberately and much time is wasted in useless discussion, but the system seems to suit the people and I allowed it to be continued with some small modifications. When transport is required, the panchayat sits to select the coolies, and after that is done there is a curious custom of drawing lots for each man's load gone through. Each one gives a garter to the headman, who puts them all together in the inside of his boku or outer garment. He then goes round to the loads, drawing out a garter and placing one on each load, and the owner of the garter has to carry that load. This is all a little tiresome when one is anxious to be off, but once the formalities have been gone through, the loads are picked up and quickly carried away without another word. The people of these valleys are a particularly nice lot, jolly and bright and of splendid physique. I have travelled with them often and never had the least trouble. They are of Tibetan origin, but came into Sikhim from Hah in Bhutan. Lachung itself is a beautifully situated village of about eighty houses, with enormous cliffs overhanging it on the opposite side of the valley, and it is not very wet—probably about fifty inches of rain in the year—and with an elevation of nearly 9,000 feet, it has a delightful summer climate.

Between Chungtang and Lachung there is probably as good gural (Himalayan chamois) shooting as anywhere, and I managed to get some excellent sport on the cliffs immediately above Lachung, though it was very difficult climbing, but with the help of one of the villagers I succeeded in getting up and bagged three or four. I saw many more, but it was not possible to get within shot.

At Lachung a valley comes down from the Tanka-la, and up this, very good burhel shooting is to be had,

TYPICAL SIKHIM SCENERY

especially in the winter months, when the animals come down to graze.

I marched slowly back to Gangtak accompanied by the Phodong Lama, and was not sorry to arrive there after an absence of eleven weeks. We had work to do in every camp, and that and the state of the track necessitated short marches ; the paths were so bad it was only with the greatest difficulty any four-footed animal could be taken over them. Now there is a good road the whole way from Gangtak to Lachung, and the distances can easily be covered in two days, while at that time a week was the quickest it could be done in.

CHAPTER X

EXPEDITIONS AND EXPLORATIONS IN SIKHIM—*continued*

Demarcation of the northern boundary between Sikhim and Tibet. Difficulties of transport. Mountain sickness. Survey work. Caught in a storm. Durkey Sirdar. Ovis ammon. Photographing the glaciers. A ride at 21,600 feet. Evidence of former size of the glaciers.

My exploration of the northern boundary between Sikhim and Tibet was undertaken in 1902 under very different circumstances to my other explorations. The object on this occasion was, under instructions from the Viceroy, to lay down the boundary between the two countries as defined by the Tibet Treaty of 1890.

I took with me an escort of the 8th Gurkhas under command of Captain Murray and Lieutenant Coleridge, with an officer in medical charge, and Major Iggulden accompanied me as Intelligence officer.

We left Gangtak on June 15. It was my first experience of entire dependence upon local resources for the transport of so large a body of men, as well as their rations and other impedimenta, and I had some difficulty to commence with, especially at Tumlong, where the populace is very scattered, in finding a sufficient number of men and animals, and I was obliged to halt to collect them. In addition, the weather was abominable, rain coming down in torrents and wetting the tents through and thereby enormously increasing their weight. But after a short delay I got everything off and followed myself the next day. Major Iggulden caught me up just before I reached the Samatek Bungalow, wet through, and we were very glad to get into its shelter and to dry our clothes. I continued to have difficulty with transport until we reached Lamteng in the Lachen Valley, where we could get yaks, and then my troubles ended. Travelling in these very sparsely populated valleys, where only coolie transport is available, has many difficulties when a large party has to be moved. Above Lamteng the road is much easier, the gradients are better and the hot steamy valleys are left behind. Yaks, if properly treated, make excellent beasts of burden and throughout the trip I had no difficulty with them; they even crossed almost inaccessible passes with remarkable ease, and it was quite wonderful to see them picking their way through ice and snow where it was difficult even for a man to find a foothold.

After spending some days at Thangu, where I left half the escort under Lieutenant Coleridge as a reserve, and after sending on ahead rations, firewood, &c., we started for the higher lands and camped the first night at Gochung at an elevation of about 14,500 feet. I have always found from 14,000 feet to 15,000 feet a critical height in climbing, and men often feel the effects more at this elevation than higher up; also if they do not feel the height then, they are unlikely to feel it much, even at very much higher elevations. Many of the escort fell out, suffering from mountain sickness and violent headaches, nothing would induce them to go on, and they were so bad next morning we were obliged to send them back. All these men were Nepalese hill men and ought not to have felt the height at all. After this weeding out, although I took several to an elevation of over 20,000 feet, and two of them to 21,600 feet, not a man fell out.

The next day we moved on to Giaogong, a point in the Lachen Valley lying within the boundary, and claimed by the Tibetans. According to the Sikhim-Tibet Treaty of 1890, the boundary between the two countries is defined as the watershed of the river Teesta and its tributaries, and as Giaogong lies some eight to nine miles south of the watershed, it was difficult to see on what grounds the Tibetans claimed it, and it was in order to settle the disputed question and to finally demarcate the boundary, as defined in the Treaty, that I had come.

My plan was to traverse personally the whole disputed line from east of the Donkia-la to the head of the Lonak Valley. This was not a very easy undertaking as in one place only did the line come as low as a pass of 17,700 feet, while all the other passes were very much higher. We found it possible to march along the boundary, from a point north of Panhunri to a point just north of Chomiomo, across rolling downs rising to 19,000 feet, but for the remaining distance it was only possible to reach the boundary at a few scattered points on high and very inaccessible passes. My explorations to ascertain exactly where the watershed—the proper boundary—actually lay, commenced from Giaogong.

From the camp I made for the west, for the ridge running north from Chomiomo, accompanied by Iggulden and Mr. Dover and a few Gurkha orderlies. We rode as far as we could and then had to dismount to negotiate a very steep climb before reaching the ridge. Before we had gone very far, Iggulden was attacked by such a severe mountain headache he was obliged to return to camp. I went on, and on reaching the ridge, turned south towards Chomiomo and eventually reached a height of 20,700 feet, where I was stopped by ice and snow and also by the advancing day from going further.

At this elevation I sat down and ate my lunch. It was a magnificent afternoon and the view over Tibet was glorious. Khamba-jong was distinctly visible and also the Everest Group. The power of the sun's rays at this height and in the very clear atmosphere was extraordinary, and I have never before or since felt it in the same way. I was obliged to keep my hands in the shade of my sun helmet, for, though they are very hard, I could not stand the heat and was afraid of being blistered. But there is something very exhilarating in these high altitudes, the tremendous expanse of snow around gives a feeling of freedom not experienced at lower elevations, while there is always a fascination in arriving at a summit of a mountain, particularly when the unknown is on the other side. After sitting for some time drinking in the delightfully fresh atmosphere and admiring the view, we reluctantly started down the ridge on our return to camp by a somewhat roundabout way, but one which appeared a little easier. We had not gone far, however, before the weather changed, clouds came up and in a few minutes it began to snow with a light wind; this soon changed into a blizzard, and we had the greatest difficulty in reaching the camp, where we did not arrive till long after the dinner hour. It was a very nasty walk in the dark in the teeth of blinding snow over unknown country. Murray and Iggulden were getting anxious and thinking of sending out search parties, but they had no idea from which direction I would come. A change to dry clothes and some dinner was very acceptable.

Next morning everything was a sheet of snow, which luckily soon melted in the sun, but it had been a cold night for the sentries. I was expecting some of the Tibetan officials to come along the disputed boundary, and soon heard that they had arrived at the Sebu-la and were on the way to my camp. I was also informed that the Lhasa Government had sent as one of their representatives a man named Durkey Sirdar, a Darjeeling rascal, who had been obliged to fly to Tibet to escape the attentions of the police. The Tibetans gave as their reason for sending him that he "knew our ways." Of course, I absolutely refused to have any dealings with the man, and gave orders he was not to be allowed to enter the camp, and told the Tibetans I could have no dealings with them until they sent a proper representative. I mention this incident to show the curious methods on which the Tibetans work. I have no doubt Durkey, who was a clever scoundrel, had impressed the very stupid Tibetan officials in Lhasa, but it was extraordinary they should believe that a man of his character, which they knew, would be accepted by us as their representative. Durkey held a minor post under the Tibetans in Yatung, and on my visits I had invariably refused to receive him, and our Government ought never to have allowed him to remain there.

From Giaogong I moved camp to Gyamtso-na, a lake about four miles up the valley. It was a very exposed and cold camp, but no better or more sheltered place was to be found. From this camp I surveyed the boundary from Chomiomo, working east. It was bitterly cold work for the native surveyors who had to take theodolite readings at elevations up to 20,000 feet. All the work had to be done by day, and during the day, and all day, the wind blew a small gale, it never stopped for a moment till the sun went down, and then mercifully we nearly always had quiet nights, but only to have the same howling wind next day. It commenced as early as eight o'clock and was never later than ten-thirty. It was a veritable curse, and I was often glad to lie down in some hollow or to crouch behind stones so as to be out of it even for a few minutes.

Murray stayed in camp with his escort, but Iggulden always came with me and we had some fine rides over the wind-swept heights. There was not much game to be seen, but we generally managed to get a Tibetan antelope or a brace of Tibetan sand-grouse, and occasionally we came across a solitary male kyang. They are pretty creatures, but shy when not in herds, and they generally made off in a bee line for the plains in Tibet across the border.

On one of our rides we were lucky enough to come across some fine male ovis ammon. Iggulden saw them first up a side valley, so we divided, he going up one ravine and I up another. I had crawled most carefully for quite 1½ miles, seeing no signs of them, and was crouching behind

NUNS FROM TA-TSHANG NUNNERY

a rock, having almost given them up, when suddenly the whole seven charged past me not thirty yards off. I knocked over two and hit a third, when my rifle jammed and I could do nothing except watch the remainder make off into Tibet. I only succeeded in picking up one of those I hit, where the other got to I never knew. A little later we came upon the flock of females, who were quite tame and did not mind us, but of course we left them alone.

I afterwards found that there were one or two flocks that remained permanently in the valley, and even in the summer, when the Tibetans drive their flocks of sheep up to these heights to graze, they do not leave.

What a flock of 1500 to 2000 sheep could find to eat in these parts was a marvel. Casually looking at the ground you would say there was no grass on it, but on close examination a few blades appeared. To watch the flock grazing on these few and scanty blades was a curious sight. The sheep literally run over the ground, those in front eating and those behind running on ahead to find an ungrazed spot. In spite of this, the sheep at this season fatten quickly and are excellent eating, which proves that the sparse pasturage provides a great deal of nourishment.

From this point almost the only habitation visible was the Nunnery of Ta-tshang which stood out against a limestone hill and across an apparently enormous plain. We often wished to visit it, but of course could not cross the boundary, though I subsequently did visit it when encamped at Khamba-jong with the Tibet Mission in 1903. That was a red-letter day to these poor creatures who live here always with not a single other habitation in sight. They are grossly ignorant, and live in absolute filth, but they are good-natured and the abbess has a good face. The photograph shows them wearing a curious woollen head-dress, as their own heads are shaved.

Our next camp, Yeum-tsho, was in a much more congenial spot, lying right behind Kangchenjhau and sheltered from the south-west monsoon and winds, and consequently dry. It was situated on a flat sandy plain with a river meandering through it and with many round pools, surrounded by rushes. It was an interesting camp—ducks of many varieties were breeding in these little pools, and the sandy plain was covered with larks' nests, while the old moraine terraces were full of marmots and hares. There were also a good many foxes and I saw one wolf. Another day, climbing along a ridge of moraine about six miles from camp, I came across a Tibetan lynx with two cubs. I fired at the lynx, but missed it, and they all three got into inaccessible holes amongst the stones and I saw no more of them. It was a handsome animal and no doubt lived well on both the wild and tame sheep in the vicinity.

A round hill to the north above the camp was also the run of a flock of ovis ammon. The whole hill was lined with their tracks, and they would come out in the evenings and look down on the camp, but they were all females with not a head amongst them.

Our doctor was a hopeless individual, who hated being at this elevation and loathed the cold, and I could not induce him to do anything. He would not even attempt to collect plants, butterflies, birds or geological specimens —generally lay in bed until the bugle sounded for meals, when he turned up only to go to bed again till the next meal. It seemed a terrible waste of opportunities, and greatly to be deplored, that on an occasion like this a better selection could not have been made. Any number of keen young officers would have given a great deal to be allowed to accompany me, and would have thoroughly appreciated so unique an experience, and it seems extraordinary that such an officer was not sent.

While I was encamped here I received formal visits from the small Chinese official stationed at Giri, and also from the officials from Tashi Lhunpo, who came to pay their respects.

I again moved camp to near the Cholamo lakes, a more exposed position on account of the keen high wind blowing across the Donkia-la, but it was more convenient for my work. The Khamba Jongpen paid me a visit soon after my arrival.

I left the escort in this camp for a few days and moved with Iggulden, and very light loads, to a higher camp at an elevation of 18,600 feet. We pitched our tents on the lateral moraine above the magnificent glacier from which the river Teesta springs. This is one of the most beautiful glaciers I have ever seen, with its magnificent sweep down from the perpetual snows. It also shows the stratification of the ice most clearly almost the whole way down.

I waited for hours to get a good photograph, and in the end I was successful, although I was nearly frozen in the attempt. The wind swept down the glacier and was most bitterly cold and with it some light clouds kept blowing almost continuously across the glacier from a small gap on the left, and I had to wait for a clear moment. The result, however, repaid me for my trouble.

Next day Iggulden and I started out to climb a snow peak which looked like the watershed at the head of the valley. We rode our mules and got on well till we came to almost the last rise, when it became so steep we had to dismount. The mountain side was not only very steep, but a mass of loose rounded stones, and very difficult for the mules, so Iggulden left his behind. I, however, stuck to mine, and was able to ride up the last 500 or 600 yards, which were comparatively flat. The peak proved to be 21,600 feet high, and I fancy few people have ridden a mule at that elevation. The sun was terribly hot during our climb as we were ascending the southern face, and also there was a tremendous glare off a huge snow field coming down from Panhunri.

At some remote period, the whole valley, lying between us and Panhunri, must have been filled with ice, as by no other means could the hill opposite have been covered, as it is, with gneiss moraine *débris*, the mountain itself being shale.

All along these mountains there is everywhere evidence of the former enormous size of all these glaciers, both on the north and south. To the north, moraine *débris* is found fifteen to twenty miles within Tibet, and boulders of gneiss are found on limestone hills with nothing now but huge flat plains between them and the peaks of the Himalayas. To the south, along all the valleys, old lateral moraines extend for many miles and in many places are quite distinct, 1000 feet to 1500 feet above the present river level. It seems almost impossible to take in the fact that these valleys were once filled with ice, or to imagine what these mountains were like in former days, as the moraine *débris* now showing, would by itself form mountains as high as those we have in England without taking into account the enormous quantites of silt carried down by the rivers during these ages.

The rainfall in these parts is very heavy, and this very great alteration in the glaciers can, I suppose, only be accounted for by the gradual change of temperature, although theoretically, in accordance with the scientific opinion held by many authorities, that the Himalayas are still being elevated by the contraction of the earth's surface, the mountains must in those days have been more massive if individual peaks were not higher. From this point we had a splendid view of the Bam-tsho and Yeum-tsho lakes, of which I had known for some years, but had not seen before, with Chomolhari in the background, standing up splendidly against the blue sky. The panorama of interminable ranges in Tibet was also very impressive, although gloomy, and I wished I could march into the then forbidden land.

The survey of this portion of the boundary finished, I returned to Thangu in order to reach the Lonak valley *viâ* the Nangna-la. It was a very roundabout, and very difficult route, and took several days longer than if I had

LONAK VALLEY

gone direct to the Naku-la, crossing a small portion of Tibet, but as I was debarred from entering Tibet, I had to make the best of the bad track.

I reconnoitred the Nangna-la and found it deep in snow, with large snow cornices on the western side, where the snow lay deep to nearly the bottom of the valley. At the best of times the pass is a difficult one, especially for yak transport, as the descent is over a succession of terraces which were covered with snow and exceedingly dangerous. At this time of year the snow was, of course, melting, and yaks cannot travel over soft snow. However, we were obliged to go on, and taking as many coolies as I could muster to help us, we set out. The ascent was comparatively easy, but soon our difficulties commenced. On reaching the pass, the snow cornices had to be cut away to make a passage for the yaks, and the soft snow on the west side had to be trampled down to enable them to go over it. It was a wonderful sight to see the loaded animals cleverly negotiate these huge steps, and they eventually got down, somewhat late, but with no mishap. It was a difficult climb even for a man, and in one place I came upon the doctor, very miserable, who had got himself into rather a tight corner, and with some trouble I got him out of his difficult position and down some rather nasty smooth, slippery rocks, when he cheered up a little.

We pitched our camp at Teble, again in a dry climate, but I did not remain long there, but moved on to Pashi which, lying further up the valley, was more convenient for survey work. While surveying and exploring the valley and its offshoots, I discovered many lakes of glacial origin, in one place a fine chain of five, called the Kora-tsho.

There were numbers of burhel (*Ovis nahura*) in this valley, but no ovis ammon, and very little else, with the exception of marmots, of which there were some large warrens, and a few duck and solitary snipe on the marshes, in the beds of the old partly silted-up lakes.

By this time I had again left behind me the undulating

hills so characteristic of parts of Tibet and was again to the south of the main Himalayan range. The peaks in this part of the boundary are magnificent, and all the way up the valley of the Lungpo-chhu the scenery is splendid. To the north lies the chain of hills which bound Sikhim, and to the south the magnificent peak of Kangchenjunga, with the range running from it to the north, which, combined with the huge glaciers coming down on all sides makes up a splendid picture which is not easy to surpass in any other part of the world.

From my camp in the Lungpo-chhu I went up to the Chorten Nema-la, a difficult pass, but occasionally used by Tibetan graziers bringing their flocks and herds to graze in this valley. The southern side is a scree for some thousands of feet, and the northern is a glacier, and I should think a difficult one to climb. It was a very weird spot, and the pinnacles of bare rock starting out of the snow on the top of the pass gave it a very wild and most distinctive character.

One of my most interesting journeys from this camp was to the head of the valley. This I found filled by an enormous glacier which I suddenly came upon looming out of the mist, a sheer wall of perpendicular ice some forty to fifty feet high. I managed to climb this in one place, and went for some miles along the top, which was almost quite flat, but the weather was bad, and it commenced to snow, and I had to retrace my footsteps. Unfortunately I never had the time or opportunity to explore further up. Coming suddenly upon these glaciers on a misty day, they look very weird, standing out in ghostlike shapes, the stratification of the ice adding to their peculiar appearance. In sunlight they are quite different and look very beautiful, as the colouring in the ice is then seen to perfection. Once, while exploring down the glacier, I came upon the most beautiful sight I have ever seen. The glacier was cut up into a succession of huge ice waves and looked exactly like an angry sea suddenly frozen solid. The ice hummocks were

GLACIAL LAKE, LONAK VALLEY.

in many places fifty to sixty feet high, and between them were the most enchanting ice lakes of an exquisite turquoise blue, while the colours in the surrounding ice varied, as the sun's rays caught it, in all shades of deep blue, green, violet, and almost prismatic colours in places. Some of these little lakes might have been in fairy-land they were so lovely, and my photograph cannot do them justice, as it only produces the colour in shades of black and white.

As I could only demarcate certain accessible points on this part of the boundary, I soon finished my work and returned to Thangu, to find that Coleridge had been working hard during my absence on the road leading towards Nangna-la and had made quite a passable path. I only remained a few days in Thangu, just long enough to settle accounts and to pay the head men of the district for transport, &c., and then returned to Gangtak, having completed the object for which I had been sent on the expedition.

CHAPTER XI

DEPARTURE FROM SIKHIM

UNDER the rules of the Public Works Department to which I was originally appointed when I came to India, I had to retire, on reaching the age of fifty-five, in October 1908. In many ways I was glad to return to England, and looked forward to the prospect of enjoying a little leisure after my thirty-two years of almost continuous service, as, during that time, I had only been on leave for one year and five months. Again, in other ways I would have been glad to remain for a short time longer, as the time was a critical one for both Sikhim and Bhutan, and required some one at the head of affairs with an intimate knowledge of the various outs and ins, and side-issues inseparable from the administration of a native State. I had not even the satisfaction of knowing I was leaving matters in the hands of an officer whom I had trained to the special necessities of the case, as I have never had an officer deputed as my general assistant, although for years I have corresponded with Government on the subject. The assistants I did have, Messrs. O'Connor, Bailey, and Campbell, were each in turn placed in charge of Tibetan and Trade affairs and had nothing whatever to do with Bhutan and Sikhim. Quite apart from the fact that, as the work and responsibility had increased so enormously, it was impossible for one man to carry it on properly, it was bad policy not to have some one ready to fill my place should I wish to go on leave or in case of illness or breakdown. If you consider that single-handed I had to deal, in Sikhim alone, with the various departments which in other districts are placed, each in charge of a special officer and staff, Police, Revenue, Forests, Education, Excise, Agriculture, Public Works, Judicial, Administrative, in addition to the whole of the Tibetan and Bhutan correspondence and negotiations, it is not surprising I applied for an assistant officer, but the Government of India considered my request superfluous, and I had to manage as best I could with my office staff under Mr. Hodges the superintendent and the services of a State engineer. Mr. Hodges served under me for eighteen years, and the office was always in a state of efficiency and good order, while I was exceptionally fortunate in my two engineers, Mr. Dover, who accompanied Mr. Douglas Freshfield on his journey to the snows, and later Mr. Hickley, than whom one could not find a more energetic and painstaking officer.

The time was critical for Sikhim in several ways: the industries I had introduced, apple growing, cloth weaving, carpet manufacture, still required careful fostering, while the mining industry was barely in its infancy. The Maharaja and Maharani had at last been aroused and were keen to improve their country, but perhaps the most serious matter was the approaching return of the Maharaj Kumar, who had spent a couple of years in England and part of the time at Pembroke College, Oxford. Relations had never been quite satisfactory between him and the Maharaja, partly, I think, owing to his jealousy of the influence exercised over his father by his stepmother, the present Maharani, and at this juncture more than ever a strong hand was needed in addition to full sympathy with the lad and an intimate knowledge of former events, and I fear my successor has a difficult task before him.

In Bhutan new relations, which, at the risk of being considered conceited, I must I am afraid put down as greatly personal to myself, had been opened up after many years of complete isolation, and the Maharaja was full of schemes for the improvement and betterment of his country, and I would have given a great deal to see him put on his way before leaving.

As soon as they realised the time for my departure was drawing appreciably near, the Maharajas and people of both countries sent petitions signed by all members of the community to the Viceroy, praying for an extension of my services, and when the first petition was rejected, they appealed more than once against the decision, and the Maharaja and Maharani of Sikhim travelled to Calcutta and personally made their request to Lord Minto.

Had the Viceroy's answer to the petition been favourable, I might have remained on for a year or two more, but my health had begun to fail, and the hard work and exposure to tell on me, and I was really anxious to return to England, so in April, 1908, I took leave preparatory to retirement, and was succeeded by Mr. Bell, I.C.S.

For weeks before my departure the house was besieged by the people from far and near, all anxious to bid me good-bye, or to ask some special favour before I gave up the reins of office. I knew them all and their affairs, their family histories, their small quarrels, and their ambitions, and they always came freely to me for advice and redress, knowing I was always accessible and would not refuse to see any one, Lepcha, Bhutia, or Paharia. I knew their ways and they trusted and liked me, and never thought of withholding anything from me, and in consequence a mutual confidence and affection had sprung up between us which made the parting hard. I was leaving a people I loved, and in whose service I had spent the best years of my life, and they felt they were losing a trusted friend on whom they had learnt to rely.

At last the time came for my final departure, everything was packed and despatched to England, and the house stood bare and dismantled, but the garden and flowers were more beautiful than usual. But we were not to leave even that behind us, for on the last afternoon a terrific hailstorm came on, the worst I have ever experienced in these hills, and before nightfall not a vestige of blossom or leaf was left. It sounds an exaggeration, but many of the hailstones were the size of golf-balls and weighed two and three ounces. When morning came the trees stood up bare and wintry against the sky without a leaf; tree-ferns, rose-bushes, everything, were nothing but leafless stems where twenty-four hours before there had been a wealth of blossom. Even the lawns were pitted all over by the force of the hailstones. The conservatory, built of ¼-inch-thick ribbed glass, which had stood all former storms, was smashed to atoms, and so were the lights in the verandahs. The Maharaja and Maharani were with us at the time, and exclaimed that the gods were showing their displeasure at my departure, an opinion endorsed by all the natives.

So it was a scene of sad desolation to which we bid good-bye next morning, as, accompanied by the Maharaja, and preceded by the pipers of Mr. Hickley's Sikhim Pioneers, we took our way down the hill for the last time, with the whole populace lining the roads to bid us godspeed and filling the air with lamentations.

Throughout the journey the same scene was enacted, the headmen and villagers of every village we passed coming out to kiss my feet and weep over me, and I was glad when we were at last in the train at Ghoom.

The night before I left Gangtak I received no less than two coolie-loads of letters from Sir Ugyen Wang-chuk and his family, and from all the Bhutan officials, both great and small, expressing the hope that I would some day return and visit them as a private individual if I could no longer come officially. Rai Ugyen Kazi Bahadur and his sister met us below Kurseong with Bhutanese refreshments of tea and fruit, laid out by the roadside for the last time, and we parted with many expressions of mutual goodwill, while Rai Harri Das Bahadur, Lambodar, Luchmi Narain, and all the leading Paharias saw me actually into the train.

The different communities subscribed to present me with farewell addresses, which under the Government rules I was unable to accept until after my retirement, and they were sent to me in England later on.

And so ended my twenty years' connection with the little State of Sikhim; but I still hope some day, should my health allow of it, to revisit both Sikhim and Bhutan, in which countries and amongst whose people I have spent so many happy years and whose people I have grown to love.

CHAPTER XII

HISTORY OF THE FOUNDING OF BHUTAN

THE early history of this remarkable country is enveloped in great obscurity, for unfortunately, owing to fire, earthquake, flood, and internecine wars, its annals, which had been carefully recorded, were destroyed. The burning of Poonakha in 1832 and the widespread destruction of buildings by the earthquake of 1897 were particularly noticeable in this connection. The latter disaster is responsible for the almost total destruction of the library of the present Tongsa Penlop, only a few MSS., from which I have gathered some information, having escaped. Their great printing establishment at Sonagachi was burnt down about eighty years ago.

The earliest legend we hear of is that one Sangaldip, emerging from the environs of Kooch (whether from Bhutan or Assam is obscure), subdued the countries of Bengal and Behar, fighting against Raja Kedur of Lakhnante, or Gaur, and was in his turn defeated by Piran-Visah, general of Afrasiab, King of Turan, or Tartary. This was about the seventh century before the Christian era.

We next hear that in the middle of the eighth century A.D. the Indian saint Padma Sambhava converted Bhutan to the Buddhist faith. The chief rúlers at that time were the Khiji-khar-thod of Khempalung, in Upper Pumthang, and Naguchhi, King of Sindhu. The site of the latter's palace, Chagkhar Gome (the iron fort without doors), is still visible. Naguchhi, the second son of King Singhala of Serkhya, founded the kingdom of Sindhu, while his sons extended his realm to Dorji-Tag and Hor in Tibet and as far as Sikhim. In the course of a war with Raja Nabudara, who lived in the plains of India, the eldest son was killed, and Naguchhi was consequently plunged into grief. It was at this juncture that the saint Padma arrived on the scene, and with the aid of the king's daughter, Menmo Jashi Kyeden, who possessed the twenty-one marks of fairy beauty, restored the king to happiness and saved his soul. The struggle with the demons lasted for seven days, and at the end of that week marks of the saint's body appeared in the solid rock. The legend further goes on to say that the fir-tree growing beside the cave was the alpenstock of the saint, who, like St. Joseph at Glastonbury, made the stick to grow. Naguchhi appears to have been a second King Solomon, as it is recorded that all the most beautiful women of India and Tibet were taken to wife by the king, and that they numbered a hundred in all.

The rival King Nabudara was also converted to Buddhism by the saint, and peace was restored to the land, and a boundary pillar set up at Mna-tong. This kingdom, however, lasted only another hundred years, and was destroyed by Tibetan hordes in the time of Lan-darma, the apostate King of Tibet, who reigned about the years 861–900 A.D. Some two centuries later Bhutan was occupied by the followers of King Tiral-chan.

The subsequent fate of Bhutan is wholly connected with the origin and the spread of the Dukpa sect, founded by Yeses Dorji at Ralung. Yeses, or Gro-Gong-Tshangpa-Gyal-ras, was born in 1160 and died in 1210 A.D.

A young lama from China came to his successor, Sangye-on, and was given the name of Fago-Duk-gom-Shigpo. After studying at Ralong for some years he was sent to Bhutan, and settled at Cheri Dordam, where he lived with his wife and family. His fame soon spread, and aroused the jealousy of Lhapha, a rival lama already resident in

Bhutan. Quarrels arose, and Lhapha, after an unsuccessful attack on Cheri, was totally defeated, and had to fly. In his flight he came to the Am-mo-chhu Valley, where he was warmly received by the villagers, who submitted to him. Lhapha, however, treacherously betrayed them to the Tibetans, who thereupon seized the valley. Lhapha's settlement is recognised in the valley to this day.

Having got rid of his rival, Duk-gom's power increased greatly, and the conversion of the Bhutanese to Buddhism was further assisted by the advent of four other lamas, who belonged, however, to different sects, and were not Dukpas. But although so many saints visited Bhutan and settled there, founding temples and monasteries, yet they only served as heralds to symbolise or portray the final auspicious advent of the peerless Dukpa Rimpochi, Nawang Du-gom Dorji, who brought Bhutan under one ruling power and control.

Du-gom Dorji, better known as Shabdung Nawang Mamgyel, was the son of Dorji Lenpa Mepham Tempai Nymia, a man of noble lineage, by the daughter of Deba Kyishöpa, and showed remarkable intellectual precocity; even as a child his carvings were marvellous in beauty and symmetry of workmanship. The date of his birth is supposed to be 1534 A.D. He studied under the Dukpa lama, Padma Karpo, at Ralong, and bid fair to succeed to the Hierarch's chair; but a rival claimant, Kerma Tenkgong Wangpo, backed by Deba Tsang-pa, was too strong for him, so the Shabdung, in disgust, started on a long pilgrimage, and finally entered Bhutan by the Lingzi Pass in 1557 A.D., in his twenty-third year, and lived to be fifty-eight. During these thirty-five years he was continuously engaged in warfare and in consolidating his temporal as well as his spiritual power. The opposition of the Deba Tsang-pa, of the Ralong Hierarch, and of the descendants of the four lamas mentioned before constantly involved him in serious fighting. The Tibetans five or six times attempted unsuccessfully to conquer Bhutan, and even penetrated as far as Simtoka, but each time were driven back or captured *en masse*. The booty obtained from the vanquished greatly increased the wealth of the Shabdung Rimpochi, whose fame spread to India and as far as Ladakh. Raja Padma Narayan of Cooch Behar sought his friendship and sent presents, as did Drabya Sahi and Purandar Sahi of Nepal.

It was at this time that some foreigners from a distant country beyond the ocean called Parduku (Portugal) brought some guns and gunpowder of a new sort and a telescope, and offered their services, which were, however, refused, as to accept them would have been against the religious principles of true Buddhism.

Most of the big monasteries and forts date from his reign, although few of them have escaped fire and earthquake. Practically Simtoka, first built in 1570, but rebuilt in 1572, after its recapture from the insurgents, is the only building now existing in its original form. Perhaps the next oldest is Paro-jong, originally started as a school of medicine, but burnt down in 1907. All other buildings have either been rebuilt or enlarged. Poonakha was founded in 1577, and designed to accommodate 600 monks. The Dharma Raja, when remonstrated with for planning such an enormous house, replied that the building would in time be found much too small. When I was there in 1905 there were at least 1500 monks in residence. Angduphodang was begun in 1578, and Tashi-cho-jong in 1581, and the Shabdung's quarters still exist in the western end of the fort at Tongsa.

The lama Du-gom Dorji was something of a humorist. During the rejoicings at a notable victory over the Tibetans at Poonakha he was asked if he thought it likely they would return or send any more expeditions against Bhutan. He replied: " Oh, there is no assurance they will not come again, but as they never do any harm to us it will be all right. This time we have a sufficiency of armour and weapons; we will in future indent for some tea and silks." The saying subsequently turned out to be a prophecy.

To quote the Tibetan chronicler: "In the intervals of peace the Dharma Raja devoted himself with full energy to his various State duties, founding a body of priesthood, providing for and controlling them, giving instruction to those who were serious seekers after truth; in short, he was pastor, abbot, psalmist, rector, superintendent of carving (for printing purposes), architect of State and monastic buildings, overseer of bookbinding and other embellishments of the Kagyur library, settlement officer, chief commandant of the forces for quelling foreign aggressions, chief protector and ruler of his own adherents and followers, chief avenger and punisher of those who were inimical to the cause of Buddhism and the public peace. He was all these in one person, and fulfilled the duties right thoroughly and efficiently. He introduced law into lawless Bhutan. His boast was that he never wasted any time in idleness or selfish ease." For the better ecclesiastical and temporal administration he appointed two of the monks who had come with him from Ralong, one, Nay-tan-Pay-kor-Jungnay, to be the chief Khempo, or abbot, whose duties were to enforce the strict observance of priestly vows among the priests, direct their studies, and preside at the ceremonies; the other was Tenzing Dukgyag, the Amsed or prior of Ralong, who was the first Dug Desi or Deb Raja, whose duties were to attend to the general administraton of the State, to deal with foreign Powers, to manage income, revenue, and other resources of the State, to provide the lamas with food, and, in short, to look after the State, while the Dharma Raja and the Khempo devoted themselves to the Church. This dual administration must be borne in mind when considering foreign relations; and it must also be carefully realised that Bhutan is wholly an ecclesiastical State, that the Church is all in all with the Bhutanese.

Such was the character of the first Shabdung Rimpochi. After his death three reincarnations appeared; that of his body became the Dharma Raja, that of his voice the Chole Tulku, and that of his mind the Thi Rimpochi—an incarnation now dying out, owing to the misconduct of the present incumbent.

CHAPTER XIII

MY FIRST MISSION TO BHUTAN

From Gangtak to Tashi-cho-jong. Choice of routes. The Natu-la in bad weather. Deputation in the Chumbi Valley. Entering Bhutan. The Hah-la and Meru-la. Punishment for murder. Leather cannon. Paro. The Penlop's wives. Paro-jong. Turner's description. Eden's description. Dug-gye. Weeping cypress at Chalimaphe. The quarrel between Ugyen Wang-chuk and Aloo Dorji. Murder of Poonakha Jongpen. Tashi-cho-jong.

One of the most pleasant duties I had to perform while holding my appointment was when the Government of India deputed me to proceed to Bhutan in 1905 to present the insignia of a Knight Commander of the Indian Empire to my friend Ugyen Wang-chuk, the Tongsa Penlop, as a recognition of the services he had rendered to the British Government at the time of our mission to Lhasa. Major F. W. Rennick accompanied me to represent the Intelligence Department, and Mr. A. W. Paul, C.I.E., late of the I.C.S., came out from England in response to the Tongsa's invitation. I also took, as my confidential clerk, Rai Lobzang Chöden Sahib and an escort of twenty-four sepoys, with some pipes and drums of the 40th Pathans under Subadar Jehandad Khan, two Sikhim Pioneers and two Sikhim police, in addition to the usual following of chupprassies and servants.

This was the first occasion for forty years that an Englishman had visited Bhutan, and was a sharp contrast to the visit paid by Eden in 1864, when every obstacle was placed in his way and every discourtesy shown him. I had more than once received the most hospitable and pressing invitations from the Tongsa to visit him on the first possible opportunity, and was only too glad now to be able to accept his hospitality.

I had in the first instance to make a selection of the route by which it would be best to travel, making due allowance for the season and state of the roads. There were at least four known routes:

1. The Buxa-Poonakha route, used by Bogle in 1774 and Turner in 1783, when they entered Bhutan, and by the Bhutanese officials when they came for the annual subsidy paid to Bhutan by the Indian Government; but on a previous visit to Buxa I had ascertained that the first few marches were extremely bad, and also that the Bhutanese themselves did not recommend it.

2. That *via* Dewangiri, which leads directly to Tongsa, and was traversed by Pemberton in 1837–38; but this I found would be hot and difficult, and, as the most easterly one, too far removed from headquarters.

3. The road *via* Sipchu to Hah and Paro, along which Eden travelled in 1864. The first portion of this was reported to be in very bad order and impracticable for laden animals, added to which the crossing of the Tegon-la would probably be more difficult than crossing the higher pass, the Natu-la.

4. I therefore decided on the route which, on leaving Gangtak, crosses the Natu-la into the Am-mo-chhu Valley, thence over the Massong-chung-dong range into the Hah Valley, and thence to follow Eden's route.

I originally proposed starting in February, to avoid the heavy storms usual in March, and to arrive at Poonakha before the summer heat and consequent migration of the Court to Tashi-cho-jong. But unforeseen circumstances delayed me till the very end of March. All the previous week there had been heavy storms, and the snow and wind were so bad that Colonel Burn, of the 40th Pathans, commanding at Chumbi, took thirteen hours between Champitang and Chongu, a distance of ten miles, and had to abandon his transport; and two days later my party found the bodies of two coolies out of a batch going to work on the Am-mo-chhu Survey, who had perished from exposure to the cold on the top of the Natu-la.

We finally left Gangtak on March 29, travelling for the first six miles over an excellent road, which during the late expedition to Lhasa was widened sufficiently for wheeled traffic, and for the remaining distance to Karponang, our first halting-place, over a good mule road. Karponang was the first stage for the coolies carrying supplies over the Natu-la during the Lhasa Expedition, and we put up for the night in the small, inconvenient huts still standing, glad to get out of the wet and gloom which had come down as the day waned. This part of the road is particularly beautiful in fine weather, which we fortunately had the next morning, for the road winds gradually up through forest-clad hills, with white magnolia and scarlet rhododendron in full bloom, and the sides of the road were carpeted with primulas in every shade of mauve and purple; but this year the feathery foliage of the blue bamboo was missing, and replaced by melancholy, dried-up sticks, for the bamboos had flowered and seeded the year before and then died. We crossed some fine precipices on the older and more difficult track, from which we had a magnificent view over a sea of hills stretching in one uninterrupted panorama to the plains of India, perfectly distinct in the clear atmosphere only to be met with at this time of the year after rain. As we mounted higher we came to snow, at first not very deep, and the mules had no difficulty in getting through it, but from Lagyap onwards the whole country was a smooth white sheet, and it was impossible to realise that Tani-tso was a lake. By the afternoon the usual blizzard commenced, and drove the drifting snow through the chinks in the plank walls of our miserable huts, the smoke down the chimneys, and reduced us all to a state of discomfort, as our only shelter was another abandoned transport station. The road on which we were travelling was that commenced by the Indian Government during the Tibet Mission, leading from Gangtak to Chumbi *via* the Natu-la, and is without doubt the best and easiest route between Sikhim and Chumbi, a fact recognised by the military authorities. The greater portion of this excellent road had been finished at an expense of several lacs of rupees, when, on the signing of the Lhasa Treaty, Government, in spite of my repeated remonstrances, decided to abandon the undertaking, ordered work to be immediately stopped, and rather than incur the small extra expenditure threw away the large amount already expended, by leaving uncompleted a few miles in the middle of a road, the greater part of which had already been finished and was well aligned the whole way to Chumbi.

We had great difficulty in crossing the Natu-la, 14,780 feet, next day, owing to the deep, soft snow, and although I had every one on the road before six in the morning it was 12.30 before I reached the top of the pass with the first few coolies, it having taken us three hours to do the last 1½ miles; but that year was an exceptionally severe and late one, with 65 inches of snow registered at Chumbi, against 20 the year before. During the year of the Mission I used to cross 450 maunds of stores daily with my Sikhim Coolie Corps, which, at the special request of General Macdonald, I had organised under Captains Souter and Muscroft, who, one or other, almost daily crossed with their men. On many other occasions I have always ridden across the pass, but this time I had to walk the whole distance, and had such weather occurred in 1904 the consequences might have been disastrous. From the pass we reached Pema, 9600 feet, in the Chumbi Valley, halting for a night at Champitang, without further misadventure than that nearly one-third of my coolies were suffering from snow-blindness, and Major Rennick also, as he had incautiously taken off his smoked glasses.

BRIDGE OVER THE AM-MO-CHU AT PEMA IN THE CHAMBI VALLEY.

London: Edward Arnold.

The day was fine, and Yatung, where the treaty mart had been established for over ten years, was well in sight for some time. Viewing it from the Kagui Monastery, Mr. Paul thought the real site for the Yatung Trade Mart, to which he had agreed when the subject was discussed after the Sikhim Treaty in 1890, was where the Chinese village is; but the time is long past for this to be of anything but academic interest. I visited the Kagui Monastery, and found that the Incarnate Lama who supplied our officers with information as to the Tibetan forces and numbers in 1881 had died some two years later, and had been succeeded by an Incarnation found at Hah, and the rumour that he had been murdered by the notorious Durkey Sirdar was based on the fact that Durkey Sirdar murdered another monk belonging to the monastery. I found the monastery in excellent condition; it had not been looted by either side in either expedition, and there were about it a number of merry acolytes, who, however, were so ignorant that they did not know to which of the two sects, Dupka or Gelukha, they belonged.

In the valley I was met by Ugyen, who had come by the Jeylap route, and complained of a very difficult crossing. Mr. Henderson, of the Chinese Customs Service, kindly placed his house, which boasted of one large chimney and several panes of glass, and had formerly been rented for the use of the Sikhim Coolie Corps during the expedition, at my disposal, and we halted here for a couple of days, while I made final arrangements in connection with my escort and baggage, instructed Mr. Bell with regard to carrying on the administration during my absence, and the Superintendent of Field Post Offices to send a weekly post after me. While I was there a deputation of headmen from Galingka and the other villages situated in the Am-mo-chhu Valley waited on me to complain of the serious dilemma they were in. Under recent orders from the Government of India, they were forbidden to take orders from the Chinese and Tibetan authorities or to supply them as formerly with free carriage, &c. If it was the intention of Government to eventually restore the Chumbi Valley to the Tibetans (in reality to the Chinese) and to abandon them, the villagers, what would their ultimate fate be? Could I give them any guarantee that the Government of India would protect them and ensure their safety? With the fate of the late Sinchen Rimpochi, forced to throw himself from a cliff into the river, the Pala family disgraced, in consequence of assistance rendered to Surat Chundra Das, the Shape Lhalu banished, the threatened punishment of the Phodong Lama and Kangsa Dewan because they expressed friendly feelings towards the British, to say nothing of the more recent catastrophes which befell the late Shapes, banished on account of supposed friendliness to the Mission at Lhasa, and my two Lachung villagers carried off and imprisoned in Lhasa as spies and only released on the Mission's arrival, before their eyes, it was only natural that the people should be inspired with a dread of severe retribution should they again find themselves in the power of the Tibetans. I did my best to reassure them and to point out that matters would be satisfactorily arranged, but it was neither a pleasant nor an easy task to have to deliberately deceive people who trusted you, as I had to do, for I was only too well aware that at the first opportunity Government would throw them over and leave them in the hands of the Chinese (nominally the Tibetans), than whom there are no more cruel or revengeful people. And subsequent events prove my forecast to have been only too true, for two years later, on January 1, 1908, under the orders of a Liberal Government, the Chumbi Valley was handed back to the Tibetans, our troops and civil officer withdrawn, and the people left to the mercy of the Chinese, who are now the actual rulers in Tibet, since by our recognition of China as the paramount Power we have placed Tibet completely under her sway. With the evacuation of the Chumbi the curtain was finally rung down on the Mission to Lhasa in 1904, and our Government voluntarily resigned all that had been gained by those long months of hardship and stress, by vast expenditure of money and the loss of valuable lives.

It was instructive, in view of the then disputed question as to whether Chumbi, as the people themselves maintained it ought to be, should be restored to Sikhim, to note the close intimacy that exists between Chumbi and Sikhim. The wealthiest man in the valley was the headman of Pema, whose grandfather and great-grandfather had lived in Gangtak, whither their forefathers had migrated from Chumbi. According to local tradition, Chumbi itself came into the possession of the Sikhim Raja a little more than a hundred years ago as the dower of a Tibetan wife, the people of the valley below Galing paying him no rent, but carrying for him and his amla free. I tried to trace the previous history of the valley, but I could find no one with any knowledge of or interest in the subject.

Next day, after concluding my arrangements, we commenced our journey on the right bank of the Am-mo-chhu as far as Rinchengong. Ugyen Kazi, the Bhutanese agent, who was the bearer of the Viceroy's letter to the Delai Lama in 1903, pointed out the house in which the late Durkey Sirdar used to live, and poured out a repetition of his wrongs; that doubt should have been thrown on the fact that he had delivered his Excellency's letter to the Delai Lama himself had sunk deep into his heart, and still rankled sorely. "There," he said, with dramatic action, "lived and flourished my enemy; he maligned me to the Tibetan Government, who denied me access to Lhasa, and, through his Kalimpong friends, to the Indian Government, who doubted my honesty. I was alone with but few friends, and what was I to do? I sent money and presents to the great oracle at Nachung, and told the Shapes [Tibetan Council] at Lhasa that I was an honest man and placed my case and my trust in the gods of my fathers. If I had been dishonest and disloyal to either Government, if I had not to the best of my abilities striven to do my duty to both Governments and consulted their interests alone, let the divine vengeance fall on me. But if I were honest and true, let it be meted out to my traducers. Sir, Durkey Sirdar and his two wives died within a short time of each other, and their house knows them no more. That has been my answer to the Council at Lhasa; they have accepted it, and I am free to go to the Holy City. What my Indian masters will do is their own good pleasure."

At Rinchengong the road crosses the Am-mo-chhu by a substantial bridge, and our path opened out most lovely views, with splendid timber. But unfortunately the track, which is capable of great improvement at little cost, had been much neglected of late, and opposite Assam-Ro-tsa a rock nearly stopped us altogether, though after the expenditure of much time and labour we got all our transport safely across, with the exception of one pony, whose leg was broken and who had to be shot. That, with the loss of two of the mules, who died on the way from eating the poisonous leaves of a small rhododendron fatal to animals, was a heavy toll for the first day's march. After passing Assam-Ro-tsa we got on fairly well, but I found the map was wrong, and that the stream marked Langmarpu-chhu is really the Kyanka, a second stream which we had already crossed higher up being the Langmarpu-chhu. Over the Kyanka there was a good new bridge, which we crossed, and passed under a cave, or rather two overhanging rocks, named Tak-phu, which were pointed out as being in Bhutanese territory. At the head of the Langmarpu-chhu there is said to be a large lake and good shau (*Cervus sinencis*) shooting. Turning up the Kyanka, the narrow track ran some way above the stream, and, gradually ascending, brought us to our camp, which was pitched in a somewhat confined glade close to the stream at a place called Lha-re (height 9900 feet), in Bhutan. After a fine night, with the thermometer registering only 30°, we started early, and found the path improved as we ascended the Kyanka, which we twice crossed within two miles on bridges of the cantilever order in good repair. After passing the second bridge we came to two caves, Pyak-che and Au-pyak, formed by overhanging rocks, but of no great depth. These " robber caves," as their name implies, were formerly used by the Hah-pa folk as a base from which to issue to rob and terrorise peaceful merchants. At one time the Hah-pa were amongst the richest people in Bhutan, but, as Eden relates, they took to evil ways and fell on evil times. But in justice to the Hah-pa it must be acknowledged that for the last fifteen years their winter grazing-grounds near Sipchu and the lower hills have been seriously curtailed by the increasing irruption of Nepalese settlers, and thus the chief source of their wealth—cattle-rearing and dairy produce—has begun to fail, while the constant quarrels arising between them and the Paharias entail much worry and expense.

A little further on we crossed the Chalu-chhu, and the valley widened out into the most delightful glades and upland swards, forming rich grazing-grounds; in fact, Chalu-thang would form a perfect site for a summer sanatorium, for it is a well-wooded, gently sloping park, spreading for several miles up the vales of the Chalu-chhu and Tak-phu-chu. Growing in abundance were spruce, larch, silver fir, holly-oak, various pines and rhododendrons, interspersed with grassy slopes, while the main valley had the appearance of a gigantic avenue leading up to the snowy pyramid of Senchu-la. Out of the valley a somewhat steep ascent round a grassy knoll brought us to the Dong-ma-chhu, up which runs another track, meeting the head of the Langmarpu-chhu, and thus by a more northerly but difficult path gaining the Hah road. Our route, however, took us over the Lungri Sampa, up a steep and stony path, to our camp at Tak-phu, a somewhat bare and extensive flat, an old moraine well within sight of the Kyu-la (Chula). There was plenty of timber, but we found our chief protection from the wind in the walls of the lateral moraines, of which the valley presented some excellent examples. Directly opposite I counted four distinct moraine terraces, one above the other, forming gigantic spur works which keep the present river within bounds. At the same time, so far from the moraines being barren, stony walls, they were luxuriantly covered by virgin forest right up to the parent ridge. Our night was not a very comfortable one, as it snowed all afternoon and most of the evening. The road from Rinchengong was capable of being made into a good one without any great difficulty, and Ugyen Kazi has since greatly improved it. There were no insuperable obstacles, and the streams were already well bridged, but we experienced considerable difficulty, owing to the surface having been injured by recent frosts and snows. The surrounding country is beautiful and well worth visiting; game is plentiful, as a bag of four Blood pheasant, two Monal pheasant, and one, burhel, without really leaving the road, clearly evidenced; and it would make an ideal place to spend a holiday in.

The night before crossing the pass was the coldest we had experienced, the thermometer registering 18° of frost, and my breath actually congealed and formed a coating of ice on my blanket. With no knowledge of what might be before us, as no European or even properly qualified native explorer had crossed the passes of the Massong-chung-dong range, I had the camp roused at 4 A.M., and the main body well on the way by 5.45 in fine bright weather. We soon entered a fairly level amphitheatre, which, however, contained no lake, and where high up on the northern slopes we saw a large flock of burhel, and Rennick bagged a fine female. It was quite possible to ride to the foot of the last ascent to what we thought was the pass, an ascent very deep in snow, which luckily was hard frozen; and as a matter of fact my cook, a Mugh from Chittagong, and a great character, rode the whole way from camp to camp without dismounting, a feat that even the hardy

Bhutanese looked upon as marvellous. The real pass, Kyu-la, 13,900 feet, lay a little way off with a small lake to the east, and we reached it about 7.15 A.M. Looking back over the valley we had ascended, we had a grand view of the Jeylap range behind a finely wooded foreground. Turning round, the aspect entirely changed; about a mile and a half away was the Hah-la, which was wrongly marked on our maps as the Meru-la; between the two passes was a hollow dip, flanked on the north by precipitous cliffs and on the south by a deep snowdrift ending in space, and somewhere between the two our track lay—verily, as our guide called it, "a Bridge of Death." Woe to the poor traveller caught between these two horns, should the wind rise and the snow fall; for him there was no shelter from the storm, no means by which to light a fire to warm him, not a tree or a shrub to be seen over the wind-swept fields of snow, only bleak and bare outcrops of rock. But in our case the little wind there was soon died down, and in perfect weather we climbed down the snow-slope to the bottom of the hollow, where we found we could ride for some distance, and finally reached the Hah-la about an hour later. On the top were many "obos," offerings to the spirits of the pass, a fact that bore significant testimony to the story of our guide, and looking back, as I cast my contribution on the nearest cairn and threw my "airy horse" (Lung-ta) aloft, I breathed a silent but fervent prayer that though my horse could not materialise, the spirits of the air might remain still and grant a safe and sure passage to the next wayfarer. Climbing a knoll to the south, I had a fine view of an unknown snowy ridge, which ended suddenly on the north-west in an enormous precipice, apparently giving outlet to the Am-mo-chhu, and, as far as I could gather, called Tso-na. To the north the fine mass of Chumolhari was seen in the distance, and nearer the snow-peaks of Massong-chung-dong, which dominate the head of the Hah valley, and about which there runs a legend that there once lived in Hah two men so powerful that they were able to uphold the mountain, and that their spirits still have their dwelling-place somewhere in its icy fastnesses. On the east was a well-wooded but rather steep valley, down which we had to descend by a very rough precipitous track, which at first, owing to the snow, could hardly be called a road; it, however, improved by the time we reached a small open glade called Damtheng, though the frozen snow still made our footing insecure. Soon after we were met by the Tongsa Donyer, who accompanied the Tongsa Penlop to Lhasa in 1904 and was formerly the Donyer of Angdu-phodang; he brought the usual scarf and murwa in the name of the Tongsa, and informed me he had been detailed to accompany me during my stay in Bhutan and to arrange for the comfort of my party, and these duties he carried out most satisfactorily. From Damtheng, after crossing a good bridge, we slightly ascended before reaching Tsangpa-pilam where the traders' branch road to Phari joins that from Hah-la, and where we found three small but excellent riding-mules, which proved most useful and satisfactory animals, sent by the Paro Penlop, in charge of the Paro Gorap (gate-keeper).

The road now became quite good, and about midday we rode into Damthong (10,400 feet), where we found a zareba of fresh pine boughs encircling a well laid-out camp. Words fail me to describe the beauty of the scene. Grassy glades, gently sloping, opened on a series of wide valleys in the far distance, while on either side and at our back was a deep fringe of fine trees of every age, from the patriarch of the forest down to young seedlings. The Bhutanese seem to have acquired the secret of combining in forests self-reproduction with unlimited grazing, for from the time we left Rinchengong we passed through forests which, without exception, were self-reproducing. When we were comfortably settled in our tents the Tongsa and Paro officials, accompanied by the Hah Zimpon and Nerpa, brought us a further salutation from the Penlops, in the shape of a piece of silk for myself and rations for the whole party. The arrangements were so good they augured well for the future welfare of our Mission.

After a comfortable night we started in the morning along a very good road, which soon brought us into an open valley, leading through most magnificent scenery, with often a small gompa, or chapel, perched high above us, in accordance with the practice, more or less universal here, of planting one on every commanding promontory. The first village of note was Ke-chuka, which possessed a good chuten, built by a former Hah Jongpen, and fine water-mills. We went into the village gompa, and found a curious custom prevailed, which I have not come across elsewhere, namely, that most travellers offered a small copper coin, and then tried their luck with three dice kept in the alms-bowl.

At Kyengsa a road leads up through a thickly wooded side valley, through Talong and over the Saga-la, and so down to Dug-gye-jong, on the main road between Paro and Phari. It was here the horse-dealer Aphe formerly lived, who supplied some years ago a batch of ponies to the Assam Government, which was then commencing a tonga service between Gowhati and Shillong. He later died in Lhasa, and this shows how widely ramified is the trade between India and Lhasa.

On a beautiful flat, called Gyang Karthang, an annual dance and fair is held in December and January, and a more suitable site could hardly be imagined. Yangthang, a large village, is situated on the left bank of the stream at the broadest part of the valley, and as the Hah-chhu runs where the irrigation channels lead, a great deal of stony, barren land which would otherwise be the bed of the river is exposed. The road ran across a bridge through the village, and out again over another bridge, but as these bridges were said to be dangerous we continued our journey along a temporary path on the right bank, and at every village we passed the inhabitants turned out to receive us and had hot tea always ready on the roadside. Many of the Darjeeling gwallas, or cattle-owners, come from Yangthang, and the village seems to be a dividing line, as the people living above it are known as notorious robbers and thieves, while below they are supposed to be more reputable.

Holly-oak (Pi-shingh, locally) was now conspicuous by its presence, and the formation of the hills was markedly of crystalline limestone. After passing some mineral springs we came to the twin forts and village of Tomphiong (8370 feet), and, crossing a strong bridge, reached our camp, pitched on a large level maidan, flanked with willow-trees, and ornamented by a long mendong, or wall of prayer. The Hah Tungba, a brother of the late Aloo Dorgi, paid his respects, accompanied by one of his younger sons, and brought rations for the party. After lunch I visited the main fort, which was dirty and dilapidated, and where perhaps the most notable article was a Westly Richards rifle, with a Whitworth barrel, dated 1864, which the local blacksmith had converted into a muzzle-loader; while the Tungba showed me some excellent sword-blades manufactured in the village by the same man. I was also shown two curious hollows in the limestone formation which connect some subterranean lake with the river; the villagers place baskets at the outlets, and the rush of water at times brings out a number of fair-sized fish, though I saw no fish in the Hah stream itself.

My party were now the guests of Bhutan, and we were relieved of all trouble with regard to transport and camping-grounds, as this was in the hands of the Tongsa Donyer, whom I have already mentioned as having been sent to meet us by the Tongsa, and who was unfailing in his efforts to secure our comfort. Next day we rode up to the chief monastery, Tak-kyun Gompa; at least, we rode as far as we could, as the monastery is situated on a flat with almost precipitous sides, and we had to struggle up the last ascent on foot. The buildings were in good order, but of no great interest, although the view both up and down the Hah-chhu is magnificent. Near this is the Poisoners' Gompa mentioned by Eden, but it was closed, and I did not think it worth while to send for the key.

In the afternoon a severe thunderstorm sprang up, and it snowed heavily nearly all night ; so much so that in the morning I was doubtful about starting ; but, learning that the road was easy and in good order and that the coolies were already assembled, I decided to go on. While the loads were being portioned out amongst the coolies I saw a man being led off between three others, and thinking that he might have lost or spoilt something, and anxious that he should not be unnecessarily punished, I inquired what was the matter, and learned, to my astonishment, that he had a year ago killed one of the Tongsa's servants, and, escaping, had been wanted ever since. According to the custom of the country, the punishment for the offence was that his right hand should be cut off and the tendons of his legs severed ; and what could have induced the man to run the risk of such a punishment I cannot imagine, for he probably got nothing in payment for his three days' labour in carrying my things. It sounds very barbarous, but when the state of the country and its condition is taken into account it somewhat alters the appearance of things. There are no jails, and this is a severe method of deterring hardened criminals from committing such offences and then absconding.

Our route took us over a very good bridle-path, and we rode nearly the whole way to the top of the Chiu-li-la, which we reached about an hour after leaving our former camp. As we rode we had occasional glimpses of the Hah valley as far as the Dorikha, where Eden camped, but the weather was unfortunately very damp, windy, and chilly. On the pass I was met by an orderly from Paro with murwa, which in the cold was most acceptable and refreshing. On the way up I noticed that a small patch of forest had been burnt, the first trace of a jungle fire I had seen. On several occasions I had noticed men carefully extinguishing the remains of their night's fire, and now learnt that any carelessness in the matter of fire in the forests was most severely punished by the Bhutanese authorities.

Descending the other side, our path, owing to the frozen snow in the shade and to melting slush in the sun, would have been very difficult had not the villagers thickly strewn it with thick soft moss, which made walking quite pleasant. High above on our right was the nunnery of Kyila, built on the face of a very steep precipice, and said to contain sixty nuns; but as I counted twenty-five houses, the majority quite large, I fancy the number of inhabitants must be considerably greater. The road leading to it must be very difficult, and as it lay some distance off, across a small valley, I did not attempt to visit it. The rule forbids any male creature to remain in the precincts of the establishment.

We arrived at Cha-na-na, a small hamlet of half a dozen houses, mostly in ruins, about midday, and camped there for the night. Our experience in crossing the Chiu-li-la was so different in every respect from that of Eden that I cannot but suspect that he was deliberately guided away from the proper route to some mere cattle-track, and my boiling-point readings, which are about 600 feet lower than Eden's, point conclusively to this theory. While here I nearly lost my best riding-mule from the effects of a poisonous herb which it had eaten; but after the native remedy, bleeding from the ear, had been resorted to it sufficiently recovered to leave camp with us. We soon emerged on a spur, whence we obtained a grand view of the valleys of the Pa-chhu and its tributaries. There we found a broad, well-cultivated, level country, which under good management ought to produce all temperate crops in abundance. On a distant mountain to the south-east was situated the monastery of Danka-la, visible, I believe, from Poonakha; on a hill a little to the north-east was Beila-jong, close to which our future road ran; while away up the Pa-chhu the fort of Dug-gye dominates the route to Phari, and takes its name from a notable defeat of Tibetan invaders. Soon we came upon the monastery of Gorina, which a former Shabdung Rimpochi used to make his summer retreat. The chapel was clean, and gaily decorated with fresco paintings in good taste, while the hangings round the altar were overlaid with wrought brass open-work superior to anything that I had seen in Lhasa, but in sharp contrast the side altars were adorned with four gaudy green porcelain parrots. The chuten was a very fine one, and on the face was a figure of Buddha embossed on a large brass plate. There was also a subsidiary gompa, but we did not go inside. On the ridge below we were greeted with salvos of artillery, fired from iron tubes bound with leather; and I wondered whether these could be the leather cannon of which we heard so much in the Chinese-Gurkha war. The Paro Penlop's band was also waiting, with three richly caparisoned mules in attendance, and we slowly descended a clayey slope which must be absolutely impassable in wet weather, and thence rode along the plain, past the fort and its bridge, through a quadruple avenue of willows, to our destination that day, Paro, where our camp was pitched on a large level maidan. A large square had been marked off by a strong lattice fence of split bamboo, and at the entrance a new Swiss cottage tent was pitched, and in it I found waiting to receive me the Penlop's small son and the Paro Donyer, who offered us tea, oranges, and fruit for our refreshment. The Donyer was particular in reminding Paul that he had formed one of the Penlop's party some sixteen years before, and had then been photographed, and was very pleased when I promised to take him again that afternoon. I was particularly struck on the day's march by the total absence of rhododendrons, which always love a peaty soil, and the change from gneiss to crystalline limestone, sandstone, and dark shales, then to heavy red clay deeply impregnated with iron, and again to bluish-grey limestone.

In the afternoon, while wandering round the camp, which was very well laid out, I watched the curious Bhutanese custom of feeding mules with eggs, which I had never come across elsewhere. All our mules, as well as those belonging to Ugyen Kazi and to the Penlops, each had a ration of two or three raw eggs. The eggs were broken into a horn, the mule's head held up, and the contents of the horn poured down the animal's throat, and, strange to say, they seemed to like the unnatural food. The Bhutanese always give this to their animals when they have any extra hard work to do, and say it keeps them in excellent condition; and certainly all their mules were in first-rate condition.

The next morning the Paro Penlop, accompanied by his young son, paid me a formal visit, at which we exchanged ordinary compliments. The Penlop was then about fifty-six years of age, a fair man, with a weak, discontented, though not unhandsome face. His first and lawful wife, Ugyen Zangmo, was a relative of the Tongsa Penlop, but as she was childless he married his present consort, a woman called Rinchen Dolma, from a village near Paro, who bore him a son, at the time of our visit about twelve years of age, and a most ill-mannered young cub, who would have been all the better for a good thrashing. His mother, Rinchen Dolma, though elderly and crippled with chronic rheumatism, is a pleasant, clever woman, who completely rules the Penlop. In order to preserve her influence as she grew older, and to prevent him bringing a stranger into the house, she gave him her own daughter, Tayi (by her first husband), as his junior wife, and they both lived amicably in a pretty house across the valley. The wives have a dwelling outside the Jong, on account of the strict regulation that no female is allowed to remain in the fort after dark. The gates of the fort, as well as those of the bridge across the Pa-chhu, are regularly closed at sunset, and, as in China, are not opened until morning on any pretext whatever; even the Penlop himself is not admitted, and consequently, if he wishes to

CHORTEN AT GORINA MONASTERY

remain with his wives, must stay for the whole night in their house, where his apartments command lovely views both up and down the valley.

When Dow Penjo, the Paro Penlop, came to Kalimpong some years ago he was accompanied by his sister's son, then scarcely out of his teens. This person had now become the Paro Donyer, in name the chief official after the Penlop, but in reality a low, drunken, ignorant fellow, and the only person with whom I had any trouble. Going about in a state of maudlin intoxication from early morning, it was difficult to keep him in his place, for under the pretext of friendliness and relationship to the Penlop he used to walk into one's tent at most inconvenient times, asking for anything from an old solah topee to our mess kit. Finally I had to purchase a temporary respite with the present of a pair of binoculars that he badgered every one for, and at last we parted from him almost sober; but he was the one exception, as the other officials and the people throughout the journey were extremely well behaved and very friendly.

Next morning I rode to the fort, which is situated on a limestone bluff overhanging the river, to return the Penlop's visit. There is only one entrance from the hillside, and that above the third story, the lower stories being used entirely as storehouses for grain, &c. Crossing a foss, which separates the outer courts from the fort, by a heavy drawbridge, we entered a huge gateway, and, turning to the left, found ourselves in the eastern courtyard, in the centre of which is the smaller of two citadels, equal in height, and occupied by petty officials. A series of rooms and verandahs overlooking the river are built against the inside of the east and north outer walls, with a covered verandah, one story in height, occupying nearly the whole west front. The Penlop's rooms are situated in the south-east corner on the floor above, and we entered through a long, low room filled with retainers seated in four rows, two on either side, facing each other, a scene which made one think of an old baronial hall in bygone English days. To add to this impression, the reception room was large and handsomely decorated, and the walls hung with arms of all descriptions, shields, spears, matchlocks, guns, bows and arrows of every imaginable kind, all well kept and ready for use.

The Penlop received us in a large bay window looking down the valley, but the visit was dull and uninteresting, as he seemed to know little of the history of his country, and what information we did extract was vague and inaccurate. I made him some presents, including a rifle and ammunition, and gave his son a knife, binoculars, and a magnifying glass, with which the lad was immensely pleased, and shortly after took my leave, receiving permission to inspect the fort, and to pay a visit to his wives in the house across the valley.

The fort is said to have been built in the time of the first Shabdung Rimpochi, and does not seem to have suffered from the earthquakes that shattered part of Tashi-cho-jong and Poonakha. On the first floor is the temple, the gompa, or public chapel, a very finely proportioned hall, well lighted, and with two galleries running round the main building. It is a much larger room than the one in the Potala at Lhasa where the Tibetan Treaty was signed, and all its decorations are good, a hanging latticework of pierced brass in front of the altar especially being very effective and unusual. At the other end of the west verandah is the private chapel of the Ta-tshangs, the State monks, where we were received by their head, Lama Kun-yang Namgyal, who went to Lhasa with the Tibet Mission and exercised a good influence amongst the monks there. We were pleased to meet again, and he gladly showed us all there was to be seen. The larger of the two citadels is in the centre of the western courtyard, at the north-west angle of the building, and while I was going round I noticed old catapults for throwing large stones carefully stored in the rafters of the verandah. In the north-east corner are rooms for distinguished guests, and there is also a guardhouse in the parade-ground beyond the drawbridge. The fort and its surroundings have been described by both Turner and Eden, from whom I give the following extracts.

Turner writes :

"The castle, or palace of Paro, known also by the appellation of Paro Jong, and Rinjipo, is constructed, and the surrounding ground laid out, more with a view to strength and defence than any place I have seen in Bootan. It stands near the base of a very high mountain ; its foundation does not decline with the slope of the rock, but the space it occupies is fashioned to receive it horizontally. Its form is an oblong square ; the outer walls of the four angles, near the top of them, sustain a range of projecting balconies, at nearly equal intermediate distances, which are covered by the fir eaves that project, as usual, high above and beyond the walls, and are fenced with parapets of mud. There is but one entrance into the castle, which is in the eastern front, over a wooden bridge, so constructed as to be with great facility removed, leaving a deep and wide space between the gateway and the rock.

"Opposed to the front are seen, upon the side of the mountains, three other buildings, designed as outposts placed in a triangular position. The outer one is most distant from the palace, and about a double bowshot from those on either side, as you look up at them. The outer building and that on the left defend the road to Tassisudon, which runs between them ; that on the right the road from Buxadewar and passage across the bridge. On the side next the river, from the foundation of the castle, the rock is perpendicular, and the river running at its base renders it inaccessible. The bridge over the Patchieu, which is at no great distance, is covered in the same manner as those at Tassisudon and Punakha, and has two spacious gateways."

Eden writes :

"The fort of Paro is a very striking building, and far surpassed the expectations we had formed from anything we had heard of Bootian architecture. It is a large, rectangular building, surrounding a hollow square, in the centre of which is a large tower of some seven stories, surmounted by a large copper cupola. The outer building has five stories, three of which are habitable, the two lower stories being used as granaries and stores and are lighted with small loopholes, while the upper stories are lighted with large windows opening in most cases on to comfortable verandahs. The entrance to the fort is on the left side, by a little bridge over a narrow ditch ; the gateway is handsome, and the building above is much higher than the rest of the outer square ; it is ornamented and painted, and has a number of well-executed inscriptions engraved in stone and iron, some of them gilt. At the gateway are a row of cages in which are kept four enormous Thibetan mastives. These beautiful animals are very ferocious ; they are never taken out of their cages ; they are said, however, to be less dangerous than they otherwise would be from their overlapping jowls, which prevent their using their teeth as freely as ordinary dogs. The first thing which catches the eye on entering the fort is a huge praying cylinder, some ten feet high, turned by a crank ; a catch is so arranged that at each turn a bell is rung. The gate of the fort is lined with light iron plates. On entering the fort you are surprised to find yourself at once in the third story, for the fort is built on a rock which is overlapped by the lower stories and forms the ground base of the courtyard and centre towers. . . . After passing through a dark passage which turns first to the left and then to the right, a large well-paved and scrupulously clean courtyard is reached ; the fine set of rooms on the left is devoted nominally to the relations of the ladies of the palace, in reality, I believe, to the ladies themselves, who, however, are supposed to live outside the fort, in accordance with the

PARO-JONG

theory that all in authority are under obligation of perpetual celibacy. Beyond these rooms is a second small gateway, and the first set of rooms on the left hand belong to the ex-Paro Penlop ; they are reached by a very slippery and steep staircase, opening into a long vestibule, in which the followers lounge ; this leads into a large hall in which his sepoys mess, and in which one of his amla is always in waiting. Beyond the hall is the Penlop's state room ; it is somewhat low, but of great size and really very striking, for the Bootanese have derived from their intercourse with Tibet and China in old days very considerable taste in decoration. The beams are rudely painted in blue, orange, and gold, the Chinese dragon being the most favourite device, the roof is supported by a series of carved arches, and all round the room and in the arches are suspended bows, quivers, polished iron helmets, swords, matchlocks, coats of mail, Chinese lanthorns, flags, silk scarves consecrated by the Grand Lama of Tibet, arranged with the most perfect taste."

Eden also mentions other forts, of which only three now exist, viz., Tayo-jong, Doman-jong, and Suri-jong, as the very large one, Chubyakha-jong, is entirely in ruins. The large wooden bridge across the Par-chhu is kept in good order, and on the river-bank below the fort, close to where a covered way from the castle meets the water, is a very picturesque chapel, built into a recess of the rock, and dedicated to the tutelary deity of the place.

The Penlop, his senior wife and son, came to lunch with me the following day ; but it was a dull proceeding, for my guests would eat and drink nothing, their excuse being that it was the 8th of the Tibetan month, and therefore a fast day, an excuse I had to accept, although it happened to be the 9th, and not the 8th. The lady tried to make conversation, and showed great interest in a stereoscope, but also said it gave her a headache. My clerk's attempt to entertain the smaller officials at the same time was not much more successful, as although religious scruples did not prevent them making a hearty meal and taking away with them the wine they were unable to drink, after their departure the air thermometer of my boiling-point apparatus could not be found, which was annoying, as it left me without a second instrument to verify my readings. During lunch the band of the escort and the gramophone provided music for our guests' entertainment.

The next day we determined to visit Dug-gye-jong, and although it was cloudy we had a very pleasant ride up the valley over a road ascending very gradually, though in many places we found the soling of large stones very troublesome both for riding and walking. At Long-gong, about five miles from Paro, there is a pretty village and orchard of walnut-trees, where the Thumba or headman of that part of the valley lives, and on the cliffs opposite, to the east, is the more than usually inaccessible monastery of Paro-ta-tshang. We also saw in the distance the monastery of Sang-chen-cho-khor, from which the present Deb Raja came. At the end of nine miles we rode up to the fort of Dug-gye, also built in the days of the first Shabdung in commemoration of a victory over the Tibetans.

I cannot describe it better than Captain Turner does; the scene does not seem to have altered in the least. "We entered Dug-gye-jong, a fortress built upon the crown of a low, rocky hill, which it entirely occupies, conforming itself to the shape of the summit, the slope all round beginning from the foundation of its walls.

"The approach to the only entrance is defended by three round towers, placed between the castle and the foot of the hill, and connected together by a double wall, so that a safe communication between them is preserved even in times of the greatest peril. Around each of these towers, near the top, a broad ledge projects, the edges of which are fortified by a mud wall, with loopholes adapted to the use of the bow and arrow or of muskets. On the north of the castle are two round towers that command the road from Tibet. On the east side the rock is rough and steep; and

PARO TAKTSANG MONASTERY.

close under the walls on the west is a large basin of water, the only reservoir I had seen in Bhutan.

"The castle of Dug-gye-jong is a very substantial stone building, with high walls, but so irregular is its figure that it is evident no other design was followed in its construction than to cover all the level space on the top of the hill on which it stands. Having ascended to the gateway at the foot of the walls, we had still to mount about a dozen steps through a narrow passage, after which we landed upon a semicircular platform edged with a strong wall pierced with loopholes. Turning to the right, we passed through a second gateway, and went along a wide lane with stables for horses on each side. The third gateway conducted us to the interior of the fortress, being a large square, the angles of which had three suites of rooms. In the centre of the square was a temple dedicated to Mahamoonie and his concomitant idols."

I found the whole of the premises very clean; the Jongpen, who was appointed by, and is a staunch adherent of, the Tongsa Penlop, and who had been to Lhasa in his suite, received us most cordially, and entertained us with a Bhutanese lunch of scrambled eggs and sweet rice coloured with saffron, accompanied by murwah (beer) and chang (spirit), also coloured with saffron, fresh milk, and a dessert of walnuts and dried fruits. His wife, who prepared the meal, was one of the cleanest and best-looking women I have seen in Bhutan, and her little boy, wearing an exact copy, in miniature, of his father's dress, was a nice little chap.

The Dug-gye armoury is said to be the best in the country, and is contained in a fine room with a large bow window facing south and looking down the valley—in the Tongsa Penlop's opinion, the best balcony in Bhutan. In the outer courtyard men were making gunpowder. A silversmith and a wood-turner were also at work, and in the inner courtyard were piles of shingles (pieces of flat wood) ready for re-roofing the castle, which has to be entirely re-done every five years. Altogether there was an air of bustling activity which was pleasant to meet with. Up the valley lies the nearest road to Phari, a short three days' march for a laden coolie, and it was along this route the Chinese Mission passed when bringing a decoration for the Tongsa Penlop in 1886.

We struck camp early the next morning, and on our way bade the Paro Penlop farewell at the entrance to the castle. The ascent, which I think must have been a short cut, and not the regular road, was very rough and steep up to the Tayo-jong, the curious rounded fort described by Eden.

"One of them is a curious building formed of two semicircles, one large and the other small, built up one against the other for about five stories high."

The road beyond was very good, and ascended gradually to the pass, 8900 feet, near the Beila-jong. A steeper road on the other side led us down to Pemithang, the seat of an inferior official who calls himself a Penlop, where we camped under walnut-trees. The so-called Penlop was a pleasant, stout man, who did his best to make us comfortable. We found some of his boys playing quoits, a very favourite game amongst the Bhutanese, and close by a curious succession of mendongs, or prayer-walls, which was most unusual, as the mendong ordinarily consists of one long wall, but here there was a succession of three.

We left Pemithang early, and instead of going to Tashi-cho-jong *via* the Pami-la, we followed the Pemi-chhu to its junction with the Tchin-chhu, the road, a very good one, never being far above the water. The hills on either side were thickly wooded, with beautiful masses of flowering pear and peach, but at the junction with the Tchin-chhu, where we turned east up the stream, the whole aspect of the country suddenly changed to barren hills, with sparse and stunted trees, chiefly *Pinus longifolium*.

On the left bank, about two miles up, we saw a house conspicuous for its cared-for appearance, and found that it belonged to the ex-Paro Penlop, who was for years one of

DUG-GYE-JONG

our pensioners at Kalimpong. It says a great deal for Sir Ugyen Wang-chuk that he allowed this man, one of his most powerful enemies, to return to his old home and die there in peace, and then allowed the widow and daughters to remain on unmolested in the pretty place.

We reached our camping-ground at Chalimaphe after rather an uninteresting march, and pitched our tents round one of the largest weeping cypresses I have ever seen. It measured fifty feet round the trunk five feet above the ground. This would have been a pleasant halting-place but for the howling wind that roared up the valley and nearly blew our tents down, so we were not sorry to be off the next day, more especially as this proved to be quite the most interesting day I had yet spent in Bhutan.

Mounting our mules, we started early, and almost at once came in sight of Simtoka, the oldest fort in the country. Turning to the left, we rode along the left bank of the Tchin-chhu, where, about half a mile further on, I saw a fine cantilever bridge carrying a large wooden channel with a stream of water across the Tchin-chhu to irrigate a succession of rice-fields on the opposite side. I have particularly noticed during my travels in the country how remarkably skilful the Bhutanese are in laying out canals and irrigation channels, and the clever way in which they overcome what to ordinary people would be insurmountable difficulties in leading the water over steep, difficult places on bridges or masonry aqueducts, often built up to a great height. Riding on, the plain opened up into cultivation, extending its entire width and far up the mountain slopes, which were only sparsely clothed with forest. We crossed the Tchin-chhu, and shortly passed on our right a conspicuous knoll in the very centre of the plain. This marks the scene of an act of treachery on the part of the present Paro Penlop that materially changed the course of events in Bhutan, and was the beginning of the Tongsa Penlop's power.

In 1885 Gau-Zangpo was Deb Raja, and Aloo Dorji the

Thimbu or Tashi-cho-jong Jongpen, while Sir Ugyen Wangchuk, then about twenty-four years of age, had succeeded his father, Jigme Namgyal, better known as Deb Nagpo, or the Black Deb, as Tongsa Penlop, and Dow Penjo, first cousin to Deb Nagpo, was and still is Penlop of Paro. Two factions formed. On the one side were Deb Gau-Zangpo, Aloo Dorji, the Thimbu Jongpen, and the Poonakha Jongpen, brother-in-law to Aloo Dorji, and who naturally supported him. On the other side were ranged the Tongsa and the Paro Penlops, assisted by some of the smaller Jongpens. The cause of the final rupture was the action of Aloo's party, who, taking advantage of Ugyen Wangchuk's youth and supposed weakness, withheld from him for three years his rightful share of the British subsidy; in return Ugyen refused to pay his quota towards the maintenance of the Ta-tshang, or Government monks, who belong to the five monasteries of Poonakha, Tashi-cho-jong, Paro, Angdu-phodang, and Tongsa, in number about 3000 souls. This, however, was a losing transaction, as the Tongsa's share of the subsidy was a much larger sum; so, failing to receive an account or satisfaction of any kind, Ugyen collected his followers, to the number of about 4000, and, crossing the hills, came down near Chalimaphe. He himself went boldly to Tashi-cho-jong, where the Deb and the Thimbu were residing, and bearded them in their den, demanding satisfaction and accusing them of base ingratitude to their benefactor Deb Nagpo; and, when his demands were laughed at, retorted that if they wished to fight he was quite ready. Returning to his men, he attempted to surprise Tashi-cho-jong by crossing the mountains to the south-east; but his enemies discovered his move, set the grass on the lower slopes of the hills on fire, and the Tongsa had the greatest difficulty in saving his men from being suffocated by the smoke; and how choking and pungent the fumes from such fires can be I have had painful experience myself. He next attempted to storm the fort at Simtoka, which was strongly held by the Thimbu's men, the Jongpen himself keeping well out of the way at Tashi-cho-jong; but the day went against the eastern party, and they were beginning to waver and fall back, whereupon Ugyen Wang-chuk himself rushed into the van, upbraiding and even striking his men, and made such an impression on his leaderless foes that they fled panic-stricken, and left the fort of Simtoka with its granaries an easy prize in his hands. After waiting a day or two to recruit, the Tongsa's troops moved up the right bank of the Tchin-chhu, and there were more skirmishes, indecisive, but attended by much loss, principally the burning of houses, destruction of crops, &c. At this juncture the Paro Penlop appeared on the scene, and suggested to the Poonakha Jongpen, Aloo's chief supporter, that if they held a conference they might be able to settle the dispute and prevent further bloodshed; and Poonakha, suspecting nothing, came to the knoll we were looking at. The conference lasted some time without much result, when an adjournment was made for lunch; and while the soldiers belonging to the Jongpen were busy preparing their food on some level ground near the river to which they had been inveigled, the Paro's followers, taking advantage of their opponents being off their guard, rushed on the defenceless men. The Poonakha Jongpen was stabbed to death as he sat on the ground, and many of his men were massacred. The Tongsa's army then marched unopposed to some villages on the west of the castle, and during the night Aloo Dorji, who seems to have been a cowardly braggart, in alarm for his own safety, abandoned Tashi-cho-jong and fled over the hills to Poonakha, and from thence, after gathering up such of his property as he could lay hands on, continued his flight *via* Ghassa-la into Tibet, when he appealed to China and Tibet for help. The Chinese and Tibetans despatched envoys with the object of mediation, but their overtures were rejected by the Bhutanese, and soon after the Sikhim Expedition of 1888–9 broke the power and influence of the Tibetans, and the cause of Aloo Dorji, who fought on their side in the attack on Gnatong in May 1888 was lost. All subsequent attempts at interference by the Chinese and Tibetans were frustrated by the closer relationships with the Penlops which we maintained henceforth, and thus Ugyen Wang-chuk's influence in Bhutan was firmly established.

Paul has, however, told me that, when he was informed of the occurrence at the time, the death of the Poonakha Jongpen was not ascribed to the result of a deliberately planned scheme of treachery; that the meeting was honestly held for the purpose of arranging a compromise, but a quarrel arose between the followers of the rival factions, in which one of the Paro men had his arm sliced off, and on his rushing into the presence of the leaders his comrades avenged him by stabbing the Jongpen with their daggers. But whatever may have happened, there is nothing to show that the young Tongsa was cognisant of the plot, and when the castle of Tashi-cho-jong was abandoned the Tongsa himself had the gates firmly secured, and, standing before the main entrance, prevented his soldiers from breaking in and looting the palace. He had even to shoot one of his own men before order could be restored, and that was hardly the action of a man who would lend his countenance to so mean an act of treachery.

After leaving this knoll, called Changlingane-thang, with these interesting historical associations, we soon arrived at the castle of Tashi-cho-jong, an imposing edifice in the form of a parallelogram, the sides parallel to the river being twice the length of the other two. It differs from other forts in one particular; it possesses two large gateways, one on the south; the other, on the river-face, and protected on the west and north by a wide fosse filled with water, is only opened for the Deb and Dharma Rajas, and was closed at the time of my visit. Unlike Paro and Poonakha, the bridge across the Tchin-chhu was not connected with the castle, and just below it was a wooden structure, cleverly designed to catch the timber floated down the river from the distant hills for use in the castle. The interior of the castle is divided into two unequal portions by a high, strong wall, the larger section, to the south, containing the usual square tower, measuring about 85 feet each way, and in it are situated the chapel and private apartments of the Dharma Raja. The original tower was destroyed by the earthquake in 1897, and the present structure was finished about 1902; but it has been badly built, as the main walls were cracking already and the interior showed signs of unequal subsidence. The decorations, of course, are quite modern.

In the south-east angle of the courtyard beyond are the public or living quarters of the Dharma Raja, and on the west front those of the Thimbu Jongpen, where we were hospitably entertained. The northern and smaller section of the castle is occupied entirely by the Ta-tshang, or State lamas, and is not usually open to laymen. The dividing wall is surmounted by a row of white chotens, protected from the weather by a double roof, and in the centre of the inner courtyard is an extremely fine hall of audience or worship, 120 feet square and at least 50 feet high. It is well lighted, and decorated with fresco paintings, and when the silken ceiling-cloths and embroidered curtains and banners are hung it must look extremely well, but the lamas were absent at Poonakha, and all the decorations were either carefully put away or taken with them. A succession of chapels was built on the west side, one of which, a splendid example of good Bhutanese art, the door-handles of which, of pierced ironwork inlaid with gold, were exceptionally beautiful, had been presented by the Deb Nagpo. It was said to contain 1000 images of Buddha, and the number is very likely correct, as I counted more than 600, while the pair of elephant's tusks supporting the altar, which I have remarked as an essential ornament to the chief altar in every Bhutanese chapel I have visited, were larger than usual.

A short distance further up the valley we passed

Dichen-phodang, the private residence of the Thimbu Jongpen, which appeared to be a fine building, but I did not visit it. Above, on a commanding height, is the very large monastery of Pha-ju-ding, formerly one of the richest houses in Bhutan, but which has now fallen on evil days and is out of repair, while most of its ornaments have either been stolen or have disappeared, and I could not find time to visit it. We had a pleasant ride back to camp, but in the evening a more than usually strong gale of wind blew, with some rain, and two or three miles down the valley it seemed to fall in torrents.

CHAPTER XIV

MY FIRST MISSION TO BHUTAN—*continued*

From Tashi-cho-jong to Tongsa-jong. Simtoka-jong. Entry into Poonakha. The Deb Raja. Presentation of K.C.I.E. Description of Poonakha Fort. Expedition to Norbugang and Talo Monasteries. Visit of the Tango Lama. So-na-ga-sa the Zemri-gatchie of Turner. Farewell visit to the Deb. Angdu-phodang. Death of my dog Nari. The Pele-la. Tongsa-jong. Bad roads. Water-power prayer-wheels. The ceremony of blessing the rice-fields.

We left Tashi-cho-jong early next morning in lovely weather, with the thunder of a salute of thirty guns reverberating through the air, and soon arrived at Simtoka-jong, which is situated on a projecting ridge, with deep gullies separating it from the main hill. It looks old, and is not in very good repair. On the four sides of the central square tower, instead of the usual row of prayer-wheels, we found a row of square slabs of dark slate, carved in low relief with pictures of saints and holy men. It was a wonderful collection of different types, with no monotonous repetition of the same figure, whence derived I cannot imagine, unless, indeed, of Chinese origin, as the variety reminded me of the 1000 statues in the temple in Canton, where one figure is pointed out as Marco Polo. In Simtoka one face is a very unflattering likeness of the German Emperor. In the chapel itself, beneath a magnificent carved canopy, was one of the finest bronze images of Buddha that I have seen; it was supported on either side by a number of standing figures of more than life size.

From Simtoka a good road led us up the Lhung-tso Valley to the Dokyong-la (9570 feet), through beautiful glades of oak, chestnut, and rhododendron, while on the higher slopes forests of *Pinus excelsa* reappeared, in pleasant contrast to the barren slopes of the past two days. But on reaching the east side of the pass we seemed suddenly to come into a completely changed climate, and the valley we were entering might have been in Sikhim, not Bhutan. It was evidently a wet zone, and with a very bad path leading to our camp at Lungme-tsa-wa, we were glad when our march was over.

Next day we continued our descent down a steepish lane overhung by rhododendrons in full bloom, until we reached a bridge across the Teo-pe-rong-chhu. After crossing we gradually ascended a fair road on the side of hills quite different from those on the opposite side, sparsely clothed with *Pinus longifolia*, and a remarkable contrast to the flowering thickets on the way down. High above us were the monasteries of Norbugang and Ta-lo, and after rounding a ridge which parts the Mochu-Pochu from the Teo-pe-rong-chhu we again began to descend to our camp at Gang-chung-Dorona (5800 feet), the last before reaching Poonakha. Neither Poonakha nor Angdu-phodang were at any point visible.

It was in heavy rain next morning that we had to make our entry into the capital of Bhutan, along a road of heavy clay, on which it was almost impossible to keep one's footing. Close by a choten built at the junction of two valleys, and commanding a most picturesque view of the castle, I was met by a curious collection of musicians, dancers, &c., in gay clothing, sadly out of keeping with the constant rain and mud. Preceded by them, we managed in time to reach the bridge across the Mo-chhu, and after a little pause to cross, under a salute of guns—fifty now instead of thirty—heartily glad to reach the shelter of our camp, where a wooden house of two rooms was prepared for us.

In the camp waiting to receive me were the Tongsa

POONAKHA-JONG

Penlop, the Thimbu and Poonakha Jongpens, Zung Donyer, and Deb Zimpon. The first three I had met in Tibet, and the last two at Buxa. They greeted me most cordially and condoled with me on the weather, making many inquiries about our journey and whether we had encountered much difficulty; then, in a short time, the rain having ceased, they took their departure and left us to settle down in our quarters. For myself a large, comfortable Swiss cottage tent had been pitched, and a smaller one, dyed blue, with an embroidered top, for Major Rennick, in addition to a very good cook-house and some ranges of fine mat-sheds, and these, with my own tents and camp equipage, provided us with a luxurious encampment. I also had a great compliment paid me, as the Deb Raja's band played in front of us all through the outer courtyard right into the camp, an honour not paid even to the Tongsa Penlop himself beyond the entrance to the bridge.

The next day I spent receiving visits of ceremony from the Tongsa, the head Ta-tshang lamas, and other officials, and in disposing of an accumulation of official work. Whilst paying my return visits to the Tongsa Penlop and the officers in the fort I also paid my respects to the Deb Raja, who received me in his private apartments with great cordiality, and thanked the Indian Government for having sent me on such a friendly visit to his little country, while hoping his people had obeyed his instructions to look after my comfort in every way.

The Deb Raja is a great recluse, and occupies himself entirely with the spiritual affairs of the country, although, owing to the failure to discover a reincarnation after the death of the late Dharma Raja, he holds both offices; but meanwhile all temporal affairs are managed entirely by the Tongsa Penlop and his council, while in the Deb Raja all spiritual power is vested.

In the afternoon I had a long interview with the Tongsa Penlop, who came to see me unofficially, and we discussed many matters, and amongst others the question of extradition. He informed me that Bhutan had lately made an arrangement with Tibet regarding refugees, who were not to be returned unless some crime was proved against them, although formerly either State was obliged to send back all refugees. The Penlop dined with us, and we arranged that the presentation of the insignia of his Knight Commandership should be made on the following morning in open Durbar, presided over by the Deb Raja himself.

Unfortunately, on the morning of the Durbar it rained heavily, but cleared up before the ceremony, which was held in the Palace of Poonakha in a large hall. As soon as we learnt that everything was in readiness we formed a small procession from the camp, Major Rennick and myself in full dress uniform, preceded by our escort under Subadar Jehandad Khan, 40th Pathans, and proceeded to the fort, where we were ushered with great ceremony into the Durbar Hall.

This is a fine, handsome room, with a wide balcony overlooking the river Po-chhu, and with a double row of pillars forming two aisles. The centre or nave, a wide space open to the lofty roof, was hung with a canopy of beautifully embroidered Chinese silk. Between the pillars were suspended chenzi and gyentsen hangings of brilliantly coloured silks, and behind the Tongsa Penlop's seat a fine specimen of kuthang, or needlework picture, a form of embroidery in which the Bhutanese excel, and which compares favourably with anything I have seen in other parts of the world.

At the upper or north end of the room was the high altar and images always to be met with in Bhutanese chapels, and in front of this was a raised daïs, piled with cushions, on which sat the Deb Raja, in a rich yellow silk stole over his red monastic dress, with the abbot of the Poonakha Ta-tshang lamas in ordinary canonicals on his left. To the right of the daïs was a line of four scarlet-covered chairs for myself, Major Rennick, Mr. Paul, and the Subadar, and in front of each chair was a small table with fruit and refreshments. Close behind us stood my orderlies with presents. On the opposite side of the nave, facing me, was a low daïs with a magnificent cushion of the richest salmon-coloured brocade, on which Sir Ugyen Wangchuk sat, dressed in a handsome robe of dark blue Chinese silk, embroidered in gold with the Chinese character "Fu," the sign emblematical of good luck. Below him were ranged the chairs of all the officials present, the Thimbu Jongpen, the Poonakha Jongpen, the Zung Donyer, and the Deb Zimpon. The Taka Penlop had come to Poonakha, but was too ill to leave his bed; the Paro Penlop was unable to travel owing to the state of his leg, and had made his excuses personally on my way through Paro and had sent a representative; and the office of the Angdu-phodang Jongpen had not been filled. In the aisles were double and treble rows of the chief Ta-tshang lamas, seated on white carpets, while four flagellants, carrying brass-bound batons of office and formidable double-thonged whips of rhinoceros-hide, walked up and down between the rows to maintain order. At the lower end, by which we had entered, were collected the subordinate officials of the court, standing, with my own escort formed up in front of them, facing the Deb at the lower end of the nave. It was altogether a brilliant and imposing scene.

After my party and the high officers of state, who had risen on my approach, had taken their seats there was a short pause for order and silence to be restored. I then rose and directed Rai Lobzang Chöden Sahib to read my short address in Tibetan, which I had purposely curtailed, as I foresaw that the Bhutanese portion of the ceremony would be a lengthy one. My remarks seemed to give general satisfaction, and at their conclusion I stepped forward, with Major Rennick carrying the Insignia and Warrant on a dark blue cushion fringed with silver, in front of the Deb Raja as the Tongsa Penlop advanced from his side to meet me. With a few words appropriate to the occasion, I placed the ribbon of the order round his neck, pinned on the star, and handed the warrant to Sir Ugyen Wang-chuk. Major Rennick and myself then returned to our seats, while the Penlop, still standing before the daïs, expressed his thanks for the honour the King-Emperor had conferred on him. I again advanced, and presented Sir Ugyen with a rifle, my photographs of Lhasa and Tibet, and among other things a silver bowl filled with rice, the emblem of material prosperity, in commemoration of the day's ceremony, and, finally, placing a white silk scarf on his hands, offered him my hearty congratulations and good wishes. Major Rennick and the Subadar also offered scarves, with their congratulations; and finally Mr. Paul, as an old friend of more than thirty years' standing, in a few words wished the Deb, Bhutan, and the new Knight all prosperity and heartily congratulated them on the new era opening before them. This brought our part of the ceremony to a conclusion, and we remained interested spectators of what followed.

First Sir Ugyen Wang-chuk turned to the Deb Raja and made his obeisance. The Deb, who, as the Cholay Tulku, is also the spiritual head of the Bhutanese Church during the interval awaiting the reincarnation of the Dharma Raja, gave Sir Ugyen his pontifical blessing and placed three scarves round his neck. In like manner Sir Ugyen then received the blessing of the abbot, and afterwards reseated himself.

Now began an almost interminable procession of lamas, officials, and retainers, each bringing a scarf and presents, till the Penlop was almost smothered in scarves, while the whole nave from end to end gradually became filled up with heaps of tea, bags of rice and Indian corn, fabrics—silk, woollen and cotton—of all colours and values, with little bags of gold dust and rupees appearing on the top. As each present was placed on the floor the name of the donor was announced by the Zung Donyer. I had no means of judging, but I should think there were at least two hundred donors. It was amusing to watch the emulation amongst them and the flourishes some of them gave as they dumped their presents with a bang on the floor and whipped out their scarves to their full length.

When these congratulations came to an end tea and refreshments were offered to all the company of guests, including the lamas in the aisles, who at each course intoned a sort of grace. Finally betel and pan were distributed.

At the commencement of the feast a large cauldron of murwah, or native beer, was placed at the lower end of the nave, and an unusual ceremony—at least, it was unusual to me—was gone through. The Zung Donyer, with a long, bowl-shaped ladle, mixed the liquid three times, and, holding up the bowl full of beer in one hand, raised the other in prayer. This ceremony he repeated three times, and then advanced with his ladle full to the Deb Raja, who blessed it; he then turned to the Tongsa, upon whose hands a small portion was poured; and finally the Donyer returned and poured the remainder into the cauldron, which was then removed, doubtless for the refreshment of the crowd of onlookers who were not of sufficient importance to share the tea and refreshments dispensed in the Durbar Hall. Next, with great ceremony, a wooden spear, with a piece of red cloth and a white silk scarf fastened to the base of the head, was carried to the Deb and blessed; it was then waved over the Tongsa, who reverently touched the end of the shaft. The spear was then sent to the Tongsa's apartment. The final act in the ceremonial was a short prayer, led by the Deb and intoned by the lamas, and with this the proceedings ended and we returned to our camp.

It was a most interesting ceremony, and was conducted throughout with the greatest order and reverence, and passed off without a hitch of any kind. It says a great deal for the change in the conduct of affairs in Bhutan and the anxiety to show respect to the British Government that they should have made the presentation of the decoration to the Penlop the first occasion of so public and elaborate a ceremony, as I understand that hitherto it has been the custom of the recipient of an honour to go to the Deb and head lamas to receive their blessings, while congratulations and presents are received at his private dwelling.

One of the pleasantest incidents during my stay in Poonakha was an expedition to the Norbugang and Ta-lo monasteries; but equally full of interest was the inspection I made of the fort and palace of Poonakha, which I will try to describe. Poonakha is a typical example of the Bhutanese forts, which throughout the country are built after one common plan. The site selected is always a commanding one, generally on a ridge, with the primary object of defence. In the case of Poonakha, however, the building is situated on a tongue of land running down between the rivers Mo-chhu and Po-chhu just above the junction, and as both rivers are unfordable three sides of the parallelogram are most efficiently protected from attack. Access to the Jong on the river side is by means of two substantial cantilever bridges, strengthened by strong gateways of heavy timber studded with iron, with strong defensive towers at each end, through which the roadway runs. On the only land side the fort is protected by a massive masonry wall, built from river to river, commanding the open plain, which the enemy would have to cross to approach the Jong. There are two strongly defended gateways in the wall.

Poonakha, lying between the rivers, is easily supplied with water, but other forts built on a ridge have some difficulty, and are in many cases, as at Dug-gye, obliged to build sunk passages zigzagging down to the valley, and protected by towers at each turning, to ensure a supply of water in the event of a siege. Where a fort is built on the side of a hill, as at Paro and at Tongsa, protecting towers are always built above it.

The plan nearly always followed in the forts is that of a rough parallelogram divided into courts. The main entrance in Poonakha is approached by a steep flight of wooden steps about 20 feet in height, which in time of emergency can be easily removed, leading to the gateway, a massive wooden structure, easily closed, and invariably shut at night.

Through the gateway the first court is reached. The main citadel is situated in this at the south end, a square building, about 40 feet at the base and 80 feet high, and flanking the court on all sides are the two-storied buildings used as residences by the lay officials. Beyond the citadel there is another court, also surrounded by double-storied dwellings, and in the building dividing this court from the next is the larger Durbar Hall, which stretches across the whole width, the smaller Durbar Hall, where the presentation was held, lying to the east. Next comes another and smaller court, within which, to the south, stands the second and smaller citadel, enclosed by more buildings. Beyond comes another court, given up entirely to the Ta-tshang lamas, numbering about 3000, the large temple standing in the centre. The lamas' cells occupy two sides of the court, the third side overlooking the junction of the rivers. Underneath these courts are a few store-rooms for the housing of grain, but the greater part is filled in with earth and rock. All the buildings are roofed with shingles made of split wood, and in this the great danger, that of fire, lies, as the shingles are easily set alight, but otherwise, in the days of bows and arrows, such forts were practically impregnable, and this one could, if necessary, house 6000 souls, or even more. I did not find it as clean as some of the other forts I visited, but that was probably owing to the large numbers who had been in it for the past six months; and it must not be imagined that it was anything like as dirty as the accounts of previous travellers would lead one to anticipate. A great deal of damage was done by the earthquake of 1897, and many of the frescoes were seriously injured by having large strips of plaster shaken off, but the embroidered banners and brocade hangings were magnificent, and a feature of the palace; but Poonakha looks its best and is most picturesque from a distance.

I gave a dinner party in the evening, at which the Tongsa and Jongpens and other officials were present, and seemed to enjoy themselves. They were particularly pleased with the magic lantern, and asked Major Rennick to give a second display in the fort. We did so a few evenings later to a vast crowd, I should think of at least a thousand people, who, from the remarks I at times overheard, took a keen and intelligent interest in the performance. In addition to slides made from my Tibetan pictures, I had several of India and Europe, and we wetted the screen thoroughly to enable the audience on both sides to see.

My hospital assistant was in much request, and amongst other cases was called to attend the murderer captured at Hah about ten days before, who had suffered the usual punishment; his right hand had been cut off and the tendons of his right leg severed. The process by which it is done is slow, and intended to be merciful, as the skin of the hand is turned back, and the wrist then separated at the joint by a small knife, not injuring the bones of the fore-arm, and also allowing some flesh to form a flap. Medical aid was not called in early enough, but the doctor was able by repeated dressings and applications to give the patient some relief, though he did not remain long enough to ensure a complete cure.

On a lovely day I started with Paul to visit the Ta-lo and Norbugang Monasteries, situated high up a mountain to the west. The track, if it deserves even that name, must be absolutely impassable in wet weather, as it runs entirely over red clay. As it was we had to walk a great portion of the way going there and the whole distance returning. As far as Norbugang, about two hours' march, the hillside was bare and uninteresting, but afterwards we passed through one or two pretty glades, and the pear and clematis blossom were beautiful. After three hours of hard climbing we reached the colony of Ta-lo. The situation was charming. Small, well-built two-storied houses, with carved verandahs and painted fronts, were scattered, each in its little garden of flowers and trees, all over the hillside, with here and there a decorated choten to break anything like a monotony of houses. The large temple seemed to crown all by its size, with its background of cypress and *Pinus excelsa.* But we afterwards found, 200 feet higher, the small, but beautifully decorated, private residence of the late Dharma Raja, which was an even more fitting crown. The head lama had sent his band, with oranges and other refreshments, for us some way down the hill, and when we emerged on the large platform on which the great temple is built he, with his chief monks, met us and conducted us to a Bhūtanese embroidered tent, where he regaled us with several kinds of tea and liquor, none, I fear, very palatable to our European taste. Out of compliment to us, I suppose, the most potent spirit was served in a very curious, old-fashioned cut-glass decanter, with a flat octagonal stopper. After partaking of this kindly hospitality, the head lamas, one of whom was eighty-one years of age, insisted on showing us round themselves. The chapels were scrupulously clean, and possessed some glass window-panes, of which they were evidently very proud. Nothing could exceed their civility; they never hesitated to break seals or open cupboards if we manifested the least curiosity.

The principal objects of interest were the miniature chotens or caskets in which rest the ashes of the first and the late Shabdung Rimpochi; these are made of silver, highly chased and jewelled, but the jewels not of any great value from our point of view—mostly turquoises and other semi-precious stones. The sacred implements of the late Dharma Raja were also on view, and were fine examples of the best metal-work. The pillars and canopies were beautifully carved, and then in turn overlaid with open hammered metal scrolls. The whole impressed me with a very high opinion of Bhutanese art and workmanship, which is both bold and intricate. It is a thousand pities that the present impoverishment of the country should give so little encouragement to the continuance of the old race of artificers. The head lama himself complained of the difficulty he was labouring under in completing the memorial to the late Rimpochi.

He then conducted us through the pine forest to the private residence of the late Dharma Raja, where from the top of the hill above there is a beautiful view. It is a perfect little dwelling, charmingly arranged, and full of fine painted frescoes and carved wooden pillars and canopies. We were shown into the room or chapel where the late Lama died and lay in state for some days. I noticed that my attendants and others who were allowed to enter kowtowed to the ground three times and to the altar, and three times to the daïs on which the Lama had lain, and from this I gathered that a high compliment must have been paid me by being taken into the room. We went back to the tent, where we found a lunch provided by the ladies of the Ta-ka Penlop and Thimbu Jongpen, who were related to the late Delai Lama. They pressed us warmly to stay the night, and though I should have liked to do so I did not find it possible to accept the invitation.

On my way back I visited the temples at Norbugang, and was very glad I did so, though the lower one looked so dilapidated and neglected from the outside that I almost resolved not to risk the steep and rickety ladders that do duty for staircases. Luckily I went in, and found the chapel was full of excellent specimens of both metal and embroidered *appliqué* work. I also found three kinds of incense in process of manufacture. It is a very simple process—merely a mixture of finely powdered charcoal, aromatic herbs, and rice-water made into a paste, then spread on the floor and cut into strips, rolled between the hands and formed into the sticks seen burning in the temples. The different qualities depend on the ingredients, the more expensive having musk added as well as herbs.

After a day of pouring rain the morning opened brilliantly, and for the first time I saw the snows at the head of the Mo-chhu Valley, but it soon clouded over. The ladies who had entertained me at Ta-lo came to Poonakha and paid me a visit. After listening to the gramophone, with which they were much pleased, they went away, taking with them some silks for themselves and toys for their children. With them came the head of Ta-lo, the Tango Lama, a man about forty, and his younger brother, Nin-ser Talku, about eleven years old. In the evening the lama came back to dine with us, accompanied by the Thimbu Jongpen, but I do not know that on this occasion the dinner itself was an actual success, as the lama was not allowed to eat fowl or mutton, our principal stand-bys, and the Thimbu excused his want of appetite by saying he had already dined.

I have always found the Bhutanese, as well as the Sikhim people, very appreciative of English food, and as they are Buddhists, with no question of caste, they consider it an honour to be asked to meals, and are most anxious to return any hospitality they receive, in marked contrast to the natives of India, who are defiled and outcasted by such intercourse with strangers. It is a great factor in helping forward friendly relations, and although, out of politeness, they never refuse to taste wine, nearly all the officials are extremely abstemious. At Poonakha the others jocularly remarked that the Zung Donyer, being so much older, was a seasoned vessel, and must drink for the rest of them, and often passed the half-emptied glasses on to him to finish, but at the same time they kept a strict watch to see that the strange spirits whose strength they were unaware of should not overcome him.

After dinner I showed the Tango Lama a stereoscope, with views of Europe, and he so enjoyed it that I gave it to him when he called to take leave. He asked me if I had not brought with me any toy animals, mentioning in particular an elephant, as he wanted them to place before a new shrine they were making at Tango. By a great piece of luck I had a toy elephant that waved its trunk and grunted, also a donkey that gravely wagged its head, and a goat that on pressure emitted some weird sounds. He was greatly delighted with them, and bore them off in triumph, but whether to assist his worship or amuse his children I do not know. Next day, on leaving, he asked if I had not a model of a cow, but that, unfortunately, was not forthcoming. It was an excellent idea, bringing models of animals and simple mechanical toys amongst the presents, and they are most popular as gifts, a jumping rabbit being in great demand. It shows the simple nature of the people that they should be interested so easily.

The Tango Lama, in wishing me good-bye, made himself exceedingly pleasant, and expressed great regret that he could not persuade me to pay him a second visit and remain for the night.

One lovely morning when the snows were quite clear, I rode up the hill to the north-east, and had a fine view up both valleys. About two and a half miles up the Mo-chhu are the ruins of a small fort. It is called So-na-ga-sa, which I think must be the Zemri-gatchie of Turner, and contained formerly the great printing establishment of Bhutan and a fine garden-house belonging to the Deb.. About eighty years ago it was totally destroyed by fire in one of the internecine wars, and has never been rebuilt, while the greater part of their printing is now carried on at Poonakha.

Not very far off is a sort of cave or arched recess in the bank formed by percolations of lime binding the pebbles, and nearly three hundred years ago it was occupied by a hermit from India known as Nagri-rinchen, whose principal claim to saintship seems to have been his power of sailing on the Mo-chhu on a skin. He probably made a coracle to cross the river in, and hence the legend arose.

The time was now drawing near for us to move camp, but before we left my escort performed a Khattak dance before the Bhutanese officials and a large crowd of onlookers, who again were absolutely well behaved. We also held an archery meeting for the soldiers in the fort. Their bows are made of bamboo of great strength, and the arrows of reed or bamboo with iron tips have four feathers, while those for game-shooting at close quarters have only two. I believe there are some extremely good marksmen in Bhutan, but the shooting on this occasion was distinctly poor.

The day before our departure I went, accompanied by Mr. Paul, to take formal leave of the Deb Raja. We were ushered into his private audience-hall, where we found him seated on piles of cushions. He showed us special honour by rising to receive us and offering us wine. Our interview was not a prolonged one, but the Deb desired me to convey his thanks to His Excellency the Viceroy for having sent me on this occasion, and to express the hope that he would continue to favour his little State, whose sincere endeavour was to carry out the wishes of the British Government. He also hoped I would visit him at Tashi-cho-jong on my return from Tongsa.

All the high officials and leading lamas came to my tent, bringing letters for the Viceroy and other high officials. The Thimbu Jongpen, acting as spokesman, made a pretty little speech, saying that as according to the Bhutanese custom a letter was always wrapped in a scarf, so they had selected the whitest of scarves, without a spot, to envelop their letter to his Excellency, and hoped that its purity would be considered an emblem of their own perfect purity of mind and intention.

Next morning we started for Angdu-phodang, the Wandipore of Turner, our first stage on the way to Tongsa. We had a charming ride along a road running on the left bank and close to the river, with a descent so gradual it was hardly felt. I found our camp laid out on a large flat to the north-east of the Jong, but as the sun was very powerful I decided to have our own tents pitched on the fir-tree-covered flat near an outer round fort. There is a curious point about this fortress ; it is built in two distinct parts, connected by an enclosed and loopholed bridge many feet above the level of the hill. There are two local legends to account for this, one that the forts were built at different times, and the other that the villagers of old were so powerful that they refused to be prevented crossing from one river to the other by the closing of the gates, so the designers of the fort were obliged to leave a passage. The most probable story, however, is that the southern and older portion was built some 320 years ago by the second Shabdung Rimpochi, and that subsequently, when one Ache-pipa, a Jongpen, wished to enlarge the building, the villagers insisted that he should leave a passage, so his addition is an entirely separate fort. It is strange that Turner has not noticed the curious way in which " Wandipore " is built.

The interior of the fort was much more picturesque than any we had hitherto seen, except, perhaps, Dug-gye-jong. My photographs illustrate the appearance of the Jong, with its picturesque corners, massive gateways, and the charming effect of its passage-way, far better than any verbal description I might attempt. Including the northern building, there are, as usual, three courts, but only one main entrance, and the damage caused by the great earthquake was still visible, though repairs were slowly progressing. The office of Jongpen was vacant at the time of our visit, for of late years there had been a heavy mortality amongst the holders of the office, and no one was anxious to be appointed, so we were conducted round by the Tongsa Donyer, formerly Donyer of Angdu-phodang, who had restored one of the chapels very well.

About forty-five years ago one of the former Jongpens, who afterwards became Deb Sangye, began cutting down the hill above the round fort, evidently with the intention of imitating the excellent flat in front of the main entrance which is well paved and contains a large choten, a masonry tank, and seats, but as his ryots objected to the expense he contented himself with levelling a large space and planting the rows of fir-trees where our tents were pitched, and it certainly was a most charming spot. I went down to the bridge so well described and illustrated in Turner's narrative. It is wonderful how the mountain rivers of Bhutan, in direct contrast to those of neighbouring Sikhim, seem to keep in one channel. No alteration of the streams seems to have taken place since Turner's visit a hundred and twenty years ago, yet there are no sufficiently solid rocks nor guiding works to retain it. In Sikhim I could never foresee the vagaries of the different rivers, which would often suddenly leave the main channel in times of flood, and later, on subsidence, take an entirely new course. I tried to get a little historical information from the lamas who came to see me here, and who appeared to be a little more intelligent than those I had hitherto met, but it was no use. I could not even get a list of the Shabdung Rimpochis or Deb Rajas for the last forty years.

On leaving Angdu-phodang on a lovely morning we followed a bridle-path very slightly ascending up the right bank of the Tang-chhu for about six miles. On the opposite bank of the river the house belonging to the ex-Poonakha Jongpen was pointed out to me. He fled to Kalimpong, and afterwards died at Buxa. High up above the road was Chongdu Gompa, the summer residence of the Poonakha Jongpen, on a beautiful cultivated site. At Chapakha we crossed the Ba-chhu (5000 feet) by a good bridge, and a stiff climb of three miles brought us to Samtengang, where our camp was pitched in the midst of pines, just above a wide grassy maidan, with a small lake to add to its picturesqueness. The early part of the day had been hot and not very pretty, but after passing Chapakha the new ridge gave us a succession of level grassy plains.

It was while on the next day's march that I had the misfortune to lose my little Tibetan spaniel Nari, who had been my companion on many wanderings in Sikhim, in

Khambajong, and in Lhasa. Just as we were commencing lunch by the Tang-chhu, which we had crossed by the Ratsowok bridge, the little chap gave a sigh, fell on his side, and expired, I suppose from heart disease, as not five minutes before he had been chasing a pariah dog. These Tibetan spaniels are delightful little dogs, and great pets of my wife's. The first one, Thibet, came into her possession at the end of the Sikhim Expedition, a puppy, which one of the telegraph signallers had bought from a Tibetan mule-driver, and ever since we have never been without some of them, though Tibbie, alas! died many years ago; but his descendants have come to England, and I hope may have many years before them. They are dainty little creatures, with beautiful silky coats of black fluffy hair, and feathery tails curled on their backs, yet full of pluck, game enough to kill rats, and the three who accompanied me to Lhasa, little Nari among the number, used to run daily for miles over the great Tibetan plain, hunting for marmots, hares, anything that came in their way.

It was a long day's march that day—quite fourteen miles—though the road was excellent and very interesting, as the scenery was constantly changing. Between Ba-chhu and Tang-chhu we seemed to be on an island hill standing alone, quite apart from the others. For some miles we gradually ascended to Tsha-za-la (9300 feet), and then equally gradually descended to a curious ravine, where, although invisible from higher up, our ridge was really joined on to the main ridge separating the two rivers. Our descent took us down to the Tang-chhu (6700 feet), and, crossing the Ratsowok bridge, a very pretty and good path took us up to Ridha, a fine open space with plenty of flat ground, the village situated on a knoll above us. There were fine views of a snowy range, whence the Tang-chhu took its rise many miles up a rich valley. It was one of our most beautiful marches, the rhododendrons in full bloom, and the oak, chestnuts, and walnuts in their new foliage giving the most vivid and delicate colouring to the scene. In every direction we could see evidences of better cultivation and more prosperity than in any valley we had hitherto traversed. Unfortunately the inhabitants are reputed to be very quarrelsome, and constant litigation, which means heavy bribes to the officials called in to decide their cases, has tended to keep the villagers more impoverished than they ought to be.

All night there was a continuous thunderstorm to the west, and we suffered from a heavy rainfall, but apart from this our camp was very comfortable, as sites had been levelled for our tents and fine mats put down, sheds erected for our followers, and—the greatest comfort of all—cows had been brought to camp, so we had fresh and clean milk.

The rain in the night had quite spoilt the surface of the road for the next day's march, and what would otherwise have been a pleasant, easy, and pretty ride through fine forests became a hard struggle for man and beast to keep their footing on the clayey soil. It took me one hour and forty minutes to get to the top of the Pele-la (11,100 feet). Then it began to rain, and a heavy fog coming on as well, we saw little and fared badly. It was very unlucky, as the country was a succession of wide, open glades, affording most excellent grazing stations. The road, too, under ordinary circumstances would have been good, and as it was showed signs of having been well aligned; portions had been paved, and other soft places corduroyed with flat timber. Another hour and a half saw us at our camp on a flat just below the village of Rokubi (9400 feet), about forty feet above the Siche-chhu, where again excellent huts had been built, a great comfort in the rain and raw cold.

Next day's march lay through beautiful country, but was marred by rain and mist, and we reached camp wearied out by an eighteen miles' march under such disagreeable conditions. A very good road led us gradually down from Rokubi through very pretty scenery to Chandenbi, passing on the way a side valley through which was a direct but bad path to Tongsa. At Chandenbi we had to halt to witness a dance on which the villagers pride themselves. In step it was very similar to the lama dances, though the dresses were not quite so gorgeous, but it was not very interesting.

Some distance further on we came to a romantic patch of sward in a gorge of the ravine where the stream was joined by another mountain torrent, and on the tongue of land thus formed, covered with beautiful cedar pines, was a fine choten, built in imitation of the Swayambunath in Nepal. For miles we continued to traverse undulating ground about the same altitude, through oak, magnolia, and rhododendrons, until we emerged on more open country. Passing Tashiling, where there is a large rest-house, we continued for three more weary miles to Tshang-kha (7500 feet), where we found our camp pitched on a fine open grassy spot, with several hundreds of fine cattle grazing close by. The village was a long way above us, and out of sight.

This was our last halting-place before arriving at Tongsa, and unluckily it rained all night, but by morning it was only misty. Our road took us up the left bank of the Madu-chhu, at a considerable height above its raging torrent, and shortly we found ourselves in very rocky country, as the gorge through which the stream flows narrows considerably, with tremendous precipices overhanging each side. We made slow progress down a road, or rather a series of steep zigzags mostly composed of stone steps, and this path continued to within a short distance of the bridge across the Madu-chhu, some 900 feet below the castle and fortress of Tongsa. The bridge was of the usual cantilever kind, flanked by defensive towers, the whole having been rebuilt within the last few years.

A second steep zigzag, with many flights of stone steps, led us under the walls of the castle, and we entered through a door in an outlying bastion overhanging the cliff up which we had been toiling, and which effectually barred further progress. Passing through the outer gateway of the castle, we emerged on a large stone-flagged courtyard, across which I rode to a gateway on the east side, and, going through this, found myself outside again on a narrow path which ran under the walls of the castle and brought us to the back of the ridge, on which was built a fine square choten. From thence a new road about one-third of a mile in length had been made along the hillside to our camp, which was pitched on an exceedingly pretty knoll, with fine trees, an excellent water supply, and a pretty round tank. This, we learnt, was the pleasaunce of the castle monks.

On our arrival at the ridge immediately below the castle we were met by a large party of retainers, leading gaily caparisoned ponies and mules for us. They were hardly necessary as we were already so well provided for, the Tongsa having placed most excellent mules at our service since leaving Poonakha, carefully selecting those we had tried and liked best; but to send additional mounts was another proof of his hospitality. Amid a salute of guns, which reverberated grandly through the rocky gorge, we emerged from the bridge, where a procession of gaily dressed minstrel singers and dancers met us, and conducted us up the hilly zigzag singing verses of praise and welcome in a curious but not unpleasant monotone. There were seven women singers, peculiar to Bhutan, four clarion players, two drummers, and two gong-strikers in addition to the dancers. We were thus ceremoniously ushered into our camp, where Sir Ugyen met us with a very hearty welcome, and gave us tea and milk, carefully seeing himself that we had all we required. He had with kind forethought sent four picked men to carry Paul, who suffered from an injured back, over the steepest parts of the journey. All Bhutanese officials are carried when the road is too steep and bad to ride a mule, but that is not often, as the mules will go almost anywhere. The orderly who carries the officer, seated pickaback in a strong cloth firmly knotted on the man's forehead, is always a specially picked and wonderfully strong man. I tried this mode of progression once, but it failed to commend itself to me, and I think Paul was wise in refusing it on this occasion. The men were, however, most useful in lending a helping hand over the worst places. I felt obliged, much against my inclination, to ride up the ladder-like steps on our way to the castle, and they held me on, one on either side, so that I could not possibly fall off. I found Captain Pemberton's description, written so many years before, exactly described the situation. "The rider, if a man of any rank, is supported by two runners, one on each side, who press firmly against his back while the pony is struggling against the difficulties of the ascent, and give thus such efficient support that no muscular exertion is necessary to retain his seat in the most trying ascents."

The castle is so irregularly built that it is somewhat difficult to describe. The building on the extreme south was erected in great haste by the first Shabdung Rimpochi to check an inroad from the east of Bhutan, and is a small, low range forming the sides of the present courtyard, and commanding beautiful views. On the north side of the court is a fine five-storied building, in which the Penlop resides when here. It was originally erected by Mi-gyur Namgyal, the first Deb, but it suffered badly in the earthquake of 1897, and the two upper stories have been rebuilt and decorated by the present Penlop. Immediately behind this building is the main tower, surmounted by a gilded canopy, while attached to the west wall is a covered way leading to a second courtyard. A flight of steps leading out of the first court to the north brought me to a large rectangular yard, at the south end of which was a very pretty, though rather small, office for the Donyer, or steward, on the east another building of five stories, each with a fine verandah, while on the first story were the very fine temples, lately repainted at Sir Ugyen's expense. There is a similar building on the west. On the north is the wall supporting

TONGSA-JONG

the last courtyard, where there is a lofty chapel, in which Sir Ugyen was erecting a gigantic sitting image of the Coming Buddha, made of stucco, and at least twenty feet high, but not then painted. A passage to the east from the third courtyard led to the north of a battlemented terrace built up from the ravine below, and a gateway on the north-west opened out on the ridge and the choten that we had reached by the lower road on the day of our arrival.

Below the eastern wall in the ravine is the building containing the prayer-wheels worked by water from which the palace took its original name of Chu-knor-rab-tsi. In it are two sets of wheels, each axle containing three manis, or cylinders, containing prayers, one above the other, the smallest at the top. They had evidently not been used for some time, so the next day, having nothing better to do, we assisted in putting them in order, by clearing out the waterways, which had been blocked with stones and rubbish, and hope it may be placed to our credit as a work of merit.

Later I received visits from the Tongsa Zimpon, who is a son of Sir Ugyen's sister and the Bya-gha Jongpen, and is married to Sir Ugyen's daughter, and also from the castle monks, who struck me as a much better class of men than usual, pleasant in their manners, clean, and educated.

Early one morning the sound of a very sweet-toned gong warned us that the spring ceremony of blessing the rice-fields was about to begin. A long, picturesque procession of men and women, led by the Donyer, came winding down the hillside until the first rice-field, into which water had been running all the day before, was reached. The field below was still dry, and, turning in there, they all sat down and had some light refreshment. Suddenly the men sprang up, throwing off their outer garments ; this was the signal for the women to rush to the inundated field and to commence throwing clods of earth and splashes of muddy water on the men below as they tried to climb up. Then followed a wild and mad, though always good-humoured struggle between the men and women in the water, the men doing their utmost to take possession of the watery field, the women equally determined to keep them out. The Donyer, the leader of the men, suffered severely, though the courtesies of war were strictly observed, and if one of the assailants fell his opponents helped him up and gave him a breathing-space to recover before a fresh onset was made. But gradually the women drove the men slowly down the whole length of the field, the last stand being made by a very stout and powerful official, who, clinging to an overhanging rock, with his back to his foes, used his feet to scoop up such quantities of water and mud that no one was able to come near him. However, all the other men having been driven off, he and the Donyer were allowed at last to crawl up on the path, and the combat for that year was over. This was looked on as a very propitious ending, as the women's victory portends during the coming season fertility of the soil and increase amongst the flocks, so they dispersed to their various homes rejoicing. After witnessing the curious ceremony we went to the castle, and were received by Sir Ugyen, who took us into the courtyard and showed us over the chapels, which he has lately renovated lavishly, but at the same time in very good taste.

From the verandah we witnessed two lama dances, the Chogyal-Yab-Yum and the Shanak, but these have been so often described by travellers who have penetrated to Leh or have seen them elsewhere that I need only say that the dresses worn were a gift lately presented by Sir Ugyen to the lamas and were most gorgeous, and the dance was excellently performed. Unfortunately, before the second dance was over the rain came down in torrents, and I had the performance stopped to save the dresses from being ruined.

CHAPTER XV

MY FIRST MISSION TO BHUTAN—*continued*

From Tongsa-jong to Bya-gha, Lingzi, and Phari. Hospitality of the Tongsa and Tongsa's sister at Bya-gha. Old monasteries near Bya-gha. Ancient traditions. Carvers and carpenters at the Champa Lhakhang Monastery. Regret at leaving Bya-gha. Lama dances. Farewell to Sir Ugyen. Reception at Tashi-cho-jong. Last interview with the Deb Raja. Ta-tshang lamas. Cheri Monastery. Magnificent scenery. Incorrect maps. Exposure of the dead to lammergeiers. View of Tibet from the Ling-shi Pass. Break-up of the Mission.

It was now time to move on again, and, accompanied by the Tongsa, we left next morning, ascending by a very steep path to the main road running above the upper fort. Thence our progress was comparatively easy to the top of the Yo-to-la (11,500 feet), and an equally easy road brought us to our camp at Gya-tsa (8740 feet), a distance of twelve miles. It was a very pretty march. The country had again changed, and we emerged from the confinement of narrow gorges into a series of broad valleys, the upper ones providing grazing for hundreds of yaks, the lower ones rich with barley, buckwheat, and mustard fields. Dotted about we noticed for the first time the temporary huts erected to shelter the cultivators during their stay in high elevations at the times of ploughing, sowing, and reaping; while lower down their substantial dwellings showed we were entering a better governed and more prosperous district than those we had left behind. In the village of Gya-tsa itself there was a fine substantial rest-house for travellers, but more especially for the Tongsa monks, who journey to Bya-gha for two months every year. On a low spur, to the north-west, a prettily built house surrounded by trees was pointed out to me as the home of a powerful family who had plotted to murder the Tongsa. The plot was discovered in time, but Sir Ugyen, although he had narrowly escaped the fate of his uncle, was merciful, and merely banished the ringleaders to a more distant valley. Nemesis overtook them, however, as their leaders commenced a drunken quarrel with their neighbours and were killed, and their adherents dispersed. Dr. Griffiths says: "Fasia [as he calls Gya-tsa] is a good-sized village, comparatively clean, and the houses better than most I have seen." He adds: "We were lodged in a sort of castle, consisting of a large building with a spacious flagged courtyard surrounded by rows of offices; the part we occupied fronted the entrance, and its superior pretensions were attested by its having an upper story."

My camp was prettily arranged on a maidan half a mile beyond the village of Fasia, or Gya-tsa, and there I was met by the Bya-gha Jongpen, who was married to the Penlop's sister.

It was difficult to select a mount next morning, owing to the large number of waiting mules, as not only were the Tongsa's animals there, but his sister and her son the Zimpon, whom I had seen at Tongsa, had also sent mules. Having made our selection, an easy and good road took us over a saddle on the Ki-ki-la (11,700 feet), and an equally easy descent brought us to an opening in the pine-forest, from whence we looked down on the broad vale of Bya-gha, through which the river Chamka-chhu flowed tranquilly. On the right bank was a large house and chapel, surrounded by trees just bursting into leaf, the home of Sir Ugyen's sister, and close by the site of the old house in which he was born. On a bluff on the central ridge, some 500 feet up, was the castle, entirely rebuilt, though on a smaller scale, after the total destruction of the old one in 1897;

while, to crown all, where the ridge widened out into broad glades edged with pine-forest, was the equally new summer house of our host. He had terraced and turfed the slope above the castle, and nothing could have been more picturesque than our camping-ground. The view everywhere, both up and down the valley, was lovely. Dr. Griffiths writes : "The country was very beautiful, particularly in the higher elevations"; and at this season, to add to the beauty, primulas, in flower in myriads, clothed whole glades in delicate violet, while above rhododendrons flamed in gorgeous scarlet. He adds : "We saw scarcely any villages, and but very little cultivation." In direct contradiction to this, I noticed that whole hillsides were being cultivated up to at least 11,000 feet, and I was so struck by the difference that I made inquiries, and found that as recently as thirty years ago, when Sir Ugyen left the valley, a boy of twelve, there was nothing but jungle either here or on the slopes opposite. The land had only been brought into cultivation since the internecine quarrels had ceased some eighteen years ago. So much for stability of government; but even now poverty reigns, and the valley is only prosperous in comparison with more unlucky ones.

A short ride brought us into camp, where Sir Ugyen awaited us. As soon as we had settled down Sir Ugyen's sister, his two daughters, and a daughter of the Thimbu Jongpen came to add their welcome. The younger ones were rather pretty, unaffected and merry girls, while the sister, although a grandmother, was full of good-nature and showed traces of good looks. They all wore the pretty and distinctive dress, which consists of a long piece of Bhutanese cloth, woven in coloured stripes, draped round the figure, and fastened on the shoulders and confined at the waist by a band of brighter Bhutanese cloth. They also wore many necklaces of large rough beads of coral, turquoise, and amber, and occasionally gold filigree beads and many bangles of gold and silver. Their hair was left unornamented, and either cut short or worn in two long plaits. The elder daughter brought her little son, to whom I gave a bottle of sweets, which pleased him just as much as it would a little Western boy, and his mother told me later that he ever after loved me for my gift.

This visit to Bya-gha, which lasted about ten or twelve days, was the most delightful part of our expedition, as we were received as honoured guests by Sir Ugyen in his private capacity; and, interesting and impressive as the ceremonial had been at Poonakha, these few days at Bya-gha gave us a much deeper insight into the life and customs of the Bhutanese, as our intercourse with our host was quite free and untrammelled. Very soon after our arrival Sir Ugyen took me all over his house. In the centre of an oblong courtyard rose a lofty square tower of many stories, the two highest, of ornamental timberwork, slightly projecting over the main walls, beautifully painted in different colours. On the south-east and north sides of the courtyard were two-storied buildings of the usual type. In the south-east corner were the Tongsa's quarters, which did not differ in any material respect from the reception rooms we had seen elsewhere; on the north-east were his eldest daughter's apartments; while between them, on the east front, occupying the whole width of the building, was a long, well-ventilated factory, where many girls were busy weaving silk and cotton fabrics, chiefly the former. The silk was in the main tussar, obtained from Assam and the northern hills. It was altogether a very charming and homelike dwelling, and evidently managed by an excellent and capable housewife in his eldest daughter, who lives with him and superintends his household.

On one occasion we breakfasted with him, and were offered several small dishes cooked in Chinese fashion in small cups, with the accompaniment of boiled rice, while in the centre of the table was a large dish of various kinds of meat. After breakfast I had to go and witness an archery contest. The distance between the butts was at least 150 yards, and the shooting was much better than what we saw at Poonakha and what Dr. Griffiths writes of. There were two teams, captained respectively by Ugyen Kazi and the Tongsa Donyer, and the former won.

Sir Ugyen took a good deal of trouble to find some books for me, from which I have gathered a fuller account of early Bhutanese history than we have had hitherto. His own story is a somewhat pathetic one. As a young man he married an exceedingly lovely girl, to whom he was devotedly attached, but after the birth of their second daughter she died very suddenly from some unknown cause. The shock was a terrible one to Sir Ugyen. He became seriously ill, and on his recovery withdrew from all gaiety, and found solace in reading and studying the history and legends of his country. As some of his followers described him, he was more than a lama. Sir Ugyen is the only Bhutanese I have come across who takes a real and intelligent interest in general subjects, both foreign and domestic, and he neither drinks nor indulges in other vices. He made a large collection of books, but unfortunately many of them were destroyed when the Dechen-phodang, near Tashi-cho-jong, was burnt down, while the earthquake of 1897, which destroyed all the principal buildings in Bhutan, ruined other archives. Paro alone escaped serious injury, but a few years later was burnt to the ground, and unfortunately the Penlop, who was a low-minded and ignorant man, could give no account of what it had contained that was of any value. I held many long private conversations with the Tongsa, and was deeply impressed by his sense of responsibility and genuine desire to improve the condition of his country and countrymen. I gave him what advice I could, and made an attempt to lay the foundation of a close friendship between him and the British Government, and only wish it had been possible to remain in my appointment long enough to see the results of my endeavours, but the time for my retirement came before any of the schemes we discussed had been even commenced.

It is much to be deplored that the proposals with respect to Bhutan made to the Government of India by Mr. Paul on the conclusion of the Sikhim Expedition in 1890 were not approved of. His suggestion that I should hold the appointment of Political Officer to Bhutan as well as Sikhim was a sound one, and had these schemes of improvement been discussed then, by this time they would have been in working order, to the great advantage of Bhutan. The loss during the last twenty years from the wholesale cutting of their forests along their boundary in the Duars alone amounts to many lacs.

The Tongsa's sister was very anxious to entertain us in her own house, so we moved some of our camp near her dwelling on the banks of the river, where a pretty flat dotted with willows had been enclosed for us. To ornament our camping-ground, they had temporarily planted it with evergreen trees hung with various blossoms—one of the little things which showed how anxious they were to do all in their power to welcome us. Sir Ugyen, his sister, and two of her daughters—the third being away in a neighbouring monastery—welcomed us most cordially.

In the evening we inspected a new Jong in the process of being rebuilt to take the place of one which was entirely destroyed in the earthquake. The new one is of the usual type, but much smaller, and Sir Ugyen explained he had carefully rebuilt the foundations for the main tower, which consequently showed no cracks or signs of settlement, unlike that of Tashi-cho-jong, which had been carelessly rebuilt on the old foundations, with disastrous results. We also rode up the valley to inspect the very old Champa Lhakhang Monastery, which is being partly rebuilt by the Bya-gha Jongpen. It is a small monastery, and only interesting on account of its age.

Further up the valley, under a rocky bluff, we came to a double gompa. The larger one was built by Sir Ugyen some years ago, and contains a very large image of Guru Rimpochi, and is called Guru Lhakhang. Close alongside is the smaller one, called Kuje Lhakhang, built on the rock itself, which forms the back wall. On the rock inside the temple is the impression of Guru Rimpochi's back as he sat leaning against it, and also of his "bumpu," or holy water bottle, which he happened to be holding up. Outside on the rock is a very fine Tsenden, or weeping cypress, which the legend relates was the Guru's staff, which he had stuck in the earth, when it immediately took root and grows to this day.

On the way back we were shown the site of the Sindhu Raja's house, now in ruins, situated on the edge of a high bluff overhanging the river. It appears to have been a square of sixty or seventy feet, and the wall apartments could not have been very wide, as there seems to have been an open space in the centre, unless this again was covered in by a floor above, in which case the building would have been an exact counterpart of the central towers we now find in every Jong. Surrounding the sides, on the level, was a well-defined ditch, with a continuation on the outer side leading to the river, and also a well-defined path. Tradition states there was also a gate at the opposite corner to the south. The Penlop has lent me a book of old stories in which there is a glowing description of the old house. On a low hill across the plain the spot was pointed out where the Raja's son was killed fighting against the Naguchi Raja, who lived in the Duars, below Wandipore, and also seems to have reigned in or near the plains. The Guru Rimpochi had heard of the constant wars between the two chiefs, and had come expressly to bring about peace. On his arrival he found the Sindhu Raja prostrate with grief at the loss of his son, and comforting him, and nursing him back to health, he persuaded him to come to terms with his rival. Before his departure, however, he prophesied that in the near future his kingdom would vanish, and not a stone of his palace would remain standing, a prophecy which has been fulfilled. The Guru is said to have married, before his departure, a daughter of the Raja named Memo-Tashi Kyeden.

When we got back to the new house the Tongsa's sister gave us an excellent lunch, but she would not sit down with us, contenting herself with a pretty speech, in which she said that, according to Bhutanese custom, some great personage would have been invited to the house-warming, but she was exceptionally fortunate and considered it a most auspicious omen that her brother's two oldest friends, Mr. Paul and myself, should have accompanied him when he paid his first visit to her new house. Later on she, with her daughters and servants, dressed in old-fashioned Bhutanese dress, in order to let me take a few photographs, and in the evening, after dining with us, the Jongpen and the eldest daughter gave us some Bhutanese music, the former on the damnyan and the latter on the pyang. The younger son and the youngest daughter live at the new Chumik Gompa, where I rode to pay them a visit. The boy was the Avatar of the Thaling Monastery, and they were bright, pleasant young folk. The boy's teacher and guardian, a Lopen of Mindoling, near Samye, was one of the most refined-looking lamas from Tibet that I have met. Next day I rode again to the Champa Lhakhang Monastery, to see the carpenters and carvers at work. The former use a square and a double-manned plane. Most of the carving tools are without handles. No iron is used, but all the pieces of timber are fitted together in the yard, and the necessary dowels made before they are carried away to the building.

Before leaving I gave a magic-lantern entertainment, which was highly appreciated, and later, at the sister's special request, my escort came from Bya-gha and gave a military display, to their great enjoyment. We then wished our kind hosts good-bye with sincere regret, for we had thoroughly enjoyed the natural, open-hearted hospitality with which all at Wong-du-choling had entertained us, and in sultry weather we rode back to Bya-gha, where we again encamped preparatory to turning our faces homewards.

The Tongsa was to see me in the morning to arrange about sending off presents to His Excellency the Viceroy and other high officials, but sent word that he was not very well. He came later on in the day, looking a little out of sorts, and laughed the matter off by saying he had eaten too many green chillies, the first of the season.

With the approach of our departure Sir Ugyen, his sister, daughters, and two of his nieces, came to take a formal farewell, and brought with them many little parting gifts, and in the afternoon, at their special request, my escort gave another military display, ending with an attack and capture of an outlying village, which greatly amused the large crowd assembled to look on. After it was over the Tongsa's sister and daughters insisted on my going to the fort to tea with them before they returned to Anducholing that evening. As my stock of presents was running short, I asked them to accept some notes, which, being in halves, like so many Indian ones, I had neatly rolled up in a leather bag. These I heard later the ladies had distributed promiscuously among themselves, when luckily Ugyen Kazi came on the scene and tried to explain that half-notes were worthless. It was difficult to make them understand, and the knotty point was solved by the ladies saying to the Kazi, " Oh, brother ! take them yourself and bring us silks from Calcutta." I found Sir Ugyen's sight was beginning to fail a little, and as my spectacles exactly suited him I was able to give him a spare pair.

With the morning the actual hour of our departure arrived, and we struck camp and commenced our real journey back. Sir Ugyen and his son-in-law left very early, intending to make one march to Tongsa, but we were accompanied by the other members of his family as far as the main ridge, where they all presented us with scarves and wished us good luck, saying how really sorry they were to bid us good-bye. I replied in similar terms, and could honestly say that all my party fully reciprocated their feelings of regret, for one and all had done their best, and had succeeded, in making our stay at Bya-gha and Andu-choling a very pleasant one.

We had a delightful ride and walk to our old camp at Gya-tsa, which is evidently a much colder place than Bya-gha; there the wheat was in full ear, here it was only a foot high. There was much more cultivation on the slopes with a north-eastern aspect than on those with a southern one. This is probably due to the former getting the morning sun, and also to being sheltered from the southerly winds that rage up the valleys. Quail abound in all the cornfields, and apparently breed in these valleys.

A fine morning turned into heavy mist as we reached the top of the Yo-to-la, and utterly spoilt our view of the Gya-tsa Valley and the hills opposite Tongsa. The yellow giant Sikhim primula was in magnificent bloom, some specimens having as many as six tiers of flowers.

On nearing the castle we were met by a bevy of songstresses, a custom peculiar to the place, as this is the only province of Bhutan in which women take part in ceremonial processions, though, according to Pemberton, the custom was much more widespread in his time. Sir Ugyen met us in camp with the information that the castle lamas were all ready and eager to finish the dances that on our previous visit had been stopped by rain, so after a hasty lunch I went on to the castle. The dance went off very well, with the dancers in gorgeous dresses of every imaginable colour, to the accompaniment of weird tomtoms and huge trumpets, flutes, and cymbals, which produce a strange and unusual but rather fascinating music of their own. But the most interesting objects to me were the masks, which, instead of being carved out of wood, as in Sikhim, were moulded from a *papier-mâché* of cloth and clay; and very well moulded they were, the heads of the various animals quite recognisable, and many with great character. The Tongsa was good enough, about this time, on learning I had become a grandfather, to make me a pretty speech, in which he hoped that as I had been a true and good friend to him and to Bhutan, my grandson would in his turn follow in my footsteps and be as good a friend to his grandson and to Bhutan, and thereupon the little chap was brought by his mother to offer his best wishes to his contemporary.

We now came in for a spell of terribly wet weather, which lasted for the next few days. I fancy Tongsa is a very wet place, and naturally Sir Ugyen's family forsake it after the cold weather. In pouring rain we marched on to Tshang-kha, and a terrible march it was; the stone steps seemed interminable, and to lead in every direction but that which took us to our camp. Sir Ugyen had started before us, and was ready waiting when we eventually arrived with welcome refreshment. He had determined to see us as far as the boundary of his province at Pele-la, and agreed to be our guest on the way. He is always very keen to find outlets for his ryots' superfluous food-stuffs, and on finding such things as Paysandu tongues and chutneys amongst our stores made many inquiries as to the best methods of preserving provisions. We had many long talks on Bhutanese affairs and new methods of government, about which he was always glad to converse and ready to ask for suggestions and improvements. After very heavy rain all night, it cleared about the time we started, so we had a very interesting, though rather slippery, ride to Chendenbi (7380 feet), about four miles nearer than Rokuhi, where we halted before, and a better distribution, as the former march from Tshang-kha to Rokuhi was too long. We rode through typical subtropical forests, until, suddenly rounding a spur, we emerged into open country and fir-trees. Opposite our camp at Chendenbi, on the other side of the river, there were cliffs of pure white crystalline limestone, which I should think was equal to the finest marble.

After dinner that evening Sir Ugyen made a speech, in

which he expressed his deep regret that on the morrow we should have to part. He hoped sincerely he should meet Major Rennick and myself again, but feared that Mr. Paul would not be tempted out from England any more. In wishing him good-bye he trusted that in his far-distant home he would not forget him or Bhutan or the good seed he had planted and nourished for the last twenty years.

We reached the top of the Pele-la along a very pretty road, where a small yellow rose, clematis, wild pear, and rhododendrons of many colours were in wild profusion, while the meadows were clothed with blue and white anemones, yellow pansies, and countless primulas.

At the top of the pass we had lunch and were photographed, and then had reluctantly to part with our friend and kind host and his son-in-law. My escort, who had a genuine respect for Sir Ugyen, presented arms and gave him three cheers before turning down the hill. We exchanged scarves and good wishes, and then also followed the path down the hill. Sir Ugyen waved us a last salute as we turned the corner and went out of sight. I think he really felt our departure as much as I can honestly say I did, and I cannot help repeating myself and saying again that no host could have been more courteous, more hospitable, and more thoughtful of his guests than Sir Ugyen Wang-chuk, the Tongsa Penlop of Bhutan, was to us, the Mission sent by the Government of India to present him with the Insignia of a Knight Commander of the Indian Empire.

The rest of the march to our camping-place, Ridha, was very slippery, but the rain kept off till most of our tents were pitched, and next day we had a fair morning and lovely day, with only one heavy shower. It was a long march to Samtengang, but very beautiful, and each day brought its new flowers, a large white rose, a white and a mauve iris, both new to me; and the giant lily (*Lilium gigantium*) appeared for the first time. It was a tiresome march on to Angdu-phodang, over a road too narrow to ride, so walking was compulsory, and in the afternoon a hurricane arose and raged till nearly ten at night, when it began to drizzle.

I now determined to try a new route up the right bank of the Tsang-chhu or Mo-chhu-Pochu, and Teo-pa-raong-chhu. The river was in full flood, and, filling its bed from bank to bank, looked very fine. I did well in choosing this route, as the road was an excellent one, with a steady ascent from start to finish, and we rode the whole way to Lung-me-tsawe. There were lovely flowers in bloom everywhere, and on the way we passed the sites where formerly two iron suspension bridges had been; the remains of the chains were lying below the Jong. Two fords were also pointed out. I found the ascent of the Dokyong-la much less difficult than it appeared on our descent earlier in the journey, and I had some lovely views until we ran into mist on the top. Luckily I had one glimpse of Kulu-Kangri, a very fine peak of 24,740 feet. On the top of the pass I saw the first yew-trees I had come across in Bhutan. We found a deputation from the Thimbu Jongpen waiting for us, with mules to ride, and chang, tea, and murwa as refreshments, not only for ourselves, but for all our following. The descent to Simtoka was very easy, and the mist soon cleared off.

Just across the bridge below Simtoka the band and dancers belonging to the Thimbu received us, and played us into our camp, nearly three miles off, at Tashi-cho-jong, on the wide maidan about a mile from the palace. With our ridden mules and led mules in their gay trappings, monks on ponies, orderlies in bright uniforms, bands of musicians and dancers, and all the rest of our varied and motley following, we made a goodly procession. It was hot, and I wished I could have headed the procession after the regal manner of King David, with an umbrella to shelter me; and, to my great relief, when we reached the chorten above the aqueduct we found a large umbrella had been unfurled, and we rested awhile under it before making our final entry. The Thimbu offered us refreshments, and made the most polite inquiries after our healths, and hoped we had not had an excessively tiresome journey. I assured him that his arrangements had been so excellent we had not known what difficulties were, and to this he replied the Bhutanese did not easily make friends, but when they did no trouble was too great to make their guests feel comfortable and thoroughly at home.

We found our camp pitched on the left bank of the Thim-chhu, where a new wooden house had been erected, with a large room with windows away from the prevailing winds. Here the Thimbu was joined by the Zung Donyer and the Deb Zimpon. The table was decorated with fruit and some of the finest peonies I have ever seen, a cauldron of murwa was in the centre, and as soon as we were all seated the Thimbu's chaplain intoned grace, in which the others joined; the murwa was then solemnly blessed, a little in a ladle was poured over my hands, and the sacred flag brought in for me to touch. Next a number of tea-pots were brought in, three at a time, each of the trio containing a different tea. These were sent by the various officials as their greeting, and when the donor's name had been announced the tea was taken away to regale our followers. We spent some little time in conversation with our hosts before going to our tents at the conclusion of this quaint ceremony of welcome.

The following day we went early to the palace to bid the Deb Raja good-bye. His reception room was very large and airy, and the Deb himself was most cordial, and came forward to receive us, and stood talking till our own chairs were brought in. In the course of conversation the Deb again expressed his sincere gratitude to the Viceroy for having sent such friends to see him, and to us for coming, and trusted that relations between his little country and the Sirkar would always be intimate and friendly, as pure as a white scarf with no blot to mar its whiteness, as indissoluble as water and milk when intermixed, and that on his part no effort should be wanting to secure so happy a result, and should any one of us at any time return he could assure him of a hearty welcome. He asked me to send him a set of photographs of Lhasa and of Bhutan, and inquired if I had any of Buddh-Gaya, as he was anxious to possess some. He sat for his own photograph, and when refreshments had been served we were dismissed with the scarf of blessing, which he placed on our arms.

From there we adjourned to the Thimbu's room, where he had a Bhutanese breakfast waiting for us, consisting principally of bowls of rice, omelettes, dishes of sausages, and pork in various forms. He too expressed his pleasure at our visit to his country, and wished our stay could be prolonged, and the least he could do was to accompany us as far as Hram, and in the meantime he asked us to gratify him by selecting anything in his hall that took our fancy.

At the conclusion of this civil speech we went to the separate court of the Ta-tshang lamas, where the Dorji-Lopon, or abbot, received us very cordially, and took us into the big hall I described on my journey up. Here we found a kind of pandemonium going on, but on closer examination discovered there were a number of dancing classes in progress, from the smallest acolytes shouting out the numbers of the little steps and arm-wavings they were being taught, to a grave collection of learned monks performing unmasked the gyrations that we had witnessed at Tongsa. When we came out we learnt that it was entirely against rules for any layman to intrude upon the monks when thus practising, and I apologised to the abbot for breaking rules through my ignorance, but he smilingly replied that "no rules applied to us, as he hoped we would consider ourselves as one with them." When giving us scarves before leaving the gompa, the abbot, who was joined by the Lopens, trusted that now that we had found our way to their abode and become their friends we would make a point of some day returning, but that whatever fate might be in store for us and them, at least our present firm friendship might remain for ever unbroken and enduring. It was very pleasant to find the same cordial wishes and expressions of goodwill repeated by every one in turn, and to be made to feel so thoroughly that our visit was looked on in the light of a compliment to their country, and that everything was thrown open to us, instead of finding obstacles and difficulties in our way.

The history of the building of Poonakha I heard from the Thimbu Jongpen, who, when a boy, heard it from a very old woman. According to him, the old palace and fort stood on the ridge where the Dechen-phodang stands. The greater part of it having been burnt down, the Deb Zimpon, who had usurped all the power, determined to rebuild it on its present site, which was much more convenient for the supply of water. The valleys were thickly populated in those days, and the Deb collected so many people that the materials were passed from hand to hand the whole way from Dechen-phodang to Tashi-cho-jong, a distance of quite a mile. It is needless to say the labour was forced, and although the palace was said to have been completed in one year the Deb became very unpopular.

The Tibetans seem to have been very fond of raiding Bhutan, as the fort of Simtoka, close by, built by the first Shabdung, was soon after captured and burnt by them. In rebuilding it the architect utilised one of the original wood pillars which had only been singed as a memorial of the saint. It stands there to this day, its damaged surface covered with elaborate carving.

We broke up camp early in the morning, and for three or four miles our path lay through open ground similar in character to that below Tashi-cho-jong. We saw several monasteries, but only entered one, Pangri-sampi-gnatsa, which was beautifully situated in the midst of the valley, but contained nothing of much interest. Turning due north over a cliff, we came to an entirely different scene, the valley narrowing considerably, and being beautifully wooded and picturesque to a degree. Throughout the march ruined houses were in a majority, most evidently deserted years ago, as big trees had grown up in and around them, and this state of things was accounted for by the following story. The monastery of Dechenphuk, founded by one of the pioneers of Buddhism, lies in a beautiful side valley about three miles from Tashi-cho-jong. The monks belonging to the monastery refused to recognise the first Shabdung when he came to the valley, and consequently there was strife between them. The ryots naturally sided with their old masters, the monks of Dechenphuk, but in the end the Shabdung won the day, and by his magic art summoned a terrible demon to his aid, and the ryots died off, and no one dared to take their place. Such was the local legend, and whatever the truth of the story may be, disease or oppression or other calamity has played havoc with the valley. Just before arriving at our destination we saw the monastery of Tango perched up a side valley to our right, the home of the Tango Lama, who received us so hospitably on our journey in. The camp was on a small flat, close to the river and beneath a cliff, on which is perched the Cheri Monastery, dating back to the first Dharma Raja. After lunch, in time for which the Thimbu arrived, Paul and myself went up to the gompa; but it is terribly difficult of access. To get from the lower to the higher temple it is necessary to climb very narrow rough stone steps overhanging a sheer precipice, over a projecting crag, and down other steps to the platform of the temple, which is literally clinging to the cliff. It is in bad repair, and did not repay me for the trouble of getting there, as it contained nothing of interest.

It rained most of the afternoon, and to the damp and unhealthiness of this camping-ground and the very long and wet march through drizzling rain the following day I attributed the fever with which most of my followers went down. An hour and a half's climbing up a steep and bad path brought us to a little glade called Aitok-keng, and we continued to climb till we came to an open side valley in which was situated the small fort of Barshong, close to which was our camping-ground. I had an attack of fever also by this time, and was glad to go dinnerless to bed as soon as the baggage came up. On the march that day both sides of the valley were thickly wooded, only the more precipitous rocks being bare. Geographically we had now left the middle third of Bhutan, and had entered the narrow gorge which leads upwards to the plains of Tibet. From the fort our path, which throughout proved to be quite good, led gently down to the bed of the stream, the Tchin-chhu, which, with a few occasional ups and downs, we hardly left. The thick vegetation of the previous day soon ceased, and we entered a gorge almost filled by the Tchin-chhu, and bordered by stupendous cliffs of most weird shapes, amongst which El Capitano of the Yosemite Valley would be dwarfed by the lowest of these monsters. These cliffs appeared to be formed by horizontal strata of sedimentary rocks, consisting of layers of limestone, sandstone, slate or shale of a dark blue colour, and quartzites. The towering rocks were cleft in numberless places from top to bottom, leaving narrow slits or fissures which I was told were often more than a mile long. One which I photographed extends for more than two miles before it opens out in a beautiful basin and forms one of the Thimbu's best grazing-stations.

Through scenery like this we rode for ten miles, crossing the Tchin-chhu no less than six times. At length we left the main stream, turned to the right into an open valley devoid of trees but of great width, and, ascending gently for another two miles, reached our camp at Byaradingka, a wide maidan of the highland character so often met with. On the slopes to the west we saw several flocks of burhel, but failed to bag any. The hills here consist of dark shales, which run right up to the east foot of Chomolhari, and are very similar to those met with at Khambajong; while the same curious concretions are also to be found here. The only gneiss I saw was that brought down by the glaciers running from Chomolhari.

On a misty morning we rode quietly up the valley, and after an hour's gradual ascent reached the Yakle-la (16,800 feet). The maps, I found, were completely wrong, as the pass is situated on the water-parting which separates the Thim-chhu from the Mo-chhu, the eastern slopes of Chomolhari thus draining into the Poonakha river. On the left of our path there lay a pretty dark green tarn, fed from a small snow-slope to the west of the pass, and from thence a somewhat steep descent brought us to the main stream of the Pim-nak-me-chhu, which joins the Mo-chhu near Ghassa. Following the valley for a few miles, we soon came in sight of Lingzi-jong on a hill apparently blocking the valley, but as we continued our march we discovered another ridge between us and Lingzi, round which we had to ride, ascending and descending for some way through lovely rhododendron scrub, of which at least eight different varieties were in flower. Crossing the stream, which separates the two ridges, and which rises in some glaciers coming down from the east of Chomolhari, we again ascended the shoulder of the Lingzi spur, and, leaving the ruins of the fort on the top, found an excellent camping-ground close to a small stream. It was, on the whole, an easy march, as there was only a small quantity of snow on the north side of the pass. We saw several flocks of burhel, but could not get a shot, although my shikari was more successful and bagged two females, which were a useful addition to the supplies of my followers. We had some particularly fine views of the Chomolhari glaciers which feed the lower streams near Lingzi. We halted at Lingzi for a couple of days, and made an excursion down the valley to try and locate Ghassa, but did not succeed, as it was cloudy and drizzly weather and we could see no distance.

We also visited the ruins of Lingzi-jong, which must have once been an imposing and very strong citadel, much larger than I should have thought necessary, but the earthquake of 1897 has reduced it to a picturesque mass of ruined masonry. The Thimbu, becoming communicative, told me that the Tibetans were formerly inclined to be very aggressive, and as this was in reality a very vulnerable spot the Bhutanese had been obliged to maintain a large garrison both here and at Ghassa. When we reached Pheu-la he would, he said, prove his words by pointing out the ruins of a strong fort the Tibetans had built on the Bhutanese side of the pass during the former troubles with Tibet. "But now," he added, "since we Bhutanese have openly thrown in our lot with the British, who have publicly recognised the services rendered against the Tibetans by the honour conferred on the Tongsa as representative of Bhutan, I shall rebuild the fort on a much smaller scale, just sufficiently strong to keep out cattle-lifters and suchlike. We now rely entirely on the good faith of the British Government to protect us against Tibet, should that nation try to revenge themselves on us." This sentiment is very flattering to us, and I only hope it may never prove unfounded. He also made a very significant remark about the Tibetan indemnity. It was that the Tibetan officials had not the least objection to promising an indemnity, as if called upon to pay by our Government they would realise more than was necessary from the poor ryots, and so line their own pockets while quibbling with us about paying in full, and thus perhaps make a little over the transaction. In this camp we had some matches at stone quoit-pitching, and great sport over games with spear, or rather pointed stick quoits, at both of which the Bhutanese proved themselves adepts.

We made a leisurely start for our short march to Gang-yul (13,600 feet), a little village in a narrow, flat valley close under the eastern glaciers of Chomolhari. While our camp was being got ready I rode two or three miles up the valley in the hope of seeing a remarkable cave which we were given to understand was in the locality. We found several indentations, before two of which were a gompa and a chorten, but nothing remarkable. We soon discovered, however, that our guide was much more anxious to show us a large flat rock of slate situated between two branches of the Tsango-chhu, at the head of which was a wooden axle, forming a rack. It was carefully explained to us that this was a holy spot on which human corpses, the head and shoulders tied to the axle to keep the body in place, were exposed, to be eaten by lammergeiers and other ravenous birds and beasts of prey. In perfectly solemn and earnest good faith we were told that the birds were fastidious and would not touch low-caste bodies, and that only three families in the valley were entitled to be thus disposed of. The Thimbu excused himself from accompanying me, as the memories connected with this spot were very painful to him, his daughter only a few years before having been laid on the slab. One of our guides lay down on the slab, while another lit a smoky fire, devices which, they said, would be sure to attract the lammergeiers from their eyries; but the deception failed, and no birds appeared. In another respect the little valley was very remarkable, as the glaciers seemed to completely close in the head, and I saw two avalanches and heard several more, caused by the increasing power of the sun's rays on the snows.

The main glacier was most beautiful, looking like a curious broad staircase of snowy whiteness leading from where we stood heavenwards. There were several fine waterfalls gushing out from holes in the cliffs high above us, and disappearing before they reached the path, the rivulets of water oozing out again from the banks of the main stream showing that the water had resumed a subterranean course. A curious feature about the falls was that as the power of the sun increased, so did the waterfalls visibly increase in size. Our camp that night was a cheery one, and we relieved the time by learning, to the great amusement of the bystanders, to play Bhutanese backgammon, our implements being two wooden dice, a collection of little wooden sticks of varying length, and a handful of beans.

In anxious fear of the unknown pass, the Pheu or

Lingshi-la, and its difficulties, we made a very early start along a fair bridle-path, which led us past the Tsango-chhu and then turned to the left above a small, flourishing valley, absolutely blocked at one end by a cliff extending from side to side in a perfect level, over which a very fine waterfall fell. This little valley was excellently cultivated, and had a great many large, fine fir-trees on its sides. Our path brought us at an easy gradient to the top of the cliff, which we discovered was the lower edge of another long level valley. In this way we progressed by a succession of steps, as it were, until we came to the last tread of the stairway, which was an almost precipitous slope of stone and rocks, up which our laden yaks and mules struggled slowly but surely, the zigzag, so far as alignment went, being so good that no one dismounted. Surmounting this, we came to a small roundish flat, in the centre of which were the walls, still good, of the fort built by the Tibetans and mentioned by the Thimbu. A short incline then brought us to the top of the Lingshi Pass (17,100 feet), where we had a magnificent view of the plains and hills of Southern Tibet. From this view I learnt more of the real geography of the great Kalo Hram-tsho plain than in my journey over it on the way to Lhasa the year before. The succession of lakes, amongst them the Rhum-tsho, was most clearly mapped out at my feet. To the north, in unclouded sunshine, lay a treeless, arid plain; to the south damp mists and clouds shut out all view of the verdant, wooded valleys of Bhutan.

After a short, somewhat abrupt descent, in places still covered with snow, we came on a rocky decline, which brought us, after a weary ride, to the sand-dunes of Hram, and finally to the hamlet of Hram-toi. In the evening we all dined together, with the Thimbu as our guest for the last time in the mess-tent, which I had promised to give him as a parting gift. We toasted the Thimbu and wished him the best of fortune, and had kindly answers from him in return, and on the morrow the Bhutan Mission would practically be a thing of the past. We breakfasted in the open, bid the Thimbu and his party a sorrowful good-bye and godspeed, and accepted from him scarves of blessing. The Tongsa Donyer, who had accompanied us everywhere throughout the whole journey, now took his leave. He was a most jovial officer, never under any circumstances put out, and ever obliging, an adept at archery and all manly games, fond of a glass but never the worse, a real Bhutanese Friar Tuck, and it was with real regret we bid him good-bye. I do not think we could possibly have had a more suitable man as our factotum, for in addition to physical qualifications he possessed a great fund of information.

A long, weary ride across sandy plains took us to the Tang-la, the monotony only broken when we missed the trail and got unexpectedly bogged. We saw several herds of gazelle and many kyang, but only succeeded in bagging a grey goose. At the top of the Tang-la my straggling caravan got divided, and the bulk proceeded to the village of Chukya, while I and the remainder kept to the main road and halted at the Chukya military encampment, so it was very late before we settled down, cold, damp, and cross. My next march brought me to Phari, ground I had already often been over, and which I have already described, so with our arrival there I will bring the account of my first mission to Bhutan to a close.

CHAPTER XVI

AN EXPLORATION OF EASTERN BHUTAN AND A PORTION OF TIBET IN 1906

From Gangtak viâ Dewangiri to Tashigong and Tashi-yangtsi, and on to Tsekang. Horse-flies. Dorunga. *Cypripedium Fairianum.* Sudden rise of the river. Tigers near the camp. Chungkhar. Borshang iron-mines. Tashigong. Stick lac cultivation. Suspension bridges. Source of the Dongma-chhu. Tashi-yangtsi. Prayer-wheels. Old roads. Chorten Kara. New flowering trees.

For some years I had been extremely anxious to explore Eastern Bhutan and its neighbouring portion of Tibet, but it was not until May 1906 that circumstances enabled me to make arrangements to do so, and I left Gangtak accompanied by Mr. Dover, the State engineer. To reach Dewangiri, the point from which I intended to enter Bhutan, I had to travel to Siliguri, thence by rail to Dhubri, and on by steamer up the Brahmaputra to Gauhati, in Assam, and from thence march to the hills. I had a good deal of camp kit in addition to my personal baggage and riding-mules with me, and on reaching Gauhati preliminary arrangements took some time. Marching at the foot of the hills at this time of the year was very trying; mosquitoes swarmed at night, and the incessant croaking of frogs kept one awake; while worst of all was the plague of horse-flies, which attacked the mules, oxen, and elephants unmercifully. They were literally in swarms, and the sides of the elephants streamed with blood from their attacks.

A little place called Dorunga lies at the foot of the hills, and is used as a temporary mart in the cold weather, but at this time of the year it is merely a collection of deserted thatched huts in the midst of a sea of grass, and by no means healthy, so instead of halting there I pushed on up the hills, beyond the fever zone. I had visited Dorunga a few months before in the cold weather, in the company of Sir Ugyen Wang-chuk, the Tongsa Penlop, and it had then presented a very different aspect. The place was full of bustle and movement and alive with traders from the hills, a striking contrast to its present appearance. On that occasion I entered the hills a little further to the west, at Subankhata, and accompanied Sir Ugyen for a few marches till we came to the Kuru-chhu, on the direct road to Tongsa. On this journey I came across quantities of *Cypripedium Fairianum* growing in masses on the magnesium limestone hills. This is the orchid of which one specimen reached England about 1860 in a consignment sent from Sikhim by Sir Joseph Hooker, but had since become extinct, and for which £1000 was offered by orchid-growers. I had been on the look-out for it for several years, and now when I did find it I was just too late, as it had been discovered during the survey of the Am-mo-chhu Valley a few months before.

At Dorunga I had a great deal of difficulty about carriage, as no arrangements had been made beforehand and I could get no coolies ; however, I had four elephants, and with them and another elephant I found belonging to one of the tea-gardens, and which I impressed into my service, I started the most necessary baggage up the track to Dewangiri, leaving the remainder in charge of the Havildar till I could make arrangements from Dewangiri. Transport difficulties were augmented by the arrival of tools for road-making lent to the Tongsa by the Government of Assam, and as the store-keeper had made no arrangements for forwarding them I was obliged to take them with me. The road we had to follow was nothing but a track running up the bed of the stream, and quite impassable during the rains. Before I had gone very far—about two miles, perhaps—I came across various articles of baggage lying in the road, and soon found that one of the elephants had bolted and strewn the road with impedimenta. A little further on I overtook the other three elephants, and the mahouts entered into a lengthy explanation that one elephant would not go without its companions, and that in order to reload the delinquent they must all go back, and then return in one party, so I had to allow them to do as they liked, and hope they might somehow reach their destination. So much for the pleasure of elephant transport.

I pushed on ahead, and it was lucky I did so, as a severe thunderstorm came on, and the river rose to such an extent the coolies were unable to cross, and had to spend the night in the jungle on the banks, while my mule was very nearly carried off its feet by the torrent of reddish-yellow mud and water. The river rose with extraordinary rapidity, coming down in regular waves of red mud. I rode on in pouring rain to Dewangiri, and was lucky to find a good hut, which had been built in expectation of the Tongsa's arrival earlier in the year, and as my orderly had kept up with me, carrying a bag, I was able to change into dry clothes in front of a good fire, and was none the worse for my adventure. Want of carriage kept me at Dewangiri for a day or two, and the first morning, on getting up, news was brought that one of the baggage mules was missing, and had been carried off by a tiger during the night. I went out and found that the carcase had been dragged at least 600 yards along a path through the dense jungle and then straight down the khud to the spot where I found it. Later in the day the remains of a sambur were brought in by a mahout, also killed by a tiger about half a mile from the camp, so tigers must be very plentiful just there, and sport ought to be good; but the jungle is very dense and game difficult to get at, and the hillsides are very steep, and in many places quite inaccessible. I had a machan put

BHUTANESE HOUSES

up, and waited for some hours in hopes that the tiger might return, but he did not do so, at any rate before dark, and I was not inclined to wait longer for him.

From Dewangiri I moved on to Rading, and for a short distance followed a path which had been made up the left bank of the Tsokhi river; but it was a hopeless track, without any attempt at alignment, and with such steep gradients over the rocks no animals could possibly use it. At Rading I was met by the Tongsa Jongpen, whom I had met when in Bhutan with Sir Ugyen in the spring. In the morning, after a very early start, I passed the large monastery of Yong-la, near the crest of the ridge, at about 7700 feet. It was very well situated, looking out over the plains, but I did not visit it, as to do so would have taken me five or six miles out of my way. The road here was good and rideable, and brought me to Chungkhar, the residence of the Jongpen, at an elevation of 6475 feet. Going down the hills from the pass the woods were full of a pretty ground orchid, and there was some very fine timber. At Chungkhar I found a good camping-ground, with extensive views, and the snows in the distance, due north. The Jongpen was living in a temporary hut, as his house had been demolished by the earthquake of 1897, and although his new residence had been commenced it was not yet finished. He had prepared some small huts for us, which we found most comfortable and cool, and used in preference to our tents.

The mules sent by the Tongsa now arrived, the delay having been caused by the destruction of the Dongma-chhu bridge on account of an outbreak of small-pox. That is the primitive method in Bhutan of checking the disease. The wrought-iron chains of the bridge are left, but the cane roadway is cut away to prevent communication from one side to the other. I had heard of the outbreak before starting, and had brought a vaccinator with me, who set to work at once and vaccinated over a hundred people in the camp. All the villagers seemed glad to be vaccinated, and men, women, and children came in willingly. I also had my mules and ponies re-shod, and this afforded some amusement as well as instruction to the villagers, who had never seen the operation before, and after it was done they crowded round to examine the animals' hoofs. There were a number of small boys smoking cigarettes, which shows that the latest vice has penetrated even into these wilds.

On leaving Chungkhar my road led straight down the hill to the Chalari-chhu, and another few hundred yards brought me to the Demri-chhu (2455 feet), where I found huts ready prepared; but it was still early, and would be exceedingly hot in the valley, so I decided to go on to Denchung, where I heard the Tashigong Jongpen was waiting.

It was a very hot ride from the Demri-chhu up the south-east face of the hill to Sari (4000 feet), on the ridge. Then the road fell again to the Tondong bridge (3000 feet), and then a very hot climb up a steep rock-face brought me to the camp at Denchung (4275 feet). The camp was a very good one, situated in the middle of woods of oak, pine, and rhododendron, with huts built for my reception and the Jongpen in waiting.

The next day's march into Tashigong was much longer than I expected, and I was over twelve hours on the road. From the first ridge I could see the famous iron-mines of Borshang, situated in a fine valley, fairly well cultivated. The ore is reported to be both red and black and easy of extraction, and it is from this mine that the iron comes from which chains are made for the bridges in this part of Bhutan. If I had only known of this a little earlier I should have paid the mines a visit, and have no doubt I should have been well rewarded for the trouble, but it was too late to do so then.

The road took me over the Yuto-la (8300 feet), and was so narrow in many places—sometimes only six to nine inches wide—and on such a very steep hillside, that I walked most of the way in preference to riding even my sure-footed mule. The alignment, however, was good, and just below the Yuto-la, to the north, there were some fine downs and very good views; but these grassy uplands were infested by ticks, and it was necessary to stop frequently to pick them off the dogs, for they absolutely swarmed in hundreds, and even occasionally attacked us.

A lama who came to pay his respects proved to be unusually intelligent, and gave me a good deal of information regarding routes, &c. From the Yuto-la the road led for some way through oak and rhododendron woods, until the village of Rungthung was passed, when the last five miles wound along a bare, steep hill-slope, and I was glad to get to my destination. The latter part of the march was very hot, and the only shade to be found was behind an occasional chorten, where I sat down and drank quantities of murwa sent by the Tongsa; but the full force of the afternoon sun was very trying. At the Jong I was met by the Jongpen. The usual form of touching a wand was gone through, and I was installed in his own room.

The Jong at Tashigong is particularly well situated on a ridge between two rivers, the Dongma-chhu and the Gamdi-chhu, and is constructed after the Bhutanese fashion, with courtyards and citadels. It has a fine temple, with an unusually large pair of tusks supporting the altar, and fittings in excellent metalwork. I was lodged in the Jongpen's own room, facing south. It was a fine, lofty room, but there was a peculiarly pungent and disagreeable smell, which I discovered came from stores of dried mutton and rancid butter kept under the floor. I asked the Jongpen to remove them, and when he had done so the surroundings were quite pleasant, as the room itself was perfectly clean. He had the skins of some very fine tigers, which he told me had been shot during the last cold weather, and that every year several tigers come up the valley and work havoc amongst the cattle, so large rewards are given for their destruction.

With regard to the geological features of the journey, as far as the Yuto-la the strata were all quartzites, but after that mica-schist was met with in small quantities.

It was a dreadfully hot camp, but my baggage had not come up, so I was obliged to halt. I started my vaccinator at work early, and before evening he had vaccinated over two hundred people, who all seemed very pleased, and flocked in for the operation. I had sent the Tongsa a consignment of lymph from Gangtak, as he wished to introduce vaccination throughout Bhutan, and his operator met us here to be instructed what to do.

From Tashigong a road runs to the small Tibetan State of Tawang, first crossing the river Gamdi-chhu, then passing over a very steep spur, and thence to the Tawang-chhu. The Tawang-Bhutan boundary is three days' march up the stream, at a place called Dong Shima, situated a little below the bridge by which the road crosses the river. The greater part of the trade from Tawang, which is, comparatively speaking, large, already comes by this route to the plains, and as soon as the Tongsa, as he hopes to do, makes a really good mule-track it will all follow this route to Dewangiri, and as the valleys are well populated and cultivated it is likely to increase rapidly.

There is a great deal of stick lac grown in the valley of Tashigong, but the Bhutanese do not carry on its cultivation in any systematic manner, which seems a pity, as if placed under proper supervision the industry might have a great future before it. Its culture is unusual, quite an interesting process, and only occasionally to be met with. Lac is an insect growth, and is cultivated on two distinct plants. Small pieces of lac containing colonies of the insect are placed on the stem of a shrub called Gyatso-bukshing in the autumn, and this plant is regularly cultivated and planted in rows in fields on the hillsides. In the spring these growths, which have meanwhile spread a few inches over the stem of the plant, are cut off and placed on the branches of a tree called Gyatso shing. On these trees during the summer it spreads rapidly over all the branches, and the crop is gathered in the autumn. With the present want of system there are no plantations for the purpose, and the cultivator has to depend on any trees he may find growing wild in the jungles, which is, of course, a hopeless method, whereas if proper plantations were made it would facilitate not only the collection and save time and labour, but also increase the output. It is a paying crop, but can only be grown in these hot, dry valleys.

It was my original intention to follow the route viâ Tawang and the Dozam-la to Lhakhang, but the Government of India did not wish me to enter that part of Tibet. I therefore had to abandon it and go round by a longer and more difficult route. Another route, the direct one, along a road running from Tashigong along the right bank of the river, and said to be fit for mules and ponies, is a very easy one, and by it I could, I believe, have reached Lhakhang in five or six days; but this also took me into prohibited country, and had to be abandoned.

From Tashigong a very steep descent of about 1100 feet took us down to the iron suspension bridge over the Dongma-chhu. These suspension bridges in Bhutan are very interesting, and merit description. They consist of four or five chains of wrought iron, made of welded links, each fifteen to eighteen inches in length. The three lower chains are tightened up to one level, and on them a bamboo or plank roadway is placed. The remaining chains, hanging higher up and further apart, act as side supports, and between them and the roadway there is generally a latticework of bamboo, or sometimes grass, in order that animals crossing may not put their legs over the side. The roadway is never more than three or four feet wide. Many of the chains on these bridges are extremely old—many hundreds of years—and appear to be of Chinese workmanship. The links are in excellent order, and very little pitted with rust. The other and newer chain bridges have been made in Bhutan.

After crossing the ridge the road wound along the hill-side some distance above the river till we came to a place called Gom Kora. Here there is a very curious little temple, with a prayer-wall completely surrounding a large stone, which has a curious water-worn hole through its centre. It is considered extremely holy, and to crawl into the small hole and out at the other side is an act of merit. Needless to say, that act of merit is not placed to my credit, though the more devout of my servants and followers performed it before being regaled by the Tomsha-Tungba.

A little further on the Dongma-chhu was left on the right, and the road, crossing the Kholung-chhu by a cantilever bridge, climbed a very steep ridge to the camp at Serpang (6450 feet). The Dongma-chhu is here a very large river, much bigger than the Kholung-chhu, and probably as big if not bigger than the Kuru-chhu, running swiftly and carrying much silt. It takes its rise in a range of snow-mountains a long way to the east, beyond Tawang. In this camp also people crowded to be vaccinated, and to be treated for various diseases. I did what I could, and Mr. Dover was indefatigable in dispensing medicines, but it would have made a very great difference if I had had a doctor with me

The road on to Tashi-yangtsi wound round the side of the hill, covered with oak and rhododendron, and the march was very beautiful, though a short one. The Jong of Tashi-yangtsi (5900 feet) is situated on a sharp spur between the Kholung and Dongdi rivers, with a very pretty view looking up the valley. In the river, with its beautiful pools and numbers of fish, there ought to be some good fishing. It ran, in places, in deep, silent reaches, very rare in any Himalayan river, with the trees overhanging and dipping in the water, much more like a river in Scotland, with a very gradual fall, and the water a beautiful blue colour. A feature of the march was the number of water-driven prayer-wheels, most of them in a state of picturesque decay, and only a few still in working order. For the benefit of my readers who are unacquainted with this practice, the following is a short description. A prayer-wheel consists of a hollow cylinder filled with written or printed prayers, and fixed to a perpendicular shaft of wood, to the lower end of which horizontal flappers are attached, against which water is directed from a shoot; the end is shod with iron, and revolves in an iron socket driven by the force of the stream. With each revolution the prayers are believed to be prayed for the benefit of the builder of that particular wheel, and count so much to his credit. They are very easily kept in order, but probably because only construction, and not preservation, is a work of merit in the Buddhist religion, no one seems to take the trouble to clear out the watercourses or to mend a broken flapper, and consequently most of them were at a standstill. It is a delightfully easy method of praying, and some enormous wheels have been erected. One at Lamteng, in the Lachen Valley, in Sikhim, contains no less than four tons of printed paper, and measures about 9 feet in height by 4½ feet in diameter; but these very large ones are seldom worked by water-power, and generally have a crank on the lever end of the shaft, which any one anxious to pray has only to turn, while a bell sounding automatically at each revolution records the number of prayers repeated. Every monastery throughout Sikhim has a row of prayer-wheels at the entrance to the temple, and as every true Buddhist passes he twirls each cylinder in turn with the ejaculation, "Om mani padmi hum."

The road along which we were travelling had evidently at one time been well made and properly aligned, although it had been allowed to go out of repair. It must have been cut to four or five feet in width, and well graded also, but though all agreed that it had been made a very long time ago, no one could tell me when. My own opinion is that it was probably built by one of the old Rajas who once gned in these valleys, and of whom some historical records remain in the manuscripts I found dealing with the reign of the Sindhu Raja of Pumthang, and have mentioned elsewhere. This march throughout was a great contrast to the last, as it was entirely through cultivated land, with small collections of houses, two or three together, not large enough to form villages. All the crops looked excellent, especially the wheat and barley; the country was thickly populated, and the inhabitants flourishing and well fed. I saw one iron-impregnated stream.

There is an easy and good trade route which runs from Tashi-yangtsi over the Ging-la to Donkhar, where it joins the route from Tashigong and Tawang and Tshona, and this is a good deal used by traders in the cold months. My shortest route was by a road branching off one day's march up the valley, and running over the hills to Singhi-jong, but I was told it was very difficult and neither ponies nor mules could be taken over it, and also that snow was lying on the pass. In consequence of this report, I decided to proceed viâ the Dongo-la, and to branch off near Lhuntsi-jong and follow the valley leading from there to Singhi-jong, if I could not get up the valley of the Kuru-chhu. While at Tashi-yangtsi I visited Chorten Kara. It is a fine specimen, and is built partly on the lines of the big chorten at Khatmandu, but, like everything else, has its origin in an unknown past. Near the chorten there were some terraced paddy- and rice-fields of a fair size, on which ploughing and sowing were in full swing, and some large villages, and in spite of the clouds snow-capped hills appeared every now and then up the valley to the right.

The road on to Lhuntsi took me up a side valley through jungle the whole way, and I camped the first night at Wangtung (10,000 feet), at the level of silver pine, on a ground so cramped that I was obliged to cut several trees down to admit some light and air; and as it was also pouring with rain and very cold it was altogether miserable and uncomfortable The morning broke very wet, but it cleared a little, enabling me to get to the top of the first pass, the Shalaptsa-la (12,000 feet), without rain. On the west side of the pass I crossed the head-waters of the Sheru-chhu, and going about half a mile further on a fairly level road, reached the Bogong-la, where I crossed the watershed of the Kuru-chhu. This double pass is known as the Dong-la. It rained hard whilst I was crossing the pass, and for some distance down the other side, where for some miles the road was as bad as it was possible to be. It then ran over some good downs, but ended in a dripping forest, with deep mud under foot the whole distance down to Singhi (6225 feet).

At Singhi I was met by the Jongpen, and stayed in a house built on a steep hillside, with some fine walnut-trees in front and a lovely view down the valley. I held a conference which lasted over two hours as to the best way to get to Lhakhang-jong, but it was very difficult to elicit any information, or even to get an answer to a simple question. I wanted to march up the Kuru-chhu, but found that would be impossible, as the season was too far advanced, and the temporary bridges, erected during the cold weather, had all been carried away by the early rains. After much discussion I learnt that there were tracks on both sides of the river, though both were reported bad and quite impassable for mules or ponies, the one viâ Singhi-jong as we should have to cross a glacier, and the other on account of precipitous rocks. It seemed rather hopeless, but I finally decided to try the Singhi-jong route on foot and to send my mules and ponies, as well as Sir Ugyen's, along a road running from Singhi, on the left bank of the Kuru-chhu, to the Kuru Sampa, and round viâ Bya-gha-jong, from whence they would cross the Monla-Kachung-la and meet me at the Lhalung Monastery.

After a very wet night I got away in fairly fine weather, and went down a very steep descent to the Kuru-chhu (4100 feet), and then for some distance along the road on the left bank, over which the mules would go, but, owing to there being no bridge over the Khoma-chhu, I had to climb up and down an unnecessary 1400 feet. Leaving the Kuru-chhu, I branched off from Pemberton's route, going north, while his led across the river and down its right bank; then, passing the village of Khoma, an exceedingly steep ascent brought me to Pangkha, where I lodged in the Angdu-phodang Donyer's house.

From the village of Nyalamdung, on the way, I had a good view of Lhuntsi-jong, standing on the right bank of the Kuru-chhu. The Jong is, as usual, built on a fine spur between two rivers, and is a large fort with two towers, but I did not visit it, as it was at least six miles out of my way. The Jongpen was much disappointed that I would not stay some days with him, but I had news that the Tongsa had already started from Bya-gha to meet me at Lhakhang, and I did not wish to keep him waiting. All the same, it took me a couple of days to get my coolies together, as they had to carry food for five or six days along with them. The Donyer's house, in which I lodged, was perched on the side of a steep hill, and on leaving it one was obliged to go either straight up or straight down, so I remained a good deal indoors. Every square yard of ground round the village had been made the most of, and all of it was terraced, manured, and well cultivated, to get the best possible crop off it.

From Pangkha I crossed the Ye-la, a mere spur, and had to descend again 3000 feet to the Khoma-chhu, which I had left only a few days before. While on the descent I saw for the first time some very fine flowering trees called, in Bhutanese, Chape and Phetsi, which were very handsome. The blossom somewhat resembles a large tea-flower, and they bear an edible fruit, which is gathered in August. This is the only place where I have come across these trees, and I have no idea what they are.

CHAPTER XVII

AN EXPLORATION OF EASTERN BHUTAN AND A PORTION OF TIBET IN 1906—*continued*

From Tsekang to Lhakhang-jong. Lhalung Monastery and Pho-mo-chang-thang Lake to Gyantse. Crossing the Bod-la between Bhutan and Tibet. Riding yaks. Welcome in Tibet. Meeting with Sir Ugyen. Wild gooseberries. Old gold-workings. Friendliness of Tibetans. Lhakhang-jong. Tuwa-jong. Dekila, widow of Norbu Sring. Lhalung Monastery. Ovis ammon. Source of the Nyeru-chhu.

I CAMPED at Tsekang in rain, and next day marched up the valley of the Khoma through dense jungle. I had intended to reach Singhi-jong, but it was too far, so I halted at Tusum Mani (10,900 feet), amongst pines and larches, on the only level place I could find. The weather cleared up a little towards evening, and I was able to see that up the stream to the north the valley was blocked by snow-hills, with glaciers running down their sides, but mist prevented me from seeing anything more. Next day was fine, and I had a beautiful ride to Singhi-jong, a very small fort, hardly worthy of the name, but well situated on a large flat, with fine snow views all round. I did not stay there, but went on through the valley to Narim-thang (13,900 feet), about four miles from the Kang-la (16,290 feet). I would have liked to camp at the foot of the pass, but there was no firewood so high, and the want of it would have entailed much extra work for the coolies. The morning broke rather threateningly, but by making an early start and riding as far as the lake below the pass, beyond which pack-animals cannot go, I succeeded in crossing before the snow began to fall. It was a stiff climb up the east side, and equally difficult going down for 1500 feet through snow, and then over a small glacier on the west. The Kang-la is the watershed, but not the boundary, between Bhutan and Tibet. Further on the road first led down to a stream, then up again, and round a spur leading into another valley, up which we marched for some miles, and just before reaching our camping-ground, at Metsephu (15,300 feet), we passed a fine lake. It rained heavily part of the way, but cleared up as we pitched our tents, and then later began to snow heavily—so heavily the tents had to be beaten and shaken at intervals to prevent their collapse. It was a cold and cheerless evening, but the snow ceased early and the night was clear, while the morning broke beautifully fine. We reached the Bod-la (16,290 feet), and crossed the boundary between Bhutan and Tibet early, and the coolies soon made their appearance, even carrying the heavy frozen tents. A Tibetan block-house, with loopholed walls, was built on the top of the pass. There were some fine views of the snow-peaks to the east, and after admiring them I started down the descent on the Tibetan side. It was a very tiresome march, over huge rocks covered with snow, and at the foot of the pass I was delighted to find yaks and coolies waiting for me, brought by the head of the nearest Tibetan village and a representative from the Lhakhang-jong, which is also in Tibet. I was tired, and it was very pleasant riding down on one of the yaks. Though slow, they are very sure-footed, and carried me most comfortably over some very steep slopes, but in one place I came to a flat rock, sloping at an angle of about 45 degrees, with nothing but a two-inch crack in the rock for the animal to find a foothold on, and I really could not face it, and dismounted and walked over, although my driver assured me there was no danger, and probably I should have been just as safe on the yak as on my own feet. On reaching a flat lower down I found both riding-

LHALUNG MONASTERY

mules and ponies waiting for me, sent by Sir Ugyen and the Tibetans, and also a message asking me to delay my arrival at Lhakhang until my camp there was prepared, so a few miles further on I pitched my tents in a beautiful glade in the midst of pines, larches, and aspens. The valley we passed through was a fine one, and the walk beautiful, with magnificent cliffs on the north side for the whole distance, nearly, if not quite, as high as those on the route above Tashi-cho-jong which I had traversed the year before on my way through Bhutan. After descending some thousands of feet we came into forests of black juniper, and below that silver pine and larch. The climate, too, was drier. The view looking down the valley across into Tibet was very fine, the hills there showing up rugged and bare, without a tree, although distant only about three miles as the crow flies, so sharp is the line dividing the wet and the dry zones.

The orderlies in charge of the yaks the Tongsa had sent took the greatest care of me whilst going over the bad places on the road, holding me on as though they were afraid I might fall off. In camp I got a letter from Sir Ugyen to say he had arrived in Lhakhang that day, and hoped to meet me in the morning.

While making my way to the Jong the following day the Jongpen met me with eggs and milk and the headman of the village with chang. At the Jong itself Sir Ugyen was waiting, and I found my camp pitched in a grove of poplars and willows, while the Jongpen had pitched his own tent for me and made all preparations for my comfort. It was a very great pleasure to meet Sir Ugyen again, and we had much to talk over and discuss.

I had hardly expected to receive such a hearty reception in Tibet, but every one vied with one another in trying to make me comfortable and in doing everything they could for me. It was most gratifying, and proved beyond dispute that the Tibetans bore no ill-will on account of the Lhasa Expedition, and also that they were genuinely pleased to see me personally. I am quite sure, notwithstanding the general opinion to the contrary, that, could the physical difficulties be overcome, there would be but little opposition shown by Tibetans generally to any one travelling in their country, so long as the immediate vicinity of Lhasa was avoided, and provided the traveller had some previous knowledge of and sympathy with the Tibetan character and that he was known to them.

Had the opportunity been taken advantage of, on the conclusion of the Lhasa Treaty, to allow a few of our own picked officers to travel in Tibet, any opposition would have died a natural death, as it existed only amongst certain members of the priestly hierarchy and the higher officials in Lhasa. The common people invariably welcomed our advent, and openly expressed the hope that they were to come under our jurisdiction. Our Government, instead of making the most of so unique an opening, has, by the most incomprehensible regulations and orders, emanating from London, raised an insuperable barrier against any fellow countrymen who may desire to travel in Tibet, while foreigners, whom they are powerless to keep out, are given every possible assistance and help. Hence, notwithstanding the vast expenditure of money, the heavy loss of life, and the many hardships endured by the Lhasa Mission of 1904, Tibet has again become an absolutely closed country to all Englishmen. In addition, Government's unfortunate subsequent policy has been the means of handing over the Tibetans, bound hand and foot, to the Chinese, and all Tibetan officials are now obliged by their virtual masters, the Chinese, to enforce the Chinese traditional policy of exclusion of all Europeans.

Up to now I had been unaware that wild gooseberries were to be found in the Himalayas, but on this march I came across them for the first time, higher up in flower and lower down in fruit. The people eat the fruit, but I fancy it would be very sour, and not like the small wild yellow gooseberry found in Scotland.

Accompanied by the Tongsa, I visited the Karchu Monastery, which is situated on a very picturesque ridge overlooking the gorge where the Kuru-chhu commences to cut its way through the Himalayas, but beyond a very good view of Kulu-Kangri there was nothing much to be seen.

I also visited some hot springs, and near them some old gold-diggings, which were said to have been worked as recently as twelve years before my visit by the late Jong-pen, who imported workmen from Tod, in Tibet, for the purpose. They were situated in an old river-bed, and are now quite abandoned, and I should think very unlikely to be worth making any future attempt to develop. I washed some of the sand, but found nothing.

Lhakhang-jong is a very dilapidated building, very dirty, and worth nothing either as a residence or a place of defence, and of no interest. The Khomthing Lhakhang, or temple, is also very uninteresting, although it had one curious feature. In one of the rooms a large apricot-tree grew through the roof, and was called for some reason, though why I could not make out, the " Mermaid Tree." But in the monastery itself there was nothing.

The fields round the fort were brilliant with the delicate green of young corn, just beginning to sprout, and the hedges were full of wild roses and pink and white spirea, while between the fields were planted lines of apricot-trees full of blossom, making a lovely picture. The crop of fruit is so plentiful that, in addition to carrying on a large trade in dried fruit, the people feed their cattle on apricots in winter; but those I tasted were not very appetising.

With all this beauty the climate of Lhakhang is abominable; situated at the mouth of the Kuru gorge, a cold, damp, violent wind never ceases blowing, while the sun at the same time is extremely hot: but even with this disadvantage the two days' rest was very welcome. The export trade consists chiefly, in addition to dried apricots, of dried mutton, sheep-skins, wool, and salt, while rice, madder, and stick lac are imported from Bhutan.

A good road through the Kuru Valley would be sure soon to become a popular trade route, as it would be a direct outlet from Tibet to the plains, with no snow-passes to cross, and from Lhakhang onwards to Tibet the present road is reported to be very easy. The few miles I traversed were broad and much used. The section between Lhuntsi and Lhakhang would be very difficult to negotitate, as it passes through an immense gorge, which would require a great deal of blasting as well as bridging; and as things have now turned out, it is very unlikely such a road will be made for many generations, if ever, though at the time of my visit it was still within the range of possibility that the Governments of India and Tibet would co-operate to improve trade routes between the two empires.

Roads already run from Lhakhang to Nagartsi and Chetang, across country in which there is said to be much good grazing and many flocks of sheep, and consequently there should be a quantity of wool to be bought. The route from Tawang also taps this country.

After leaving Lhakhang I crossed the two branches of the Kuru-chhu just before they enter, as one stream, the mouth of this magnificent gorge. The road wound along the side of the hills some thousand feet above the river, and was in some places very pretty, with hedges of yellow and red roses, spirea, gooseberry and currant-bushes, apricot-trees, and a sort of blackthorn, but for the greater part it was uninteresting. The villagers *en route* turned out to meet me, and burnt incense, and at Dur they had a tent pitched for my lunch, and presented me with chang, the native liquor, milk, and eggs. I camped at Mug (11,650 feet), in a grove of poplars, where a second messenger arrived from the Tongsa's sister with another letter of welcome and more rice, eggs, and butter.

From this village a road branches off over the Monla-Kachung-la Pass to Bya-gha, but my way led me to Singhi-jong, still in Tibet. A very hard march took me first down to the river, some thousand feet below camp, and

TUWA-JONG

then up again over a spur to Singhi-jong, a climb of 1740 feet in the full glare of the sun; then down again to a side stream, and again up to Myens-la (14,800 feet), and at last to my camp, pitched in a small side valley at Tashichukar (14,480 feet). I found the sun very trying climbing the southern slopes, but on reaching camp it clouded over, and the afternoon was wet and windy and very cold—the coldest camp I had yet been in on this expedition.

Singhi-jong is a deserted fort in ruins, situated on a fine rock, and the Jongpen does not live there, but prefers a house at its foot less pretentious and more comfortable. He was an old acquaintance of mine, whom I had met in Lhasa, where he was the official who issued rations to the Mission camp. About a year before my visit he had been transferred to Singhi, where I now met him. We had to change transport here; but everything was in readiness, so it did not take long. I had a fine view of some high snows looking up the valley on leaving Singhi-jong.

The Tibetans were not nearly so ready to be vaccinated as the Bhutanese, probably because there had been no recent outbreak of small-pox, and very few came forward, while in Bhutan the numbers already done had reached 800. From Tashichukar I made a long march and pushed right on to Lhalung, the Bhutan monastery, passing Tuwa-jong on the way. The road took me first straight down to the river, a descent of 2400 feet, and then straight up the other side in short zigzags, which were very trying. It then wound round the hillside for some distance and again dropped down to the stream at Tuwa-jong (13,000 feet). If I had only been a little earlier in the season all these ups and downs might have been avoided, as during the winter there is a path along the bed of the stream; but the glaciers had begun to melt, and the rivers were consequently in flood, so it was impracticable.

Tuwa-jong I found to be a fine building, in Tibetan style, with the fort on the top of a very steep rock, and the monastery below, also a fine building. The Tibetan and Bhutanese Jongs have a general resemblance in their architecture, particularly remarkable in the slope given to the walls, but in detail are not very similar. In Bhutan the courtyards are much larger, and the lavish use of timber gives the buildings a different aspect, especially the sloping shingle roofs invariably used there, whereas in Tibet the roofs are generally flat. The Tuwa buildings are all quite new, as they were rebuilt after the earthquake of 1897. A little before reaching the Jong we found a tent pitched, and the Nerpa, or steward, of the Jongpen waiting with refreshments. He was very anxious that I should break my journey at Tuwa, and the same request was renewed when I reached the Jong by the Jongpen and the lamas, but I told them that, if possible, and if they could make the necessary arrangements for transport, I was anxious to reach Lhalung that day. They had a camp pitched ready below the building, in a side valley, out of the wind, in a charming, fresh green garden, and the invitation was very tempting, and I should have been glad to give pleasure to my kindly hosts, but I could not manage it. All I could do was to stop and partake of the refreshments they had provided while the transport was being changed, and the arrangements were so good that by the time we had finished luncheon all the loads had gone on. I can only repeat again that I received nothing but the most unvarying kindness and attention from every one throughout my journey in this part of Tibet, and that every pains was taken, by officials and villagers alike, to make things easy and comfortable for me; and at no time, during the years I have served on the frontier, when I have been brought into contact with Tibetans, have I had any discourtesy shown me.

I was told that Dekila, the widow of Norbu Sring, is still imprisoned at Tuwa-jong, but as I only heard this at Lhalung I had no opportunity of making inquiries or trying to see her. Norbu Sring was brother to the late

Tengay-Ling, Regent of Tibet. Tengay-Ling was accused of practising sorcery on the Delai Lama, and consequently seized, and later put to death, while his brother, Norbu Sring, a layman, was also cruelly killed. His widow, Dekila, who was famous throughout Tibet for her beauty, and is a member of the highly respectable Doring family of Lhasa, and some relation to the Maharani of Sikhim, was arrested on the same charge, and, after being cruelly scourged through Lhasa, was condemned to imprisonment for life in Tuwa-jong. She is said to be even now in chains in a cell on the outskirts of the Jong, and had I known beforehand I should have made an effort to see the unfortunate woman and ascertain if nothing could be done for her. The man who volunteered this information had heard of the release of several State prisoners, and especially of the cases of my Lachung men and the friend of Sarat Chunder Das, during the Lhasa Expedition, and seemed to think the Indian Government might extend a helping hand; but I am afraid the only, and very unlikely, chance for the poor lady might have been my personal influence with the Jongpen; and even then he was responsible to the authorities at Lhasa for her safe custody, and could not, I fear, on his own initiative have done anything for her.

About two miles below Tuwa-jong the valley opens out; so far it is a deep-cut gorge, impossible to traverse except during the winter months, when temporary bridges are thrown across the stream which save many miles in actual distance and many thousands of feet in ascent and descent, but of course at this time of the year I had to follow the longer route. On leaving the Jong the road runs along the bottom of the valley—cultivated wherever water can be found for irrigation, but elsewhere a typical Tibetan valley, an arid wilderness of stone and sand, hot, bare, and dusty, with a howling wind always blowing, making it very unpleasant. The ride up this unprepossessing valley in the face of the afternoon sun was a hot one, but I was well repaid by the reception I received at Lhalung, where I was met by the Tulku, or Avatar, a nephew of Sir Ugyen's, and the monks and headmen of Lhalung. They conducted me to a charming camp, pitched in the monastery gardens, where it was pleasant to sit on the grass in the cool shade of the willows, out of the glare, and sheltered from the violence of the wind by the high wall surrounding the garden. It was a delightful place in which to rest and do nothing, and at the urgent request of Sir Ugyen I remained with him for two days, taking photographs of the buildings and of the Tulku and others, and receiving deputations from the Jongpen of Tuwa-jong, the Avatar and the lamas of Lhalung, as well as the headmen of these places. One day the Tulku entertained me at lunch, and afterwards we witnessed a Tibetan dance which was quite new to me. Most of the performers wore very little clothing—quite a new experience, as in all the Tibetan dances I have seen the dancers are rather overburdened with heavy garments. I also spent much of my time with the Tongsa, discussing the affairs of Bhutan and talking over his projects for improvements, roads, developments, &c., all very interesting subjects; and I often wonder now how he is carrying out all his schemes, and wish I had been able to set him a little further on the road towards their accomplishment before my retirement. At Sir Ugyen's request I left the vaccinator to accompany him to Bya-gha, and then to travel through Bhutan before returning to Sikhim. I also left my plant-collector, as it was still too early in the season to find plants or flowers in the high plateaux of Tibet. He made a very good collection of plants, both on this occasion and when he accompanied me on the first Bhutan Mission, and they were duly forwarded to the Botanical Gardens in Calcutta, but up to the present date I have had no news of any classification having been made. The delay seems regrettable, as there may have been some new and interesting plants among them. I certainly saw

INTERIOR OF LHALUNG MONASTERY

many plants which do not occur in Sikhim, where every valley and hill has been thoroughly explored.

The following day I continued my journey up the valley, and camped at Lung, passing *en route* the Guru Lhakhang, a very old building, surrounded by ancient poplars, but in itself uninteresting. On this march I discovered that the main stream of the Monass takes its rise in the great amphitheatre of snow-mountains, averaging 24,000 feet in height, round Kulu-Kangri. It rises from some large glaciers, and is exceedingly muddy, the water a thick yellowish-red colour. At Lyateoh, where my transport was changed, the main valley turned to the west, although the river containing by far the most water came in from the south. The quantity of silt brought down is very great, and shows what enormous disintegration is in progress. I was particularly struck by the number of ruined villages I passed on this march.

In the hills round Lung there is some fine ovis ammon ground, and I saw several large flocks. They were extraordinarily tame, and allowed me to walk, across the open, to within thirty or forty yards, and then only moved slowly away. I first saw them from my bed. I awoke early, and on looking out I saw eight grazing on the hillside not half a mile away. They have never been shot at, which accounts for their tameness.

A path from Lung, used by yaks and their drivers, leads over the snow to the head-waters of the branches of the Mo-chhu, and is said not to be a very difficult one. My route, however, took me up the valley and over the Ta-la Pass (17,900 feet), the watershed between India and the Pho-mo-chang-thang Lake basin, which has no outlet, then along high, rolling downs, and, after passing three small lakes, came to the large plain at the head of the Pho-mo-chang-thang Lake itself. The lake appears to be receding to a certain extent, and I think probably this is chiefly owing to the large quantities of silt brought down by an unnamed river from the glaciers, and its consequent filling up on the west side. We crossed the plain in a violent hailstorm, and camped in the middle of it on a bare and exposed yak station called Sagang, in sight of the lake. The Tongsa accompanied me to the top of the pass, where he took his leave, presenting me with scarves of different colours, a pretty custom which is both picturesque and at the same time expressive of the most cordial good feeling.

From the downs at Sagang I had a clear view of the snow-hills which form the boundary between Bhutan and Tibet, with the country to the north of the hills clearly to be seen and the courses of the rivers quite plainly visible. Fortunately, some of the dopkas (yak herdsmen) had pitched tents, which were most welcome, as there was a very strong, cold wind blowing, and, the march having been a long one, our things did not arrive till late. *En route* we saw some ovis ammon, but did not shoot any. We had to cross the large river which takes its rise on the north of the snows forming the boundary between Bhutan and Tibet and runs into the west end of the lake, and had some difficulty in finding a ford, as the bed was full of quicksands, but eventually a herdsman showed us one, and also told us there were only two places at which it could be crossed in safety. This man came from a very large encampment of herdsmen, who had hundreds of yaks and a few sheep in their care. They were extremely hospitable, spread carpets for us to sit on, and gave us fresh milk and Tibetan tea, as well as parched barley. It was a curious sight to watch the milking of the yaks, the method being, to say the least of it, peculiar, and one I had not seen or heard of elsewhere in Tibet.

I made a very early start from Sagang, and after climbing 600 feet came to the watershed between the lake basin and the Nyeru-chhu. These hills are nearly all rounded, with very few precipices, and are evidently much frequented by both ovis ammon and burhel, for I saw numerous fine heads lying about. The natives explained this by saying that in winter wolves attack and kill the males, who in consequence of the weight of their heavy horns cannot get quickly over the ground and out of reach. From the ridge I followed a stream which took me the whole way to the Nyeru Valley, but which is not marked on the map Ryder made at the time of the Lhasa Mission. This may be accounted for by the very narrow gorge through which it passes on entering the valley. The Bhutan boundary runs right up to the head of the Nyeru Valley, and from Nelung the Wagya-la, over which there is a trade route to Bhutan, can be seen. We had a long, weary march across a flat plain in hail and rain before reaching Nelung, where tents had fortunately been pitched by the head-man, and very welcome they were, as all our things did not come up till past eight o'clock, and it continued to rain and blow hard nearly all night, though it was fairly fine towards morning.

I discovered that the Nyeru-chhu takes its rise in the high snows not far from the source of the Kuru-chhu. It breaks through the dividing ridge between the lake basin and the Nyeru Valley under the snow, and then takes a right-angle bend to the north and comes down past Nyeru.

All the valleys I have seen to the north of the water-shed—viz., from Eastern Bhutan to some distance west of Sikhim—appear to have at some remote period been much more densely populated than at present. At every turn I came on ruins of habitations and remains of old irrigation channels; and overcrowding may possibly account for this migration over the Himalayas into the comparatively hot valleys of Bhutan, in which no Tibetan would willingly settle, though he might be forced by circumstances to do so. This also raises the interesting question of the former climate of these parts. I think there is no doubt that there must have been considerably more rain, and everything appears to support this view—the receding glaciers and diminishing streams, also the fact that all the lakes in this part of Tibet show a large amount of contraction, and to all appearances are still decreasing. On the Yam-dok-tsho several distinct old shores can be traced running round the lake, some quite sixty feet above the present lake level. Pho-mo-chang-thang, Kala-tsho, Bam-tsho, and Rhum-tsho are all drying up. What is the cause of this? Is it the gradual elevation of the Himalayas, shutting out the monsoon current, or has the monsoon current itself diminished? The migration southward might also be accounted for by diminished rainfall, the people being no longer able to support themselves and their cattle on the produce of the land, and being obliged to seek new and more productive country.

It is a very interesting subject, but requires more time and research to be devoted to it than I have been able to give.

At Nelung I lost one of my favourite mules, Kitty, whom I had had for many years, and who had served me well. She must have contracted a chill crossing in the hail, for soon after reaching camp she was taken ill with colic, and nothing I could do was of any use, and she died during the night.

From Nelung my route took me over an easy pass to the Phari–Gyantse road. At Gyantse I spent a few days making a visit of inspection to Bailey, the officiating British Trade Agent and my Assistant Political Officer. The post is a lonely and isolated one, and the work was none too pleasant, owing to the attitude of the Chinese, whc did all in their power to be obstructive, and used every possible means to prevent the Tibetans having any direct intercourse with us; but things on the whole were fairly satisfactory. From Gyantse I returned by the ordinary route to Chumbi, and thence to Gangtak, thus bringing to an end my exploration in Bhutan.

CHAPTER XVIII

MY SECOND MISSION TO BHUTAN

Severe weather. Shau. A frozen torrent. Dug-gye-jong. A visit to Paro Ta-tshang Monastery. Sang-tog-peri. Paro-jong burnt down. Arrival at Poonakha. The Tongsa's band.

MY second mission to Bhutan was undertaken at the invitation of Sir Ugyen Wang-chuk to be present as his guest and as representative of the British Government at his installation as Hereditary Maharaja of Bhutan.

I left Gangtak on November 25, 1907, accompanied by Major Rennick, of the Intelligence Branch, and Mr. Wilton, C.M.G., of His Majesty's Consular Service. Mr. Campbell, my Assistant Political Officer, I had sent on ahead to Chumbi to make arrangements for coolies and transport, and Captain Hyslop, who was accompanying me at the special request of Sir Ugyen, had not yet arrived, and was to follow, making forced marches in order to catch us up.

I travelled over the usual route viâ Karponang and Chongu, and arrived without any misadventure the third day in Chumbi, where I halted. Several days were occupied in arranging for the escort, which consisted of twenty-five men of the 62nd Punjabis, under a native officer, a hospital assistant, and the usual following of dooly-bearers, &c.

Unfortunately I contracted a chill, and was obliged to remain in bed for a few days, so I sent Campbell on with the escort and heavy baggage to Phari, and Hyslop having by this time arrived, we left Chumbi on December 2. Rennick and I went straight to Gautsa, while Wilton and Hyslop camped at Lingmathang in hopes of getting a shau of which my shikari had brought us news. It was a very cold day when we started, with the thermometer at zero and the high wind that always blows up the valley, and this shortly turned into a veritable hurricane, so the two in tents had a bad night of it. The wind was so strong they could hardly keep the tent standing; they were nearly frozen; and, worst of all, after having undergone all these discomforts, they could see no sign of the shau, although my orderly, Purboo, said he caught a glimpse of one close to the camp. The shau which the shikari reported having seen was apparently a magnificent specimen, with splendid horns, and was known to many natives by a small white patch on its forehead. I should very much have liked to stay and stalk him, but I had no time for such pleasures, and had to forego a chance I shall not have again.

Wilton returned to India from Lingmathang, as he was obliged to meet some Chinamen in Calcutta, and Hyslop came on by himself to rejoin us in the bungalow at Gautsa, where we were waiting for him. He found the road very bad and difficult, as the wind had covered it with the trunks of fallen trees.

We in the bungalow had not fared much better than the men in tents. We were a good deal higher, and the cold—26° below zero—was so intense that the river, usually a roaring torrent, was frozen absolutely solid during the night, and there was not a sound of water to be heard. It was very curious to listen to it gradually becoming less and less until it finally became silent. All our provisions in the bungalow, milk, tea, meat even, were frozen solid, and no fire would thaw them; no water was to be had, only chunks of ice; and it was almost impossible to keep warm. The wind was still blowing a hurricane, and the mule-

INTERIOR OF DUG-GYE-JONG

drivers refused to start, saying that no animal could stand against the force of the wind and the bitter cold, so we were perforce obliged to remain where we were and listen to the wind roaring through the trees.

Such a huricane was unknown so low in the valley, and the mule-men said they had never witnessed anything like it. Fortunately the storm was unaccompanied by snow, for the sky was clear and the sun shining all the time; otherwise I think it would really have been unbearable. To add to our misfortunes, Rennick had gout, and the cold did him no good.

The next morning the wind had dropped, and we marched across the plain, meeting the Katzog Kazi on the way, to Phari, where the Jongpen received us, in perfect weather, in brilliant sunshine, which in sheltered places was almost hot.

At Phari, Bailey, my assistant from Gyantse, was waiting to see me, and Morgan, of the 62nd, who had taken on the escort, was also there, and, with Campbell, we made a large gathering in the Dak bungalow. We left Phari on December 5, our party finally consisting of myself, Rennick, Hyslop, Campbell, Rai Lobzang Chöden Sahib, my confidential clerk, twenty-five sepoys of the 62nd, with three pipers and two drummers under a native officer, and 264 loads of baggage, in addition to a string of our own ponies and mules, personal servants and dooly-bearers. It sounds a large quantity of baggage, but what with presents and rations for the escort, it soon mounted up.

The day was beautiful, and we very soon reached the Temo-la (16,500 feet), about three miles from Phari, and the boundary between Tibet and Bhutan. The view from the summit of the pass looking into Bhutan was a very fine one. Our road took us over a fairly easy gradient for a few miles, and then in a sheltered little valley I was met by the Dug-gye Jongpen and a party of men with messages from Sir Ugyen Wang-chuk welcoming my party to Bhutan. The Jongpen had brought his band of drums, gongs, and cymbals with him, and they played whilst we were partaking of the refreshments he had provided for us. For a short distance further on the road was not so bad, but we then entered a very rocky gorge, down which the path led in a series of short zigzags, and was practically a rough stair, with enormous steps from rock to rock. It was exceedingly bad going both for ourselves and the mules, and was quite unrideable.

Rennick, who could hardly put foot to the ground, was carried on the back of a Bhutanese orderly, with two or three men to help, and as he weighs over fifteen stone he was no light load. However, with occasional knocks against projecting rocks, which did not improve his temper, he was safely deposited at the bottom, where mules sent by the Jongpen and the Paro Penlop were waiting for us, as the road into camp was said to be quite good.

On our way through the gorge we stopped for lunch, but none of us enjoyed it much, as the meat was frozen so hard that it was quite uneatable, and the thermos flask had gone wrong and our long-looked-forward-to hot soup was very cold. Whilst lunching, too, we dropped the top of one of the sparklet bottles amongst some stones, and it took us a long time to find it, but as we had only two bottles with us we could not afford to lose it. At the lower end the trees became very fine, and we passed some enormous specimens of larch and different sorts of pine, as well as rhododendron, birch, maple, and holly-oak.

The gaily caparisoned mules and ponies were waiting for us at the bottom, with equally gaily attired attendants. We each mounted one, and were immediately started off at a brisk trot over slippery boulders and round projecting rocks and corners, which threatened to knock our knees to pieces, but as the reins on the animals were only for ornament, and not for use, we had to submit to the syces' guidance and allow ourselves to be dragged over a horrible road. The ride was not an agreeable one; it was a marvel

BRIDGE AT SHANA

how the animals kept their feet, and I should often have liked to get off and walk; but my dignity was at stake, and for shame's sake I had to stick to my mount; but I was glad when the camp appeared round a corner and I could dismount and stretch my limbs. Just before entering camp our band was augmented by more musicians carrying "gyeling," or silver trumpets, on which they performed in the most approved style, turning towards you as they blew with a great sweep and flourish towards the sky.

We reached our camping-ground about 3 P.M., a lovely open spot in the midst of larch and spruce, with magnificent views both up and down the valley, and found our heavy baggage waiting for us. Sorting out the tents was rather a difficult task, as the coolies had thrown everything in a heap, but we soon got things into fair order, and had a roaring fire made in the middle of the camp, round which we all sat and made ourselves comfortable, although a good deal of our baggage did not arrive till midnight. We had come about fifteen or twenty miles, and the march had been a long and trying one for the coolies. We had now to change our Phari coolies for Bhutanese transport, and this, in addition to the very large amount of baggage, necessitated an early start; but my Moonshi Lobzang, who was splendid at this sort of arrangement, soon got things straight, and before we had breakfast the bulk of the piles of baggage had disappeared and was on its way to our next halting-place.

As this was our first morning in Bhutan, the escort proper thought they would play us out of camp, and, according to custom, the Bhutanese did the same, and the combined noise was awful. Hyslop was very critical about the 62nd pipers, which I suppose was natural, but as I am not a Highlander I could not see very much difference between their performance and the real thing.

A little below the camp we crossed the Pa-chhu by a very picturesque covered cantilever bridge. The march was an extremely pretty one, as it took us the whole way through forests of *Pinus excelsa*, with here and there some lovely glades, and occasional farmhouses with patches of cultivation. After recrossing the river we soon came in sight of Dug-gye-jong, which I have already said is the most beautifully situated Jong I know, and which looks well from whichever side it is approached. On arriving at the Jong I was received by the Jongpen, who took me to his guest-room, where the walls were hung with bows and arrows, shields, quaint old guns, saddle-cloths, and curious bridles. We were shown to chairs on a high daïs by the window, and an excellent omelette with spring onions was served, accompanied by milk and warm chang to drink and some very good walnuts. We stayed in the Jong till our tents were pitched and comfortably settled, when we moved across. The day had been warm, but as soon as the sun went behind the hills we were glad to put on great-coats and to sit round a good fire. We halted at Dug-gye for a couple of days, and sorted out our stores, managing to reduce them by a few loads. Some of the party went out after pheasants, but saw very few, while I enjoyed having a day off and took some good photographs.

The second day we made an expedition to the Paro Ta-tshang Monastery, one of the holiest monasteries in Bhutan, situated on the opposite side of the valley, about 3000 feet up. The road was reported to be very bad, and it certainly was, and I was glad I had not brought my own animals, but had borrowed mules from the Jongpen for all our party. The road to the top of the spur was very steep, with frozen slippery patches where it was shady and very hot in the sun. It ran in one place in a narrow path across a precipice, with a tremendous drop below, and in another became a series of steep stone steps. On reaching the top of the ridge we first came in sight of the monastery buildings, grouped on an almost perpendicular hillside in the most picturesque manner. The main temple is erected on what is practically a crack in a perpendicular rock over 2000 feet in height, and along the crack there are a few more subsidiary buildings. Each building is two stories high, and is painted, like all monasteries, a dull light grey on the lower story, with a broad band of madder-red above, and shingle roofs, on the top of which are gilded canopies. It was unquestionably the most picturesque group of buildings I had seen. Every natural feature in the landscape had been taken advantage of, and beautiful old trees clinging to the rocks were in just the right position, and, combined with the sheer precipices, made a magnificent picture.

We appeared to be quite close, but were really separated from the buildings by an almost inaccessible gorge. The only approach was by a narrow path or series of steps, where a foot misplaced would precipitate you to the bottom, quite 1000 feet, across a plank bridge, and then up another series of little steps cut in the rock. The native hospital assistant had accompanied our party so far, but this was too much for him. He said he had been in many bad places, but never such a bad one as this, and he turned back to where the mules were waiting. Natives, as a rule, have good heads and do not mind bad roads, so that speaks for itself.

Across the gorge a rope of little coloured prayer-flags was stretched, which fluttered out prayers for the benefit of those who had put them up, and this added to the picturesqueness of the scene.

On reaching the top of our ladder-like path a monk presented us each with a draught of beautifully ice-cold water in a gourd from a holy spring, and I can imagine it being much appreciated on a hot day.

The most holy shrine, the sanctuary round which all the other buildings have sprung up, was situated in a cave. The cave is not large, and in it was a gilded chorten filled with small images of Buddha in copper-gilt, each seated on a lotus, and many of very good design. The other buildings were for the most part ordinary temples, with frescoed walls and altars, with butter lamps and incense burning, and in the principal one there was a very fine brass Buddha of more than life size, surrounded by his satellites. There were also some unusually good specimens of dorjes (thunderbolts) and purpas (daggers), both of which are used in the temple services. They were supposed to be of holy origin, and to be found amongst the solid rocks near the shrine, but I could see none, although the Bya-gha Jongpen's son, a nephew of the Tongsa, had taken one away a few weeks previously. My servants were very anxious to secure one of these treasures, and climbed to an almost inaccessible point in the rocks in search of them, but without success.

In the centre of the gorge, perched upon a tiny ledge, there was a hermit's dwelling, which could only be reached by climbing a perpendicular notched pole about forty feet high. It looked diminutive against the enormous precipice, and very dreary and uninviting, with long icicles hanging from the roof, and we did not attempt to visit it. We, however, climbed to the top of the precipice to visit the monastery of Sang-tog-peri, which was most picturesquely situated on a projecting spur, with a fine old oak overhanging the entrance. It reminded me of some of the Japanese temples in Kioto in the way the natural features of the ground had been utilised to beautify the entrance.

There was a lovely view from this point. Around us on all sides were spurs with other monasteries and nunneries, but they were all more or less difficult of access, and our time would not admit of further delay, so we were obliged to return leaving them unvisited. It was a place that would take days to explore, and would well repay the trouble, especially to an artist in search of the beautiful and unusual.

We returned to Dug-gye by another road, which led down an easy spur, and were glad to rest round our campfire, as it was late and cold.

PARO TA-TSHANG MONASTERY

The next day we continued our journey down the valley to Paro, and were met half-way by Rai Ugyen Kazi Bahadur, the Bhutanese Agent in India, who had been unable to accompany us, and had travelled from Chumbi viâ Hah. He was accompanied by representatives of the Paro Penlop, bringing scarves of welcome and murwa, as well as fresh mules and ponies for all the party. At Paro I was received by the Penlop and his newly married son, quite a lad, but I did not see his bride.

Paro-jong, one of the finest forts in Bhutan, which I have already described, had been burnt to the ground a few weeks previously, and was now a heap of blackened ruins, with only a few walls standing up gaunt and melancholy. Although the ruins were still smouldering, preparations for rebuilding had already commenced, and the *débris* was being removed and new timber collected, an arduous task in these hills, especially as enormous beams are used in all Bhutanese construction. They also use a quite unnecessary amount, and make their floors far too thick.

The rebuilding of such a fort is a very great tax on the people, and is generally borne by those close at hand, but in this case, by an arrangement of the Tongsa's, the whole of Bhutan was contributing either in money or labour, thereby saving much hardship to the neighbouring villagers and expediting the work of reconstruction. It was rumoured that the Jong had been purposely set on fire, but I had no opportunity of finding out the truth, though a suspicious circumstance was that the Penlop was believed to have succeeded in saving his own property—no inconsiderable amount—while all Government property was destroyed. The Bhutanese estimated their loss at about 1½ lacs of rupees, or £12,000, and that it would take four years to rebuild the fort. There were flocks of pigeons flying about the ruins, and Hyslop and I did a little shooting.

Our next camp was in a village called Pemithang, crossing on our way the Be-la Pass (10,500 feet), from where we had a magnificent view of Chomolhari to the north. The road was fairly good, except that in a few places it was covered with ice for several hundred yards; but it was easy to have earth thrown on it, and the mules crossed safely. We were now using animals provided by the Tongsa, and very good ones they were, and as even our servants were mounted it did not take long to move from one camp to another.

At Chalimaphe our camp was again pitched round the magnificent old weeping cypress, measuring over fifty feet in circumference at the base. Unfortunately I had another attack of fever, and had to halt for a couple of days. It was bitterly cold at night, unusually so for that elevation, and water standing by my bed was frozen solid.

Hyslop and Campbell utilised the time by visiting Tashi-cho-jong, the summer capital. They found that since my last visit the Thimbu Jongpen had built a magnificent new gompa, on which he appears to have spent a great deal of money. The decorations were good, and the central figure of a seated Buddha was quite twenty feet high, and heavily gilt. Above and around it was a canopy and background of golden leaves, and the figure itself was richly studded with turquoises and precious stones. On either side were attendant female figures, and in double rows more than life-sized images of Bhutanese gods, while the walls were hung with brocades and embroidered banners; and altogether it must have cost the Thimbu a good deal.

Next morning we left Chalimaphe for the last camp before reaching our destination, Poonakha. The mornings here are always exceedingly cold until the sun rises, when one's wraps become oppressive, but the ride up the valley was beautiful. This time we visited the fort of Simtoka, which has some ancient figures and carvings in stone, but is principally interesting on account of its age. From the pass, the Dokyong-la, we had a magnificent view of the snow ranges for the first time, as on my previous visit the whole range was never visible, but was enveloped in clouds, which only occasionally lifted to allow the different peaks to be seen. It was a fine sight, as the range extended on the right as far as some peaks to the east of Kulu-Kangri and on the left to Chomolhari.

We passed our old camp at Lung-me-tsawe, and moved down to a warmer spot at the bottom of the hill, where we camped amongst paddy-fields; but even here a fire was most welcome as soon as the sun went behind the hills. From this a short march brought us to Poonakha, and about four miles out we were met by a deputation from the Tongsa Penlop. He had sent the Ghassa Jongpen, who brought scarves of welcome and baskets of fruit, oranges, plantains, and persimmons, in addition to sealed wicker-covered bamboos filled with murwa and chang. There were at least five or six gaily caparisoned mules for each of us to ride, sent by the Tongsa, the Poonakha Jongpen, Deb Zimpon, and others, so we had an abundance of choice. The Tongsa had also sent his band, which consisted of six men, two in red, who were the trumpeters, while the remainder, dressed in green, carried drums and gongs. The mass of colours of every hue was most picturesque, and we made a very gay procession as we started off again towards Poonakha. At the point where the Jong first comes in view a salute of guns was fired, more retainers met us, and our procession was joined by the dancers. The band and dancers preceded me down the hill playing a sort of double tambourine, and twisting and twirling to the beat as they descended the path. The procession must have extended for quite half a mile along the hillside. First came the pipes and drums and escort of the 62nd Punjabis, followed by some twenty led mules, most of them with magnificent saddle-cloths, with their syces and other retainers; next the bodyguard of the Tongsa, about twenty men, dressed in beautiful silks and brocades, and each with a yellow scarf. The band and dancers followed immediately in front of myself and my party, and we again were followed by my orderlies and servants, who were all mounted and wearing their scarlet uniforms. On account of the narrow path, the procession had to proceed in single file, and as we gradually wended our way across the bridge, through a corner of the Jong to the ground occupied by my camp on my visit in 1905, we must have made a brave show for the country folk, who had flocked out in thousands to watch our arrival.

At the camp entrance the Tongsa Penlop, with his council, was waiting to receive us as we dismounted, and we were conducted up a path covered with red cloth and between lines of flowers and shrubs in pots to the mess-house they had built for us, and which we entered with the council, all others being excluded. I was shown to a seat at the end of the room, with the Tongsa and his council on my left and the other members of the Mission on my right. The members of the council who were present were the Paro Penlop, the Thimbu Jongpen, the Poonakha Jongpen, and the Deb Zimpon, the other two members being prevented by illness from attending. As soon as we were seated the Tongsa, followed by his council, presented each member of the Mission with scarves, and then murwa, tea, and other refreshments were brought in. I talked for some little time to the Tongsa, who then went round to each of the party welcoming them to Bhutan and saying how pleased he was to see them.

We found a very comfortable camp laid out for us, bearing evident traces of the impressions they had brought back from their Calcutta visit, for the paths were edged with pot plants and red cloth was laid down. We each had our own little wooden house, with one room and a bath-room, raised about eighteen inches from the ground, with

GROUP AT POONAKHA, 1908

shingle roofs, and surmounted by small coloured prayer-flags. Inside, the walls were covered with thin white cloth, with a frieze of draped coloured silk. The windows were like small port-holes, of course without glass, but with a shutter to pull across at night. They had no furniture, but the mess-house, which was a big room about twenty feet square, had an excellent table in the centre, and ten wooden arm-chairs which would have done credit to any carpenter and were wonderful productions when you remember that these people have no saws, no planes, no nails, and only the roughest of tools. The walls of the mess-house were covered with wonderful pictures in colour, and a large red and yellow curtain to let down at night. The table also had a white cloth, which was carefully gummed or pasted on. Outside the houses were painted white, and a few steps led to the doors. There were also mat huts for the servants, and an excellent kitchen. The enclosure was quite a hundred yards square, surrounded by a fence, and with branches of pine-trees planted every few yards while the stables were some little distance off; so we could hardly have been more comfortable.

The next day we spent in settling down and preparing for the ceremony on the following day. I took Hyslop with me and made an inspection of the hall in the Jong where the ceremony was to be held. It was very suitable, as it was a large room on the ground floor, with a gallery running all round, and capable of holding many hundreds of spectators, and by removing part of the roof they could let in both light and air. At the main entrance to the Jong quite a little bazaar was in progress, cloth-merchants selling Bhutanese cloths and cheap down-country cottons and sweetmeats, and pan-sellers doing a roaring trade, as the Bhutanese are always chewing pan.

CHAPTER XIX

MY SECOND MISSION TO BHUTAN—*continued*

Installation of Sir Ugyen as Maharaja of Bhutan. Presentation of gifts. Tea ceremony. Oath of allegiance. Seal of the Dharma Raja. Chinese influence on the frontier. Christmas Day. Feeding the poor. Return of escort. Discussion of State affairs with Maharaja and council. I leave for Jaigaon. A Takin. Inspection of frontier. Wild animals.

DECEMBER 17, the day of the installation of the Maharaja, dawned brightly on a scene of great bustle and preparation. Punctually at ten o'clock our procession started for the Jong, all the members in uniform, preceded by the pipes and drums playing "Highland Laddie," and followed by my orderlies in their picturesque Sikhimese dress and the escort of the 62nd. At the entrance to the main gateway I was received by the Tongsa Penlop and the council, and conducted to the hall, which was gaily decorated with floating banners of brocade and gyaltsen, and with precious religious picture-scrolls embroidered in silk. At the upper end of the room was a daïs, with three wooden thrones covered with cushions and silk cloths, and in front of each a small table with a ceremonial offering of fruit.

The Tongsa occupied the centre throne, placing me on his right hand, and the Lama Khenpo, Ta-tshang Khenpo, on his left. The other members of the Mission were seated on chairs on the right of the aisle, the members of council, headed by the Paro Penlop, just below them on the same side; opposite, on the left of the aisle, was the Tango Lama and other representative lamas, in their gorgeous robes of office, and wearing brocade hats. My orderlies and the escort were lined up behind my seat and the chairs occupied by the other members of the Mission. Facing the Tongsa, at the further end of the room, was an altar covered with lighted silver butter lamps. The broad aisle in the centre of the room was kept clear, but all other available space was filled by a dense throng of spectators, monks and laymen on either side, minor Jongpens and officials at the lower end. In the gallery a band of lama musicians was stationed, and another dense mass of interested onlookers, some of whom even invaded the roof to watch through the space removed for light and air, although they were repeatedly driven off by the lamas.

The Tongsa wore a robe of blue brocade, with the star and ribbon of the K.C.I.E. and the scarlet shawl, the distinguishing mark of the council.

The proceedings were opened by the formal presentation of the Durbar gifts from the Government of India, which were brought in and placed in front of the Tongsa Penlop. This was followed by the presentation of the Ta-tshang Khenpo's gifts, which were laid on the floor by his attendants. Next came the Tango Lama, as head and representative of the monastic body. Leaving his mitre and silken cope in his place, he advanced in the ordinary red monk's garb and prostrated himself twice, then returned to his seat and resumed his vestments. After the Tango Lama came the councillors, in order of seniority, following them the Jongpens of the different Jongs in a body, and so on until all had made their several obeisances and contributed their offering to the mighty pile of silks, cloths, silver coins, and gold-dust in the centre of the hall. The Maharaja-elect and the council then presented the Mission with scarves.

When this was concluded a procession of lamas, with tea-pots and other vessels of copper, gold, and silver, appeared, and the important ceremony of tea-drinking, without which no function in this part of the world is complete, was gone through. Three kinds of tea, rice, and pan were each offered in turn, and in conclusion one of the chief lamas intoned a long grace.

The head clerk to the council now rose, and from the centre of the hall read out from a parchment scroll the oath of allegiance to the new Maharaja, which the chiefs and headmen were about to sign. The Ta-tshang Khenpo from a casket produced the great seal of the Dharma Raja, which was solemnly affixed to the document. This was a lengthy proceeding, carried out with great care, and eagerly watched by the company. The seal measures about five inches square. The paper was first most carefully damped with warm water, then the seal was painted over with vermilion, and finally the impression was taken. Then in turn the council, the lamas, the Jongpens, and other high officials each affixed his seal; but their impressions were in black, not vermilion; and the lamas, on leaving their seats, whether to present the Maharaja with gifts or to affix their seals, always took off their hats and robes of office, resuming them when they again seated themselves. The following is a translation of the document:

"*To*

The foot of the two-fold Judge.

"MOST RESPECTFULLY PRAYETH,

"There being no Hereditary Maharaja over this State of Bhutan, and the Deb Rajas being elected from amongst the Lamas, Lopons, Councillors, and the Chiolahs of the different districts, we the undersigned Abbots, Lopons, and the whole body of Lamas, the State Councillors, the Chiolahs of the different districts, with all the subjects, having discussed and unanimously agreed to elect Sir Ugyen Wang-chuk, Tongsa Penlop, the Prime Minister of Bhutan, as Hereditary Maharaja of this State, have installed him, in open Durbar, on the golden throne on this

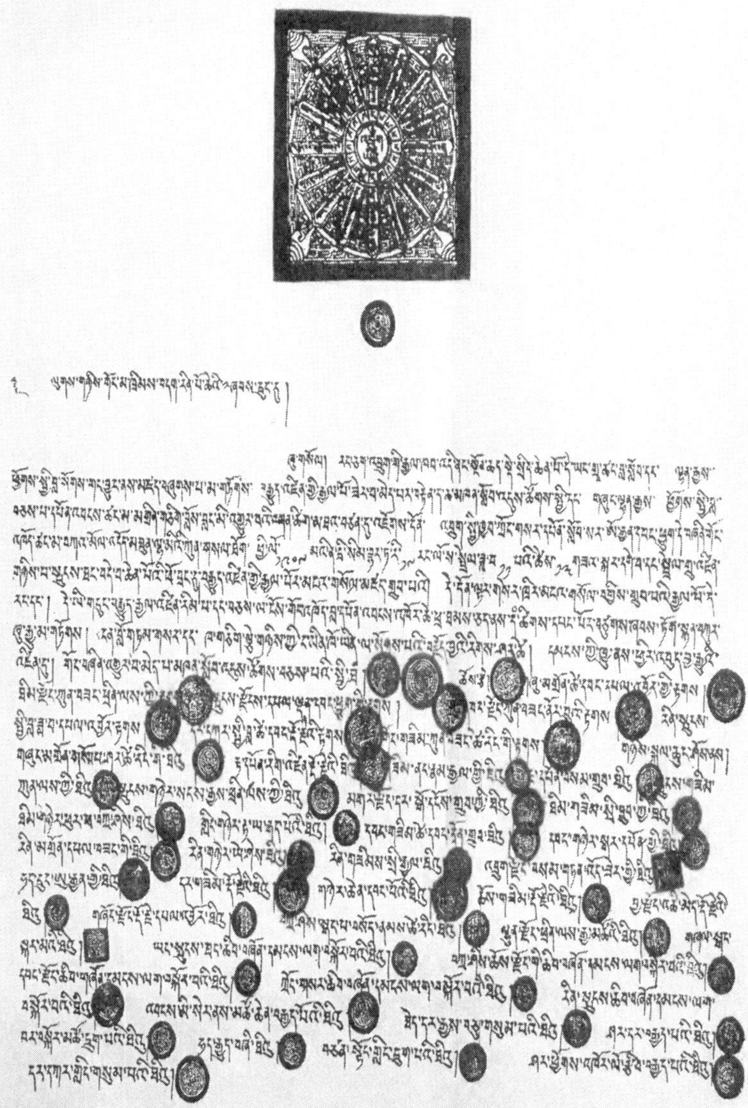

OATH OF ALLEGIANCE SIGNED AT POONAKHA AT THE INSTALLATION OF SIR UGYEN WANG-CHUK AS MAHARAJA OF BHUTAN, 1907

the 13th day of the 11th month of Sa-tel year, corresponding to the 17th December, 1907, at Poonakha-phodang.

"We now declare our allegiance to him and his heirs with unchanging mind, and undertake to serve him and his heirs loyally and faithfully to the best of our ability. Should any one not abide by this contract by saying this and that, he shall altogether be turned out of our company.

"In witness thereto we affix our seals."

Seal of the whole body of lamas, headed by the Khenpo and Lopon. Seal and sign of Chotsi (Tongsa) Chiolah. Seal and sign of Zung Donyer Tsewang Paljor. Seal and sign of Thimbu Jongpen Kunzang Tinley. Seal and sign of Poonakha Jongpen Palden Wang-chuk. Seal and sign of Angdu-phodang Jongpen Kunzang Norbu. Seal and sign of Rinpung Chiolah (Paro Penlop) Dow Paljor. Seal and sign of Tarkar Chiolah Tsewang Dorje. Seal and sign of Deb Zimpon Kunzang Tsering.

Second-class Officers.—Seal and sign of Zung Donsapa Shar Sring. Seal and sign of Zimpon Nangma Namgyal. Seal and sign of Ta-pon Rigzin Dorje. Seal and sign of Chapon Samdub. Seal and sign of Poonakha Zimpon Sangay Tinley. Seal and sign of Poonakha Nyerpa Kunley. Seal and sign of Ghassa-jong Tarpon Goley Ngodub. Seal and sign of Thimbu Zimpon Sithub. Seal and sign of Thimbu Nyerpa Phurpa Tashi. Seal and sign of Linzi Nyerpa Taya Gepo. Seal and sign of Angdu-phodang Zimpon Tsewang Ngodub. Seal and sign of Angdu-phodang Nyerpa Gharpon. Seal and sign of Rinpung Donyer Palzang. Seal and sign of Minpung Nyerpa Yesha. Seal and sign of Rinpung Zimpon Sigyal. Seal and sign of Dug-gye Jongpen Samten Wot Zer. Seal and sign of Hah Tungpa Ugyen. Seal and sign of Bya-gha Jongpen Tsemed Dorje. Seal and sign of Shon-gha Jongpen Dorje Paljor. Seal and sign of Tashigong Jongpen Sonam Sring. Seal and sign of Lhuntse Jongpen Tinley Gyatso. Seal and sign of Shalgang Jongpen Karma. Seal and sign of all the third-class officers of Poonakha. Seal and sign of all the third-class officers of Tashi-cho-jong. Seal and sign of all the third-class officers of Angdu-phodang. Seal and sign of all the third-class officers of Tongsa. Seal and sign of all the third-class officers of Rinpung (Paro). Seal and sign of Chotre Zimpon Dorje. Seal and sign of Tarkar Zimpon Dorje. Seal and sign of Nyerchen Wangpo. Seal and sign of all the subjects of Tsochen-gyed. Seal and sign of all the subjects of Thekar-kyon-chu-sum. Seal and sign of all the subjects of Shar-tar-gyed. Seal and sign of all the subjects of Bar-khor-tso-tug. Seal and sign of all the subjects of Tsen-tong-ling-tug. Seal and sign of all the Hah subjects. Seal and sign of all the subjects of Shachokhorlo-tsip-gyed. Seal and sign of all the subjects of Bar-khor-tso-tug.

Two copies of the document were prepared and duly signed and sealed, and the Tongsa Penlop was thus formally elected as His Highness the Maharaja of Bhutan, Sir Ugyen Wang-chuk, K.C.I.E. I then rose, and handing his Highness his Excellency the Viceroy's kharita, or complimentary letter, made a short speech congratulating the new Maharaja, saying:

"Maharaja Sir Ugyen Wang-chuk, Lamas, Penlops, Jongpens, and Headmen,—

"I have to-day been present at the election of Sir Ugyen as Hereditary Maharaja of Bhutan, and congratulate you, Sir Ugyen, most heartily on your accession to the gaddi, and the people of Bhutan on their choice of a ruler.

"I have known Bhutan for many years, and, with an intimate knowledge of the political questions relating thereto, I am convinced that you have taken a wise step in thus consolidating the administration of the State. Sir Ugyen has been my friend for many years, and you could not have made a better choice. His integrity, uprightness, and firmness of character commend him to every one, and his accession to the Maharajaship is not only a gain to Bhutan, but is of great advantage to the British Government, who will henceforth have a settled Government, with a man of strong character at its head, to negotiate with. My sincere hope is that you, Sir Ugyen, may long be spared to carry through the many improvements and schemes for the advancement of Bhutan which you and I have so often discussed, and I again congratulate you on your accession, and feel confident that the affairs of Bhutan under your guidance will be in the best of hands. I also have great pleasure in handing you a kharita, conveying to you the congratulations of his Excellency the Viceroy and the Government of India.

"In conclusion, I wish you long life and prosperity, and may your descendants be equally worthy to succeed you for many generations to come."

The other members of the Mission presented the Maharaja with white scarves, and congratulated him on his accession and on being the first King of Bhutan; for "Gyelpo" is the title given him by the people of Bhutan, not Maharaja, and its literal translation is "King."

The Maharaja, in return, expressed his satisfaction at the presence of a Mission from the Government of India on this eventful occasion, an occasion which he hoped would mark the opening of a new era of prosperity for his country, and his great pleasure in welcoming at the head of the Mission, as the representative of the Government of India, an old friend of many years' standing. This brought the ceremony to a close, and we left the hall in the order we had come, to the accompaniment of solemn music played by the lamas' band, the Maharaja and myself heading the procession. We accompanied the Maharaja to his private apartments, where refreshments in the shape of omelette, rice, fruit, and lychees were handed round, and after talking over the events of the day I returned to camp.

This was a momentous day in the history of Bhutan.

The country had now a recognised head; Sir Ugyen Wangchuk, the Tongsa Penlop, had been unanimously chosen by the lamas, headmen, and people as their Hereditary Maharaja. Sir Ugyen is a man of particularly strong character, who has during the last eighteen or twenty years piloted Bhutan through a series of revolutions to a state of peace and prosperity, who has the welfare of his country at heart and thinks of it before all things. He is a man universally liked and respected, and is peculiarly fitted to be the first Maharaja, and should he live long enough I am certain his rule will be entirely for the benefit of his people and their country. What he lacks to strengthen his hands are funds with which to carry on the development and improvements. The opening up of the country he has already commenced, and it is sincerely to be hoped that the Government of India may see its way to giving him the necessary assistance in the shape of a substantial loan on easy terms, or, better still, an increase of his annual subsidy. The aid is required now, not in the distant future, and I hope the fact that I am no longer on the spot or able to press the matter on Government will not mean that the proposals made will be allowed to fall into abeyance, but that the Indian Government will give, and give generously, what is required. I cannot pass over the fact that the present time is a critical one for relations between India and Bhutan, and that if we do not support the new Maharaja openly and generously grave complications may be the result. At the present moment Bhutan and its people are thoroughly and entirely friendly to the English, and wish beyond everything to enter into close relationships with them, but since the withdrawal of the Lhasa Mission Chinese influence is more active than ever on this frontier, and Bhutan, from lack of active help and sympathy on our part, may, against her will, be thrown into the hands of the Chinese by sheer force of circumstances, for China, as we know, is not likely to lose such an opportunity, when the expenditure of a few thousand rupees will gain her end, and such a departure is to be most highly deprecated from all points of view.

In honour of the Maharaja's accession I gave a dinner to Sir Ugyen and his councillors, and invited them for seven o'clock, but they all arrived about five. It was a little difficult to entertain them until dinner was served, but fortunately I had a number of mechanical toys and an electric battery to show them, and with all of them they were just as pleased as a crowd of overgrown children.

I had brought the annual subsidy of 50,000 rupees with me which, under the treaty of 1866, by which the Bhutanese ceded the Duars to the Government of India, is paid to them, and presented it in full Durbar. Our large shamianah was prepared for the ceremony, and the guard presented arms as the Maharaja entered the enclosure. Sir Ugyen and his council presented us with scarves, and a small offering of salt and cloths was laid in front of me. I then formally handed over the treasure, which was packed in boxes, to the Maharaja; at his request one box was opened and a thousand rupees were counted out. The boxes were then taken over by the Deb Zimpon and removed to the Jong. The subsidy is usually paid at Buxa, in the Duars, but it was more convenient for us both to make it over at Poonakha this year.

At the Maharaja's special request I was present unofficially, as his friend, at the first private council meeting after his election, and discussed with them and advised them on various matters connected with the administration of the State. I considered his request a great compliment, and was only too pleased to assist him in any way I could.

I prolonged my visit to Poonakha for some days, exploring and visiting the Jong, exchanging visits with the chief officials and headmen, and making one or two excursions to neighbouring monasteries. I revisited the Talo Monastery, the residence of the Dharma Raja, and found it as beautiful and charming as on my first visit, and the old Tango Lama, who, until the new incarnation is found, officiates as head of the monastery, as genial and hospitable as of old. We passed a night there, and returned to Poonakha through lovely scenery, along a road with oak, walnut, and wild pear-trees on both sides, and quantities of bracken and wild roses.

On Christmas Day the post came in most opportunely with our letters, and later the Maharaja and council arrived with their followers to be photographed. It is a great pity that in the photographs the colouring of the group does not come out, as that was the most effective part of the picture. The council were in bright-coloured silk robes, each with his crimson shawl of office; standard-bearers in gaily striped bokus; fighting men with swords, leather shields, and brightly polished steel helmets ornamented with colours; archers with bows and arrows, gun-carriers with all kinds of strange weapons, and many others, all quaintly and picturesquely dressed.

Later in the day we distributed doles to the poor in the neighbourhood. More than a thousand turned up, a most quiet and orderly crowd, who waited with the greatest patience each for his turn. I had them marshalled in double lines, sitting on the ground, and Rennick and Campbell passed down the lines, giving each person a four-anna bit. Even the babies were made to hold out their hands, though the parent speedily seized the coin. We brought an unusual Christmas Day to a close with a dinner-party, followed by a magic-lantern exhibition, at which the Maharaja and council were our guests; and with this entertainment the ceremonies attending the Maharaja's installation came to an end, and the following day our party was broken up. I sent Campbell back to Chumbi with the escort, while Rennick and Hyslop returned to India viâ the Buxa route.

I remained behind, at the urgent request of the new Maharaja and his council, to discuss with them many projects and schemes for the welfare and improvement of the country. These covered a large area—schools and education, population, trade, the construction of roads, the mineral resources of the country and the best method of utilising them, the desirability of encouraging tea cultivation on the waste lands at the foot of the hills, which are excellent for the purpose and equal to the best tea land in the Duars.

The discussions were long and earnest, and the Tongsa and all his council entered most fully into everything. The great stumbling-block to all advancement was the lack of funds, and this was clearly recognised by them all, as well as the fact that money must be raised; but the difficulty was how to do it. The sale of timber, mining concessions, and grants of tea land would all be means of bringing in a considerable revenue, and they decided to move the Government of India in the matter. After spending several days in discussing these proposals I also was obliged to take my departure, much as I regretted having to do so. Sir Ugyen was much distressed, and felt my going keenly, as, owing to my approaching retirement, it was the last time we should meet officially, though I hope some day to visit him again on my own account.

Sir Ugyen accompanied me about four miles out of Poonakha, and under the shade of a large pine-tree we sat for about two hours for our final talk, and then took a sad farewell of each other.

I have never met a native I liked and respected more than I do Sir Ugyen. He is upright, honest, open, and straightforward, and I wish it had been possible to remain in India till he had at least commenced some of his schemes of reform. He has a very difficult task before him, and at this time especially requires help given to him sympathetically and directly, without the trammels of official red tape.

My intention was to reach the plains at Jaigaon, travelling viâ Paro and Dongna-jong, and Ugyen Kazi accompanied me. After staying for the night in my old camping-ground at Lung-me-tsawe, I reached Paro, and was received by the

Paro Penlop, who had returned immediately after the installation in order to superintend the rebuilding of the fort.

While sitting round the camp-fire that night the Ghassa Jongpen's men brought me a magnificent specimen of a male takin (*Budorcas taxicolor Whitei*). The carcase was frozen hard, and it was only with great difficulty that I succeeded in having it skinned. It was a weird sight to watch the men working by the light of the fire and bamboo torches, but the operation was at last completed, and the meat distributed. Every one was eager to secure a portion, as it is believed to be a cure for many diseases and a sure panacea in the case of child-birth.

In my travels in Bhutan I have several times heard of takin in the neighbourhood, but never had time to go after them, as their haunts were always too far off my route.

On leaving Paro I turned to the south and went down the valley over a hitherto unknown route, camping for the first night at a village called Pomesa. The march up the ridge above the Hah Valley, which we crossed by the Doley-la, was good going, and we passed through some very fine forests. From the ridge I descended to the Hah-chhu by an easy road, which led chiefly through oaks and *Pinus excelsa*, passing Bite-jong on the way, but from the Hah-chhu on to the top of the next ridge, over which we crossed by the Lome-la, the road was not good. For a great part of the way there were magnificent forests of *Pinus excelsa*, *Abies Brunoniana*, and silver fir, many of the trees exceeding in size anything I have ever seen. If these forests, with the water-power at hand on all sides, were properly worked they ought to supply all the tea districts in India with boxes, and would then soon bring in some of the much-needed revenue to Bhutan; but European capital and supervision are absolutely necessary, or otherwise the forests will be destroyed.

From the Lome-la the track down to the Dongna-

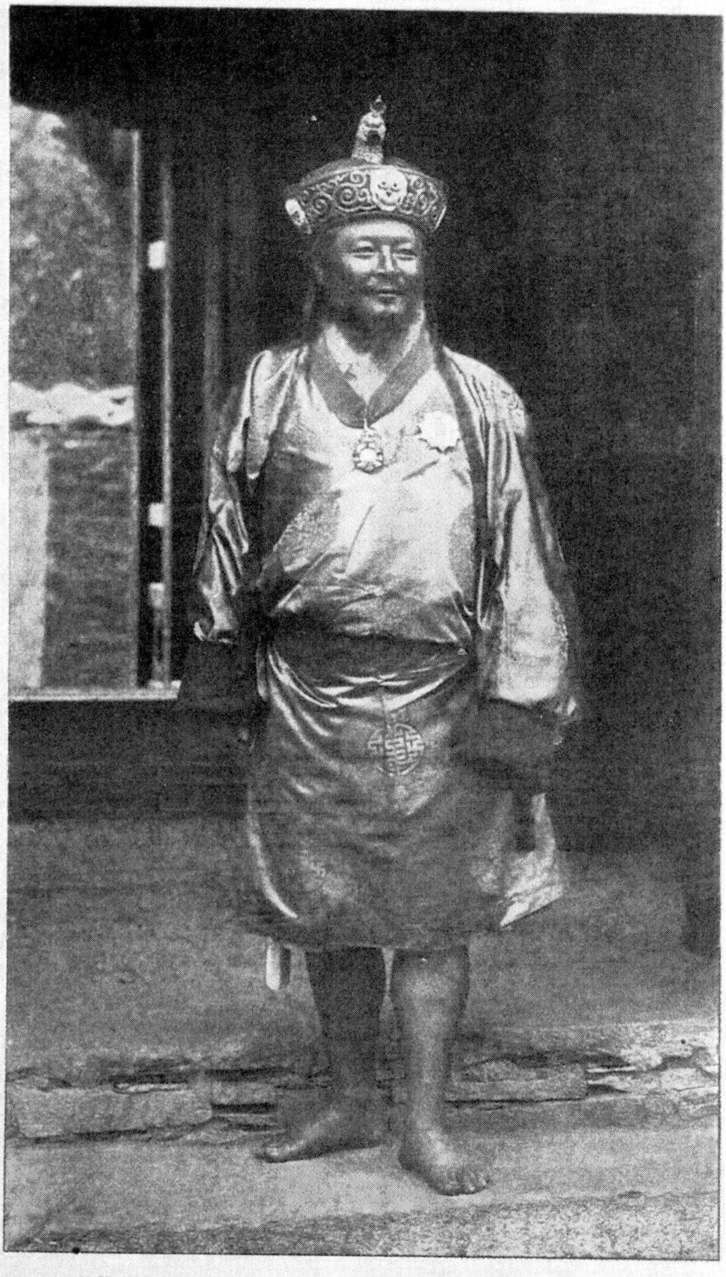

H.H. SIR UGYEN WANG-CHUK, K.C.I.E., MAHARAJA OF BHUTAN

jong, and on to the plains does not deserve the name of a road. It is nothing but a watercourse most of the way, with mere tracks along bad precipices and almost perpendicular falls, while from Dongna-jong it follows the bed of the river, and must be absolutely impassable in the rains. It was a marvel how my mules managed to get down, but with the exception of being a little footsore they were none the worse, and a few days' rest put them in condition again. One of the reasons this part of the road is so bad is that it is on the slopes of the hills immediately above the plains which receive the full force of the south-west monsoon, probably not less than 300 inches of rain in the year, and no road, unless very carefully looked after, can stand that. It is quite useless from any utilitarian point of view, but the scenery throughout is lovely.

I was not sorry to reach Jaigaon, Mr. Trood's comfortable bungalow, where I was most hospitably entertained, and where I stayed for three days to recruit and to transact some work with some of the tea-gardens on the frontier.

From Jaigaon I travelled west along the boundary to view land suitable for tea on the Bhutan side, and at the same time to look at some copper deposits which I hope may eventually prove profitable to Bhutan.

After inspecting them I turned back and went to the east of Bhutan to look at a coal-mine, travelling viâ Dhubri and Gauhati. By this time the different kinds of transport I had used during my tour had included, I should think, about every known sort. I had made use of coolies, elephants, mules, ponies, donkeys, yaks, oxen, carts, pony-traps, rail, and steamer, and the only available animal I had not employed was the Tibetan pack-sheep.

The hills where the coal is situated lie on the northern slope of the Himalayas, and are densely clothed with forests, but with practically no population, as it is too fever-stricken to allow of any one living there. They are, however, the haunt of almost every kind of wild animal—elephant, rhino, tiger, leopard, bison, mythun, sambur, cheetah, hog-deer, barking deer, &c. The river-beds are full of runs leading to the various salt-licks which occur in the hills. On one of my visits to the coal a magnificent tusker went up the valley ahead of me, and Ugyen Kazi, who pitched his camp higher up the valley, was obliged to move his tents owing to the numbers of wild elephants making it too unpleasant for him to stay on. While I was examining the coal a large tigress with her cub walked down the valley, and on my return I found her pugs, with the little one's pug inside one of her own. It would be an ideal place for shooting, but not easy to follow game, owing to the extreme steepness of the sandstone cliffs.

The elephant in its wild state can go over, or down, nearly anything, and the tusker I mentioned I found had gone up a precipice thirty feet high at an angle very little short of perpendicular.

I found the coal very much crushed and squeezed out of its original bed. The quality also was not very good, with too much ash, but it might be utilised to make gas, which could be supplied to the neighbouring tea-gardens at probably less cost than the timber now in use for fuel. After inspecting the coal I left Ugyen Kazi to attend to some timber contracts he had undertaken, and to the sale of the Bhutan lac, and fortunately finding a dog-cart available, set off to drive to the ghat at Rungamatti, a quicker way of travelling than on an elephant. There had been some rain, but the roads were in fair order. At Rungamatti I had a long wait for the steamer, which had stuck on a sandbank somewhere further up the river, and in consequence we were nearly twenty-four hours late in reaching Dhubri, the present terminus of the railway; but from there there was no difficulty in getting back to my home at Gangtak. This ended my last official visit to Bhutan; but I hope it will not be my last visit, as I look forward to meeting Sir Ugyen and his sister again, as well as all the Bhutan officials, and to revisiting the country in which I have spent so many pleasant months.

CHAPTER XX

BRITISH MISSIONS TO BHUTAN

Bogle, 1774. Hamilton, 1775 and 1777. Turner, 1783. Pemberton, 1838. Eden, 1864. White, 1905. White, 1907.

An account of the first Mission to Bhutan is to be found in the "Narrative of the Mission of George Bogle to Tibet, and of Thomas Manning to Lhasa," edited by Markham, in 1875.

Prior to this narrative, no full account of Bogle's Mission had been published. An attempt to find adequate materials in the records at Calcutta or at the India Office had failed, but fortunately Bogle's journals, memoranda, official and private correspondence were carefully preserved by his family in Scotland, and it is on these materials that Markham has based his narrative. It was the lack of these materials in the public offices that led Eden, in his account of the political missions to Bhutan, to say that Bogle does not appear to have been charged with any political functions with regard to Bhutan. Markham's investigations have proved, on the contrary, that Bogle had a mission to Bhutan, and an important one. The Mission originated in a friendly letter from the Penchen Rimpochi of Tibet, interceding with the East India Company on behalf of Bhutan after the Bhutanese invasion of Cooch Behar, and the primary cause of Bogle's Mission was Warren Hastings' desire to take advantage of this opening given him by the Penchen Rimpochi to establish friendly communications with the Government at Lhasa and open a trade with Tibet.

Eden is so far right in saying that Bogle was charged with no political Mission to Bhutan inasmuch as the treaty of 1774 had already been concluded in the April of that year, and Bogle's appointment letter is dated May 13, 1774, and in that letter no specific Mission to Bhutan is mentioned. Warren Hastings, in his letter to the Court of Directors, informs them that he is taking the opportunity of the Penchen Rimpochi's letter to employ Bogle to visit the Lama and open intercourse between Tibet and Bengal, and does not mention Bhutan.

The letter of instructions to Bogle also refers entirely to the negotiations with Tibet, though some confusion arises from the employment by Warren Hastings in this letter of the word "Bhutan." "Having appointed you my Deputy to the Penchen Rimpochi, the Sovereign of Bhutan," is the opening sentence of the letter, but Warren Hastings has used the word "Bhutan" here and in other places where it is mentioned in the letter for "Bhot," the native name of Tibet. This explanation of the use of the word "Bhutan" is to be found in Markham's note, and the context of the letter shows that it is evidently the right one. But the subsequent correspondence between Warren Hastings and Bogle proves that the latter was certainly charged with a friendly message to the Deb Raja, and with the more important duty of opening up trade with that country, and, through it, with Tibet. The main object of his Mission was to open communications and trade with Tibet, but to attain this object he was to gain the Deb Raja's consent to the passage of traders through Bhutanese territory.

Bogle was the bearer of presents to the Deb Raja, and spent some time at Tashi-cho-jong as the Deb Raja's guest, and was hospitably and civilly treated.

There must also have been some later written instructions on this point, for in writing to Warren Hastings on

October 8, 1774, Bogle acknowledges the receipt of his commands of August 9 through a merchant of Rangpur, and proceeds to say that in several conversations he has made known Warren Hastings' wish to extend the intercourse between Bengal and the Northern nations, from which Bhutan, as a channel of communications, would naturally benefit, and concludes by requesting, at the solicitation of the Deb Raja, that the annual caravan from Bhutan to Rangpur might meet with assistance and protection. The result of his visit was a very friendly letter from Warren Hastings, dated November 28, 1774, to the "Raja of Bhutan," acknowledging the kindness and civility shown to Bogle, and enclosing a perwana for the encouragement of any Bhutanese subjects who might "wish to travel with caravans to Rangpur and other districts under the Company's authority for the purpose of trade." The perwana states that strict injunctions have been given to the officers of Rangpur and Ghoraghat, in Dinajpur, not to obstruct the passage of these caravans, and to afford them every assistance. This letter was followed by another one from Warren Hastings, dated January 6, 1775, in a similar friendly tone, and promising to take steps to remove some obstructions which had been made locally to the trade in cotton between Bhutan and Bengal, and suggesting that the Deb Raja should send a vakeel to reside in Calcutta to facilitate communication between the two Governments. From the first letter of November 28, 1774, it is also apparent that Warren Hastings intended to have regular articles of trade drawn up between the two countries. A further correspondence took place between Warren Hastings and Bogle after the latter's return to Tashi-cho-jong from his visit to the Penchen Rimpochi, in Tibet, on the subject of trade negotiations. There is a letter from Warren Hastings to Bogle, dated May 9, 1775, and one from Bogle to Warren Hastings, dated May 25, which evidently crossed one another. Then we have another letter of Bogle's, of June 9, and his general report of his Mission. From this correspondence it is proved that Bogle drew up certain trade articles, to which he obtained the Deb Raja's consent, and submitted them to Warren Hastings. There is no record of these articles having ever been formally signed by the Deb Raja and Bogle, or having received Hastings' approval, but as Hastings gave Bogle a very free hand to make the best arrangements he could for trade, and as in the case of the Rangpur trade the articles were acted on, it seems most probable that Warren Hastings did approve of them.

It is curious and somewhat confusing to find that in the conduct of these negotiations both Hastings and Bogle apparently overlooked Article 4 of the treaty of 1774, which lays down that "the Bhootans being merchants, shall have the same privilege of trade as formerly without the payment of duties, and their caravans shall be allowed to go to Rangpur annually," for in Hastings' letter of May 9, 1775, to Bogle he ignores this clause altogether, and says that, to establish freedom of trade between Bhutan and Bengal, the annual caravans may continue their trade to Rangpur on the customary terms, and "you may even consent to relinquish the tribute or duty which is exacted from the caravans."

The duty is further mentioned in the letter as amounting to Rs. 2000. Neither does Bogle in his articles of trade make any allusion to the fourth article of the treaty, and in the second and third clauses of his articles provides for the free trading of the Bhutanese to Rangpur and other places in Bengal, and for the abolition of the duties on the Rangpur caravan, as if these privileges had not been already secured to the Bhutanese by the treaty. A fair was afterwards established at Rangpur under conditions which were extremely favourable to the Bhutanese. Their expenses were paid by Government, stables erected for their horses and houses for themselves. This fair continued down to 1832, when the grant for its maintenance was withdrawn.

Markham thus sums up the result of Bogle's Mission:

"Besides the valuable information he collected, Bogle's Mission was very successful in other respects. It laid the foundation of a policy which, had it been steadily, cautiously, though continuously, carried out, would long ere this have secured permanent results. Bogle formed a close friendship with the Teshu Lama (Penchen Rimpochi) and all his kindred. He secured their hearty co-operation and support in the encouragement of trade, and even succeeded, after tedious negotiations, in inducing the Bhutan Government to allow the passage of merchandise through their territory to and from Tibet and Bengal."

I have enlarged at some length on the nature of this part of Bogle's Mission to Tibet, as both Pemberton and Eden were in ignorance of the real facts, and therefore failed to recognise the importance of his visit to the Deb Raja. The same misapprehension occurs in Aitcheson's "Treaties," where it is stated: "From that time, with the exception of two *unsuccessful commercial missions* in 1774 and 1783," &c.

The Mission of 1774 noticed must, of course, have been Bogle's, and it is not fair to say that it was unsuccessful. The results of his Mission were, in fact, most encouraging at the time, and laid the foundations of what would, but for the subsequent conduct of the Bhutanese and the course events took with Tibet, have developed into a thriving trade between their country and Bengal, while the friendly attitude of Warren Hastings towards the Bhutan Government serves to show up the subsequent misconduct of the Bhutanese in their relations with us in an even more unfavourable light than it has yet appeared.

Bogle left Calcutta with Mr. Hamilton, the surgeon appointed to attend him, in May 1774, and entered Bhutan from Cooch Behar through the Buxa Duar. His route to the capital, Tashi-cho-jong, lay up the Tchin-chhu, or Raidak river, and was made in ten stages, with a computed distance of 152 miles. The route seems to have been a fairly easy one, and though the roads were too steep and rugged for the conveyance of goods except by coolies, Bogle himself was able to ride most of the way. It is interesting to notice that on his way Bogle planted potatoes at his halting-places, which he did at the desire of Warren Hastings, in order to introduce the plant into Bhutan. Between Buxa Duar and Chuka, the sixth stage, he found but few villages and scanty cultivation, but beyond Chuka and up to the capital the country opened gradually, the mountain-sides were more sloping, and the villages became more frequent. The country here is described as populous and well cultivated, the houses to be built of stones and clay, two or three stories high; there were temples and, on the last two stages, rice-fields. The temperature at Kyapcha was in June 58° in the morning and evening, and 64° in the heat of the day; at Tashi-cho-jong it was 61° in the morning, 68° to 70° at midday. The Bhutanese seem to have been adepts at bridge-making. The commonest kinds were wooden bridges on the cantilever principle, but iron suspension bridges were also met with. Bogle was furnished with a passport from the Deb Raja, and seems to have found no difficulty in getting supplies and coolies. He found the *bigari*, or forced labour, system prevalent, but says that it is so well established that the people submit to it without a murmur.

Tashi-cho-jong, the capital, is situated in a valley about five miles long and one broad, and is entirely surrounded by high mountains. The river Tchin-chhu "gallops through" the low grounds near it, which are covered with rice and well peopled. Bogle gives detailed and amusing accounts of his reception and stay at the capital, and a description of the palace of the Deb and Dharma Rajas. The palace contained nearly 3000 men and no women, and a tower five or six stories high was allotted to the Dharma Raja. The Dharma Raja apparently kept very much in the background, and Bogle's visits to him were attended with less ceremony than those to the Deb Raja. Bogle appears to have been quite satisfied with his reception, and mixed freely with the people, joining one day in a game of quoits with the Jongpen of Tashi-cho-jong and his followers. Getting tired of quoits, at which he found himself less dexterous than his entertainers, he went off and shot wild pigeons, and after that had dinner with the Jongpen. This freedom of intercourse and the friendly and cordial manner in which he was entertained by the Deb Raja and members of his court is in strong contrast to the treatment met with by subsequent Missions after Turner's, and it is perhaps not surprising that Bogle, especially considering his own gentle and amiable disposition, should give us a much more pleasing impression of the Bhutanese than is to be met with elsewhere.

In July 1774 Bogle received a letter from the Penchen Rimpochi desiring him to return to Calcutta instead of proceeding to Tibet. The excuse of which we have so often heard since in our dealings with Tibet—namely, the necessity of obtaining the consent of China to his journey—was put forward. The Deb Raja followed suit by endeavouring to persuade Bogle to return. Bogle thought that the obstacle to his journey originated with the Deb Raja, but it seems just as likely that the Deb Raja was merely carrying out the wishes of the Penchen Rimpochi. Eventually these difficulties were overcome, and he left Tashi-cho-jong on October 13, 1774, with Hamilton. The route taken was viâ Paro to Phari-jong, in the Chumbi Valley, which, after a visit to the Paro Penlop, was reached by the Mission on October 23. It would be outside the province of this note to follow Bogle in his journey in Tibet, though his account of it is full of interest. It will be sufficient to say that though he was forbidden to visit Lhasa he spent some time at Tashi Lhunpo, made great friends with the Penchen Rimpochi, and fully enlisted his sympathies with Warren Hastings' plans. Bogle left Tashi Lhunpo on April 7, 1775, and on May 8 reached Tashi-cho-jong, and apparently stayed there for about a month to carry out his trade negotiations with the Deb Raja before returning to

Bengal. The temper of the Deb Raja does not seem to have been so cordial as at the time of Bogle's first visit, but "after many tiresome conferences and further negotiations, in which the Penchen Rimpochi's people assisted," Bogle was able to obtain the Deb Raja's consent to his articles of trade. He failed, however, to obtain permission for English or European traders to enter the Deb Raja's dominions, and it was evidently on this point chiefly that the conferences were "tiresome" and ultimately "fruitless." The other difficulty he had to face was that freedom of trade in Bhutan would affect the Deb Raja's personal profits from the monopoly he enjoyed.

Bogle's Impression of the Country.—Bogle, as before noticed, carried away a much more pleasing impression of the country than any of his successors after Turner, except myself. Indeed, he gives us a picture of good government and Arcadian simplicity. It must be admitted, however, that the educated Bhutanese whom one meets outside their country, though rough in manners, are pleasant and agreeable, and that they were, as a people, never so black as they were painted by Eden, who had very good reasons for only seeing the worst side of their character. A brief account of Bogle's impressions will be interesting, as they coincide very much with the opinion formed by me during my Mission of 1906, and serve to show that the very unfavourable judgment passed upon them by Eden was hardly a true one, and was caused very much by his own treatment. Bogle found the government of Bhutan to be based on a theocracy which, while retaining a nominal, and to some extent a real, supremacy in the affairs of the country, had entrusted the administration of all temporal matters to a body of laymen. This body retained the election of the Deb Raja, the head of the temporal power, and his deposition in its own hands, made him accountable to itself for the conduct of affairs, and without its consent the Deb Raja could undertake no measure of importance in the management of the State.

As to the exact constitution of this theocracy, Bogle is not very clear, but he probably means that it was made up of the priests and heads of the monasteries under the Dharma Raja.

He divides the inhabitants into three classes—the priests, the servants or officers of Government, and the landholders and husbandmen.

The priests were formed from the body of the people, were received at an early age, and when admitted into orders took oaths of chastity. The second class comprehended the ministers and governors of provinces, tax-collectors, and all their train of dependents. They were not prohibited from marrying, yet, finding it a bar to their preferment, seldom entered that state. Like the priests, they were taken from families in the country. They were bred up in the palaces under the patronage of some man in office, by whom they were fed and clothed, but received no wages. They seldom arrived at places of trust or consequence till far advanced in life, and passed through all the gradations of service. It was no uncommon thing to see a minister as expert in mending a shoe or making a tunic as in settling the business of the nation. The landholders and husbandmen, though by far the most numerous class, and "that which gives birth to the other two," were entirely excluded from any share in the administration. Bogle evidently means that the members of the agricultural class have no chance of entering public life unless they are caught up early in childhood and trained in the households of men in office. He is not very clear in his definition of the position of the lamas. "The lamas," he says, "are first in rank, and nominally first in power. They enjoy a joint authority, and in all their deliberations are assisted by the clergy. The lamas, though nominally superior in government, yet, as they owe their appointment to the priests, are tutored by them from their earliest infancy, and deriving all their knowledge of public affairs from them, are entirely under their management. The right of electing the Deb Raja is vested in the superiors of their order jointly with the lamas. . . ." "Their sacred profession, so far from disqualifying them from the conduct of civil affairs, is the means of advancing them to it. They are often appointed to the government of provinces, employed as ministers, or entrusted with other offices of the first consideration in the State." Turner found that the governing class was educated in the monasteries. The distinction which Bogle intended to draw between the priests and the lamas was probably that the lamas were those who, having received a religious or semi-religious training in the monasteries, elected afterwards to enter the secular posts of Government, retaining at the same time a close connection with the religious side of the national life, especially in the matter of celibacy. They were represented by the Deb Raja, his governors, ministers, and councillors, in contradistinction to the priesthood, who, with the Dharma Raja as its head, concerned itself primarily with the religious administration of the country. The institution of caste was unknown, and in the absence of any sort of hereditary distinction any one might rise to the highest office.

The appointment to offices, the collection and management of the revenue, the command and direction of the military force, and the power of life and death were vested in the Deb Raja.

The provincial governors were entrusted with very ample jurisdiction. The policing of the country, the levying of taxes, and the administration of justice were committed to them. Complaints against them were seldom preferred or attended to, and their judgments were revised by the "Chief" only in capital cases or others of great consequence. They were not continued long in one station. They lived in a large palace surrounded by priests and officers, and their duties were an epitome of the court of the "Chief."

Among the non-governing class of the population, nearly every one was a landholder or husbandman. There were few mechanics, and hardly any distinction of profession. Every family was acquainted with the most useful arts, and contained within itself almost all the necessaries of life. Even clothes, a considerable article in so rude a climate, were generally the produce of the husbandman's industry. He bartered the fruits of his industry in Tibet for wool, which was spun, dyed, and woven by the females of the family, and what remained was taken to Rangpur and exchanged for hogs, salt fish, coarse linen, dyes, spices, and broadcloth. This class " live at home, cultivate their lands, pay taxes, serve in the wars, and beget children, who succeed to honours to which they themselves could never aspire."

The regular army consisted of six hundred men in pay, but all lands in Bhutan were held by military service, and every man in the country was a soldier when called upon. The taxes were moderate in themselves, and rendered still less oppressive by the simple manner of collecting them. Every family, according to its substance, was rated at a particular sum, which was often received in produce, and thus the country was unencumbered with any heavy expense for tax-gatherers. At the same time Bogle mentions the significant fact that the officers of Government received no salaries. The expenses of government, therefore, were small, and the principal drains on the public treasury were an annual payment to the Penchen Rimpochi and the support of the priests.

With regard to the general character of the people, Bogle writes :

" The simplicity of their manners, their slight intercourse with strangers and strong sense of religion preserve the Bhutanese from many vices to which more polished nations are addicted. They are strangers to falsehood and ingratitude. Theft and every other species of dishonesty to which the lust of money gives birth are little known. Murder is uncommon, and in general is the effect of anger, and not covetousness. The celibacy of a large part of the people, however, is naturally productive of many irregularities, and the coldness of the climate inclines them to an excessive use of spirituous liquor. The more I see of the Bhutanese the more I am pleased with them. The common people are good-humoured, downright, and, I think, thoroughly trusty. The statesmen have some of the art which belongs to their profession. They are the best built race of men I ever saw, many of them very handsome, with complexions as fair as the French."

In its relations with Tibet Bogle seems to have found Bhutan a dependent Power; but the Tibetan authority over the country could not have been very strong if the Deb Raja was able to exclude Tibetan traders from his country, as appears to have been the case.

The trade of the country was almost entirely in the hands of the Deb Raja, his ministers and governors, who held the monopoly of it both with Bengal and Tibet. The exports to Bengal were chiefly ponies, musk, cow-tails, coarse red blankets, and striped woollen cloths half a yard wide. The imports were chiefly broadcloth, spices, dyes, Malda cloth, coarse linen, hogs, and salt fish. The great trade with Bengal was carried on by means of the annual caravans to Rangpur, from which the Government of Bengal received about Rs. 2000 by way of duty, and there was also trade with Dinajpur. The great obstacle which Bogle found in inducing the Deb Raja to allow open trade through Bhutan into Tibet was the monopoly of it which the Raja enjoyed along with his ministers, and the profits of which, he was afraid, the admission of foreign merchants would lessen. This disinclination to admit foreign traders was not confined to traders from Bengal only; even the merchants of Tibet were not allowed to purchase goods in Bhutan, beyond exchanging salt and wool for rice.

The following were the articles of trade drawn up by Bogle with the Deb Raja:

"Whereas the trade between Bengal and Tibet was formerly considerable, and all Hindu and Mussalman merchants were allowed to trade into Nepal, which was the centre of communication between the two countries, and whereas from the wars and oppressions in Nepal the merchants have of late years been unable to travel in that country, the Governor as well as the Deb Raja, united in friendship, being desirous of removing these obstacles so that merchants may carry on their trade free and secure as formerly, have agreed on the following articles :

"That the Bhutanese shall enjoy the privilege of trading to Bengal as formerly, and shall be allowed to proceed either themselves or by their gomasthas to all places in Bengal for the purpose of trading and selling their horses free from duty or hindrance.

"That the duty hitherto exacted at Rangpur from the Bhutan caravans be abolished.

"That the Deb Raja shall allow all Hindu and Mussalman merchants freely to pass and repass through his country between Bengal and Tibet.

"That no English or European merchants shall enter the Deb Raja's dominions.

"That the exclusive trade in sandal, indigo, skins, tobacco, betel-nut, and pan shall remain with the Bhutanese, and that the merchants be prohibited from importing the same into the Deb Raja's dominions, and that the Governor shall confirm this in regard to indigo by an order to Rangpur."

Captain Turner, in the report of his Mission in 1783, alludes to this "treaty" of Bogle's, and says the Deb Raja acknowledged its validity and that there was every prospect of its provisions being kept, and in February 1786 Purangir Gosain, the Company's agent in Tibet, reported that many merchants had found their way from Bengal to Tashi Lhunpo through Bhutan.

Soon after Bogle's return to Calcutta in June 1775, Warren Hastings determined to prosecute the intercourse which had been so happily opened with Bhutan, and in November 1775 appointed Hamilton, who had been

Bogle's companion, to a second Mission to the Deb Raja. Hamilton reached the frontier in January 1776, and was invited by the Deb Raja to proceed to Poonakha. He endeavoured to enter Bhutan by the Lakhi Duar to Paro, but obstacles appear to have been raised to his doing this, and he eventually followed Bogle's route by the Buxa Duar. He reached Poonakha on April 6, 1776, and Tashi-cho-jong in the May of that year. The chief object of Hamilton's mission was to decide on the claims of the Deb Raja to the districts of Ambari Falakata and Julpaish, and he came to the conclusion that equity demanded their restoration. He also reported that if restitution were made the Deb Raja would probably be induced to fulfil his agreement with Bogle and only levy moderate transit duties on merchandise. It is not improbable that, as Eden remarks, this concession was made to the Deb Raja more in the interest of Warren Hastings' policy than on the intrinsic merits of the case, as there can be no doubt that the claims of the Bhutan Government to the Falakata and Julpaish districts were quite untenable.

In July 1777 Hamilton was sent on a third Mission, to congratulate the new Deb Raja on his accession.

The fourth Mission, under Captain Turner, took place in 1783. In 1779 it was arranged, on the invitation of the Penchen Rimpochi, that Bogle should meet him in Pekin. Unfortunately, both the Lama and Bogle died before this project could be carried into effect. Not long afterwards intelligence reached Calcutta that the reincarnation of the late Penchen Rimpochi had taken place, and Warren Hastings proposed to the Board of Directors to take advantage of this auspicious event and send a second deputation to Tibet. Turner was selected for this service, and nominated on January 9, 1783, and soon afterwards left Calcutta on his Mission, accompanied by Lieutenant Samuel Davis as draftsman and surveyor, and Mr. Robert Saunders as surgeon. He entered the hills by the Buxa Duar, and followed almost exactly the same route as Bogle to Tashi-cho-jong. During his stay in Bhutan with the Deb Raja Turner was witness to a small civil war occasioned by the rebellion of Angdu-phodang, which was ultimately quelled by the Deb Raja. The fighting, he said, on both sides gave him a very poor idea of the "military accomplishments" of the Bhutanese, and though several engagements took place between the opposing parties very few on either side were killed or wounded. He attributes this display of martial weakness more to want of discipline than to actual lack of courage. The principal weapon in use was the bow and arrow, and Turner says the arrows were sometimes poisoned. A few of the soldiers were armed with very unserviceable matchlocks. Turner considers the Bhutanese to be expert swordsmen, in which he differs widely from Macgregor's account of his experience in the Bhutan war nearly a hundred years later. Before leaving Bhutan, Turner visited Wandipore, or Angdu-phodang, and Poonakha, and ultimately entered Tibet by the Paro and Phari routes. Turner does not add much to the knowledge of the country acquired by Bogle, and says little or nothing about its political institutions. He describes the Deb Raja as a popular and prudent administrator, and seems to have experienced great kindness and hospitality at his hands. The Deb, he says, was an "intelligent man, possessed with a versatility of genius and spirit of inquiry" and fond of mechanics, and derived great amusement from Turner's electric battery. The Raja "would never venture to draw even a spark himself, but would occasionally call in parties to be electrified, and much enjoy the foolish figure they made on the sensation of a shock." The Raja also possessed a knowledge of medicine equal to any of the physicians in his dominions, and was interested in experimenting with English drugs on himself and his Court doctor. This interest, however, waned after an overdose of ipecacuanha. At Poonakha, the summer residence of the Court, there was a fruit garden of oranges, lemons, pomegranates, peaches, apples, and walnuts. Very excellent turnips were grown, but the potatoes planted by Bogle had failed. The flower garden contained hollyhocks, sunflowers, African marigolds, nasturtiums, poppies, larkspurs, and roses. At one entertainment he describes Turner had strawberries for tea, and a bull-fight closed the day's amusements. He found the monasteries the educational centres of the country. Boys were taken from the villages and educated there, and in families containing more than four boys it was obligatory to dedicate one of them to the order. The monastery was the channel to public office, and, in fact, nearly all the Government officials were chosen from men who had been trained in one. Marriage was an obstacle to any rise in rank, and but few of the official class were married; and this practice of celibacy, common to the priestly and governing classes—to the one from motives of religion, and to the other from motives of self-interest—formed a natural bar to the increase of population.

Neither from the narrative of his Mission nor from his report of it to Warren Hastings can it be gathered that Turner was charged with any particular political business in Bhutan, but Eden says that it appears from the proceedings of the Collector of Rangpur of June 11, 1789, that he was instructed to cede to Bhutan the district of Falakata, as the result, it may be presumed, of Hamilton's report. The only matter of any political interest, so far as Bhutan is concerned, to be found in his report, dated March 2, 1784, of the results of his Mission is the following opinion he records about trade relations with Bhutan:

"The regulations for carrying on the commerce of the Company through the dominions of Bhutan by means of the agency of native merchants were settled by the treaty entered into by Mr. Bogle in the year 1775. The Deb Raja having acknowledged to me the validity of that treaty, it became unnecessary to enter into another, since no new privileges and immunities appear to be requisite until the commerce can be established on a different footing with respect to the views and interests of the Raja of Bhutan, by whose concurrence alone the proposed commercial intercourse with Tibet can be made to flourish. I should be sorry to suggest a doubt of its ever receiving a check from any conduct in that Government of a hostile tendency."

There can be no doubt in the mind of any reader of the accounts of Bogle's and Turner's Missions that both these officers were well received and treated, and that the general disposition of the Bhutan Government towards the Company was cordial and friendly, and Turner's confidence that the Bhutan Government meant to fulfil its engagements was not a foolishly misplaced one at the time, as Eden would seem to imply. Hastings actually succeeded in establishing Purangir Gosain as a diplomatic agent at the Tibetan Court, and Indian merchants had commenced by the year 1786 to pass freely through Bhutan into Tibet. Thus so far it must be acknowledged that Bogle's Mission was successful, and that the Bhutan Government did fulfil its engagements. Unfortunately the Nepal war with Tibet, which broke out in 1792, destroyed all these bright prospects. The Tibetans and the Chinese Government suspected that we were covertly assisting the Nepalese. We lost their confidence, and the Tibetan passes were closed to natives of India, most probably through Chinese influence. Thus the chief object of Bogle's negotiation was defeated, while so far as the further development of trade with Bhutan itself was concerned, what had been gained was lost by the series of frontier disputes which took place between the Company and the Bhutan Government, and the consequent rupture of the friendly feeling between the two Governments which had been established by Bogle's and Turner's Missions.

The chief object of the fifth Mission, under Pemberton, was to enable the Government to enter into direct communication with the Bhutan Durbar, as it had become evident that the frontier officers of Bhutan had repeatedly withheld from the Durbar complaints addressed to it by Government on the subject of frontier aggressions. Accordingly, after the Bhutanese aggressions of 1836 had been repelled the Dharma and Deb Rajas were informed that it was the intention of Government to despatch an envoy to their capital. The replies to this communication, which was dated April 6, 1837, evinced a desire on the part of the Deb to postpone the Mission, and he had to be informed that Government was determined on the Mission and intended to send their envoy after the rainy season was over.

The conduct of the Mission was entrusted to Pemberton, with Ensign Blake as assistant and in command of the escort and Dr. Griffiths as botanist and in medical charge. The escort was to consist of fifty men from the Assam Seebundy Corps, but owing to the difficulty in supplying rations for this number only twenty-five men were taken.

Pemberton, being anxious to obtain information concerning Eastern Bhutan, determined to enter Bhutan by the Banksa Duar instead of following Bogle's and Turner's route by Buxa. This determination produced a good deal of obstruction on the part of the Bhutanese. Pemberton was detained for some time at Dum Duma, on the frontier, waiting for letters from the Dewangiri Raja, and again at Dewangiri after he had reached it, and every attempt was made to induce him to return to the frontier and proceed by Buxa Duar to Poonakha. This, however, he managed to avoid doing, and was eventually conducted through the Tongsa Penlop's country to the confines of Bhutan and Tibet, and thence by a westerly route to Poonakha. He had intended to return to Goalpara by the Cheerung route, but permission to do this was refused, and he was compelled to take the Buxa route back to India. The number of days occupied in travelling from Dewangiri to Poonakha was twenty-six, but owing to the unsettled state of the country and the difficulty of obtaining porters the actual number of days occupied on the journey was sixty-eight, and Poonakha was not reached till April 1. During his stay at Poonakha a rebellion broke out, the object of which was to dethrone the Deb Raja. Both Turner on the previous and Eden on the subsequent Mission came in for a civil war. The Mission was in its progress through the country received everywhere with marked distinction, was waited upon by the Subahs of the districts through which it passed, and was properly treated at Poonakha. Pemberton, however, did not succeed in obtaining the consent of the Durbar to the treaty he was instructed to proffer, and he was refused permission to proceed to Tibet. The Durbar even refused to forward a letter to Lhasa. The movements of the members of the Mission were closely watched, and intercourse by the villagers on the route with the Mission was so closely prohibited that it was with the utmost difficulty that any information was obtained about the country. The draft treaty which Pemberton submitted to the Bhutan Government was extremely moderate in its terms. It provided for the same privilege of freely trading in Bhutan by the subjects of the British-Indian Government that the Bhutanese already enjoyed in India; for the mutual surrender of criminals and runaway raiyats; for the more punctual payment of the Bhutan tribute for the Duars, and its payment in cash instead of in kind, and for power for the British-Indian Government to take possession of any Duar the tribute of which should fall into arrears, and hold the same till the arrears were paid off; for decisive measures by the Deb Raja to stop aggressions by the Dewangiri Raja and other of his subjects on the frontier; for the settlement of boundaries and the appointment of a Bhutanese agent at Gauhati and Rangpur. After many protracted discussions, the Deb and Dharma Rajas and other members of the council, except the Tongsa Penlop, were ready to sign the treaty, but owing to the opposition of the Tongsa Penlop, who divided the supreme power in the country with the Paro Penlop, and whose interests were affected by the arrangements for the punctual payment of the tribute for the Assam Duars, the Bhutan Government refused its consent.

But though the Mission was politically a failure, Pemberton, in spite of the difficulties thrown in his way, succeeded in drawing up an admirable report on the country and its internal government.

In 1862 it was finally determined to send a sixth Mission into Bhutan, by the most convenient route, without waiting any longer for the consent of the Bhutan Durbar. Eden was selected by the Government of India, and received his instructions in Colonel Durand's letter, No. 493, dated August 11, 1863.

In these instructions the Government of India set forth the necessity, which had arisen from the repeated outrages of the Bhutanese within our territories and those of Sikhim and Cooch Behar, of revising and improving the relations between the British Government and Bhutan, and their determination to send Eden to the Court of Bhutan for the purpose. Eden was to explain "clearly and distinctly, but in a friendly and conciliatory spirit," to the Bhutan Government the reasons which rendered it necessary for the British Government to occupy Ambari Falakata and withhold its revenues, and that the occupation would continue only so long as the Bhutan Government refused to comply with our just demands and restore the captives and property which had been carried off from British territory, Sikhim, and Cooch Behar, but that if the Bhutan Government manifested a desire to do substantial justice the district would be held in pledge for their future good conduct, and a sum equal to one-third of its net revenues would be paid to them, in the same manner as is done with the Assam Duars.

Inquiry was to be made into any acts of specific aggression complained of by the Bhutanese, arrangements made for the mutual rendition of criminals, for the reference to the British Government for settlement of any dispute between Bhutan and, the States of Sikhim and Cooch Behar. The subjects of keeping a British agent in Bhutan and of free commerce between the two countries were to be approached if it seemed advisable, but negotiations on these points were to be entirely subordinated to the main political objects of the Mission. All available information about Bhutan was to be obtained.

The above demands were entered in a draft treaty, and Eden was further instructed that if the Bhutan Government refused to do substantial justice and to accede to the main principles stipulated on he was to withdraw from the country and inform the Bhutan Government that Ambari Falakata would be permanently annexed, and in the event of further aggressions the British Government would take such steps as might be necessary to secure the safety of their own and the Sikhim and Cooch Behar territories.

Dr. Simpson was appointed to the medical charge of the Mission. The Mission was to proceed by Darjeeling, and in the beginning of November Eden arrived there to arrange his preparations. He could get no reply from the Dharma and Deb Rajas to the announcement of his intention of entering Bhutan, and it turned out that the country was then undergoing one of its periodical rebellions. The Deb Raja had been unseated by the Poonakha Jongpen and Tongsa Penlop, and compelled to take refuge in the Jong of Simtoka. The Paro Penlop was the only powerful chief who remained faithful to his cause. The insurgent party set up a sham Deb Raja to receive the Mission, but at the time it reached Poonakha there was in fact no settled Government in the country. The Government of India, however, thought that as the rebellion had been successful and a substantive Government apparently established the Mission should proceed.

This state of things accounted for the constant obstacles and interruptions which the Mission met with on its journey. It started on December 4, and Chebu Lama accompanied it as a sort of intermediary. On the 11th the Mission reached Dalingkote, and was detained there till the 29th. It had great difficulty in procuring provisions; many of the coolies, seeing the questionable manner in which the Jongpen received the Mission, ran away; the Deb sent evasive answers to Eden's letters; every attempt was made to detain the Mission indefinitely, and when Eden finally moved on on the 29th he was compelled, for want of transport, to leave most of his tents, stores, and baggage behind and nearly half his escort. At Sipchu further obstruction and difficulties in obtaining transport were experienced, and he had to consider whether to move on with a further diminished escort or to return. In view of the orders he had received from Government at Darjeeling, and its evident desire that the Mission should push on, and thinking that it was unlikely that the Bhutan Government would dare to treat a British envoy with insult or violence, Eden determined to proceed, taking with him only fifteen Sikhs and ten Seebundy sappers, and leaving the rest of his escort, all his heavy baggage, his assistant, Mr. Power, and the commissariat sergeant, moonshi, native doctor, and all the camp-followers that could be spared behind.

Sipchu was left on February 2, the ascent of the pass from Saigon commenced on the 3rd, and the party halted for the night in the snow at an elevation of 8798 feet. The next day the pass was crossed at 10,000 feet, and the descent to Donga-chhu-chhu (8595 feet) made through snow with much difficulty. The party halted the next day on the banks of the Am-mo-chhu, and Eden draws attention in his narrative to the advantage of a route into Tibet through Bhutan up this valley. The next halt was made at Sangbay, and there further obstruction was met with.

The Jongpen refused all help, as he had received no orders to allow the Mission to pass. A good many of the coolies were found to be frost-bitten. Eden had to abandon all idea of bringing on the escort he had left behind, and sent orders to Mr. Power to return to Darjeeling, taking back all the party and stores left at Sipchu and all the escort left at Dalingkote, except a guard of five Seebundys over the stores, which were placed in charge of the Jongpen. At Shay-bee, the next halting-place, the Mission was met by some Zinkaffs from the Durbar, who gave out that they had been ordered to turn the Mission back. On Eden sending for them, it turned out that they had no letters from the Durbar for him, but two to the Jongpen of Dalingkote, which they showed. One letter was full of professions of friendship for the British Government, and instructed the Jongpen to settle any dispute Eden might have with him about the frontier, but said not a word about the Mission being allowed to go forward or being turned back. The other was a most violent and intemperate production, threatening the Jongpen with loss of life for having permitted the Mission to cross the frontier, and ordering him to pay a fine of Rs. 70 to each of the Zinkaffs, and to entice Eden to return, but if he could not get rid of him, to send him on by the Samchee and Dongna road. The Zinkaffs tried to get Eden to go back to get on to this route, but as he was already only two days from Samchee, and to retrace his steps would have meant a journey of fifteen days, he declined, and left Shay-bee on February 10 for Paro. The Mission had first to cross the Saigon-la Pass (12,150 feet), and camp in snow at 11,800 feet. Though the thermometer registered 13° none of the natives, Sikhs or Bengalis, suffered from the cold. After descending into the Hah Valley the Mission was delayed in crossing the next pass on its route, the Che-la (12,490 feet), by the heavy snow. On the 19th Eden, hearing that messengers from the Durbar were on their way to stop him, determined to make the effort, though the snow was not really in a proper state for the attempt. The march was nearly ending in disaster. The snow was soft, and varying from three to eight feet in depth; men, horses, and mules were constantly sinking in it; and when the top of the pass was reached at six o'clock in the evening it was found that the descent was even more difficult on account of the snow. Evening came on while the party were still on the pass, and to have halted there for the night would have meant the death of every man in the camp, as there was no going to the right or the left. There was nothing for it but to drive the coolies on, and by eleven o'clock, after progressing at the rate of a quarter of a mile an hour, the Mission was fortunate enough to reach a forest where the coolies could bivouac. Eden, however, with some of the coolies, pushed on, and reached the nearest village at one o'clock in the morning, after having marched through deep snow continuously for fifteen hours without food. Luckily the weather had been clear, with a bright moon. The next morning the Mission was met by the Zinkaffs who had been sent to turn it back. They delivered a most impertinent message, saying that they had been sent to go back with Eden to the frontier "to rearrange with him the frontier boundaries and to receive charge again of the resumed Assam Duars"; after this had been done our further demands were to be inquired into, and if these Zinkaffs "considered it necessary" the Mission was to be allowed to go on to Poonakha. Eden said he would do nothing of the kind, but would either proceed to Poonakha or return to Darjeeling and report to his Government that the Bhutan Durbar declined to receive him. Then the Zinkaffs begged him to proceed. The letter they delivered from the Deb Raja was of the usual evasive character, declaring that the Deb never declined to receive the Mission, but that it would be better to investigate complaints on the frontier. As the letter contained no definite refusal to receive the Mission, Eden determined to push on, and reached Paro on February 22. Here again the Mission was detained, and its reception was at first unfriendly. The ex-Penlop, an old man, informed Eden that he was far from acknowledging the power of the present Deb, and that he had only suspended hostilities on the side of the ex-Deb on account of the approach of the Mission. The real power, he said, just then rested with the Tongsa Penlop, and the Dharma and Deb Rajas and councillors were mere puppets in his hands. Finally the old Penlop and his adopted son, the young Penlop, became quite friendly, and after the Mission had been sixteen days at Paro without any communication having been received from the Deb Raja the old Penlop advised Eden to proceed, gave him guides, and promised to arrange to send on his letters.

At the next stage more messengers arrived from the Durbar, and the same efforts were made as before to induce the Mission to return, with the same result. At Simtoka the Mission found the ex-Deb in retirement. He declined to receive a visit from Chebu Lama, on the grounds that any member of the Mission holding any communication with him might excite the suspicion of the Durbar against it, which was considerate of him. After crossing the Dokyong-la Pass (10,019 feet) the Poonakha Valley came in view, and on March 15 the Mission reached Poonakha. There the party were met by a messenger to say that they must not approach by the road which passed under the palace gates, and they were sent to their camping-ground by a route so precipitous that they had great difficulty in making the descent. The subsequent ill-treatment of the Mission, and how Eden was forced under compulsion to sign an agreement to surrender the Assam Duars, how the Mission narrowly escaped from worse treatment by forced night-marches from Poonakha to Paro, were reported confidentially to Government, and the details are not supplied in his general report. They are to be found in Rennie's "History of the Bhutan War." The opposition to the Mission was entirely directed by the then Tongsa Penlop, father of Sir Ugyen, who was no doubt actuated by his desire to get back the Assam Duars, which were part of his chiefship, and the annexation of which had affected his personal interests even more closely than those of the Durbar. Judging by subsequent events, it would have been wiser, no doubt, for Eden to have returned to Darjeeling instead of pushing his way to Poonakha. He had received quite enough opposition before crossing the Cho-la Pass, certainly by the time he had reached Paro, to justify his doing so. The Government of India would have had sufficient cause to annex the Duars, as they eventually did, and the indignities to the Mission would have been spared. At the same time, one cannot help admiring the courage with which Eden faced the difficulties in his way, his determination to leave the Bhutan Government no loophole by which they could evade the responsibility of the Mission not reaching them, and the patience with which he endeavoured to gain from the Durbar the terms he had been sent to obtain.

The Mission left Poonakha on March 29, and returned to Darjeeling through Paro, where it stayed one day on April 2. The same day the insurrection broke out again.

On the termination of the Tibet Mission, and to mark the approval of the British Government of the friendly attitude of the Bhutanese and the assistance rendered by the Tongsa Penlop in bringing about a friendly settlement, the King-Emperor, in 1905, was pleased to confer on Ugyen Wang-chuk a Knight Commandership of the Indian Empire. I was in consequence deputed by the Government of India to present the insignia of the order to the Tongsa at Poonakha.

The Mission was accompanied by Major Rennick and Mr. Paul, and an escort of the 40th Pathans. The route followed was from Gangtak viâ Chumbi, Hah, Paro, and Tashi-cho-jong to Poonakha.

This Mission was accorded a warm, even enthusiastic, welcome, and succeeded in establishing relations of the most friendly character with the Bhutanese, who not many years before were bitterly hostile towards the British Government. After the ceremony at Poonakha, the Mission, at the invitation of Sir Ugyen, visited Tongsa and Bya-gha, where they were most hospitably entertained by the Tongsa Penlop. The Mission returned from Tashi-cho-jong viâ Lingshi and Tibet.

In 1907 I was deputed on my second Mission to Poonakha, to be present, as the representative of the Government of India, at the installation of Sir Ugyen Wang-chuk as Hereditary Maharaja of Bhutan.

I was accompanied by Major Rennick, Captain Hyslop, and Mr. Campbell, the escort being provided by the 62nd Punjabis.

The route followed was from Gangtak viâ Chumbi, Phari, over the Temu-la to Paro, and thence by the former route to Poonakha.

Nothing could have been more cordial than my reception. The members of the Mission divided at Poonakha. I returned viâ Paro to the Hah Valley, and thence down the Dongna-chhu to the Duars, Mr. Campbell returning with the escort to Chumbi, and Major Rennick and Captain Hyslop returning viâ Buxa.

CHAPTER XXI

BRITISH RELATIONS WITH BHUTAN FROM 1772

Nepalese invasion of Tibet, 1792. The Athara Duars. Friction with Bhutan. Our occupation of the Bengal Duars. Expedition against Bhutan. Loss of guns. Treaty of Rawa Pani. Whole of Duars taken by us. Tongsa Penlop accompanies expedition to Lhasa. Sir Ugyen's visit to Calcutta. Sir Ugyen elected Maharaja.

So far as records show, the earliest relations between the Government of India and Bhutan began in 1772. In that year the Bhutanese set up a claim to Cooch Behar, invaded the State, and carried off the Raja, Durunder Narain, and his brother the Dewan Deo. The Cooch Behar family solicited the aid of the Government of India, which was at once accorded, and a small force, under Captain Jones, was sent to drive the Bhutanese across the frontier. The expedition was successful. Captain Jones drove the Bhutanese out of Cooch Behar, and captured the forts of Daling, Chichacotta, and Buxa. The Bhutanese then appealed for aid to the Tashi Lama, who at the time was Regent of Tibet during the minority of the Delai Lama. The Lama addressed a very friendly letter to the Governor-General, Warren Hastings, which was read in Council on March 29, 1774, in which he sued for peace on behalf of the Government of Bhutan, and suggested that though they deserved punishment they had been sufficiently chastised. In this letter Bhutan is claimed as a dependency of Tibet. A treaty of peace with Bhutan followed, which was signed at Fort William on April 25, 1774.

In this treaty the Company agreed to deliver up territory taken from Bhutan during the war, exacting from the Bhutan Government an annual tribute for the Chichacotta province of five Tangan horses, which was the acknowledgment paid to the "Bihar Raja." The Bhutan Government were to deliver up the Cooch Behar Raja and his brother. The Bhutanese merchants were to be allowed the same privileges of trade free of duties as formerly, with permission for their caravans to go to Rangpur annually. The Deb Raja was to abstain from encouraging incursions into the Company's country, from molesting raiyats who had come under the Company's protection, and to engage to deliver up raiyats who might desert from the Company's territories; to submit all disputes between Bhutan and the Company's subjects to the decision of the Company's magistrate; to refuse shelter to any Sunniassees hostile to the English, and to allow English troops to follow them into Bhutan; and to permit the Company to cut timber in the forests under the hills, and to protect the woodcutters.

Warren Hastings took advantage ot the Penchen Rimpochi's friendly letter to send a Mission to Tibet with the view of establishing communication with the Court at Lhasa and opening trade with that country. Bogle, who was sent in charge of the Mission, was also charged with the duty of negotiating with the Bhutan Durbar for the opening of a trade route through their country to Tibet. The Mission started on May 6, 1774, and Bogle was successful in gaining the consent of the Deb Raja to the passage of trade free of duty through his country. Articles of trade were drawn up between the two Governments, and for a few years trade from Bengal was actually allowed to pass through Bhutan into Tibet. A full account of Bogle's Mission, so far as it related to Bhutan, is given in another chapter.

Two small Missions under Hamilton almost immediately followed on this important Mission of Bogle. In

1775 Warren Hastings sent Hamilton into Bhutan to examine into the claims of the Deb Raja to Falakata and Julpaish, in the present Jalpaiguri district. Hamilton came to a conclusion in favour of the Deb Raja's rights. In 1777 he was again sent to Bhutan to congratulate a new Deb Raja on his succession. In 1779 Warren Hastings, still keeping steadily in view his policy of maintaining regular intercourse with Bhutan and Tibet, determined to send Bogle again as envoy to the Penchen Rimpochi in Tibet, but as news arrived that the Rimpochi was about to take a journey to Pekin the Mission was postponed; and it was afterwards arranged, at the suggestion of the Lama, with the consent of the Emperor of China, that Bogle should meet the Lama at Pekin. This plan was most unfortunately frustrated by the death of the Penchen Rimpochi, at Pekin, from small-pox, and not long afterwards Bogle died in Calcutta of cholera. There can be little doubt that had this meeting with the Penchen Rimpochi taken place under such auspicious circumstances the whole course of our subsequent relations with Tibet and Bhutan would have been different.

A few years later the reincarnation of the Penchen Rimpochi in Tibet was reported to Warren Hastings; the Governor-General at once seized this further opportunity offered him of prosecuting his policy with the Lhasa Government, despatched Captain Turner in 1783 as his envoy to the Court of the infant Lama, and made him the bearer of the congratulations of the Indian Government on the event. Turner was also charged with letters to the Deb Raja, and it would appear from his report that he was to stimulate the Bhutan Durbar to keep to its engagements under the articles of trade concluded by Bogle. Eden also says that Turner was instructed to cede to the Government of Bhutan the district of Falakata, in Jalpaiguri. Turner's Mission to Tibet was the last for many years. So far Warren Hastings' policy had been successful. He had succeeded in establishing friendly relations with

Bhutan and Tibet, in opening trade through the one country to the other, and in having a diplomatic agent, Purangir Gosain, at the Tibetan Court.

In 1792 the Nepalese invaded Tibet. The Chinese sent an expedition to the assistance of Tibet, the result of which was that the Gurkhas were driven out of the country, and sustained a crushing defeat from the Chinese general in their own country only twenty miles from Katmandu. The results of this war had a most unfortunate effect on our relations with Tibet. The Chinese suspected that the Indian Government had supported the Nepalese, and, in consequence, closed all the passes of Tibet to natives of India, and they have remained closed ever since. While this was the end of Hastings' policy in Tibet, our friendly relations with Bhutan began about the same time to wane, and after the year 1825, when the first Burmese War broke out, to seriously suffer from the constant aggressions committed by the Bhutanese on our frontier. The situation ultimately became impossible, and had to be put an end to by the Bhutan War of 1865. A full account of these troubles will be found in Eden's report of his Mission to Bhutan in 1863.

The earliest claim to any portion of British territory raised by the Bhutan Government was to a portion of the Zamindari of Baikantpore, including the mahals of Ain Falakata and Julpaish. From Markham's account, this claim appears to have been made as far back as 1775, and was one of the objects of Hamilton's Mission. Eden dates the claim 1787, but it was no doubt made earlier, though the territory was not ceded till 1789. Eden maintains that the claim was untenable, and it seems probable that the Government, anxious to conciliate the Deb Raja and to further their trade policy with Tibet, were too ready to accept Hamilton's report, which was favourable to the Bhutan Durbar. In 1787 claims were also raised to the mahal of Holaghat on behalf of the Bijni Raja, and to the mahal of Goomah on behalf of the Zamindar of

Beddragong; but the respective owners of these mahals repudiated the claims, and they were dropped. In 1815 some dispute arose about frontier boundaries, and Babu Bishen Kant Bose was deputed to the Court of the Dharma and Deb Rajas to settle it. He has left an interesting report of the state of the country as he found it. From this year till 1825–26 there is no account of any communication with the Bhutanese.

The first Burmese War broke out at this time. We drove the Burmese out of Assam, assumed the government of Lower Assam, and in becoming possessors of this province we also found we had inherited the very unsatisfactory relations of the Assamese with the Bhutanese. The nature of these relations must be briefly explained in order to understand what follows. At the base of the lower ranges of the Bhutan hills there is a narrow strip of country, from ten to twenty miles in breadth, and extending from the Dhunseeree River, in Assam, on the east, to the River Teesta, or frontier of the Darjeeling district, on the west. This tract, which is by nature singularly rich and fertile, was known as the Bhutan Duars, or Passes. Eighteen passes entered it from the hills, each under the authority of a Jongpen, and attached to each jurisdiction was the portion of the tract lying below the pass, and bearing its name. Thus the whole locality came to be known as the Athara Duars, or Eighteen Passes. Of these Duars, eleven were situated between the Teesta and the Monass. The other seven were on the frontier of the Darrang (Goalpara) and Kamrup districts of Assam, and were generally called the Assam Duars, those bordering on the Bengal frontier being called the Bengal Duars. The Bhutanese had managed to wrest the Bengal Duars from the Mohammedan rulers of the country, probably soon after the foundation of the present Bhutan State. They never obtained absolute possession of the Assam Duars, but by their outrages and incursions they succeeded in forcing the Assam princes to purchase security by making over their Duars to the

Bhutanese in consideration of an annual payment of yak-tails, ponies, musk, gold-dust, blankets, and knives to the estimated value of Narrainee Rs. 4785.4.

The seven Assam Duars were :

1. Booree Goomah.
2. Kalling.
3. Churkolla.
4. Banksa.
5. Chappagorie.
6. Chappakamar.
7. Bijni.

The eleven Bengal Duars were :

1. Dalingkote.
2. Zumerkote.
3. Chamurchi.
4. Suckee.
5. Buxa.
6. Bhulka.
7. Bara.
8. Goomar.
9. Keepo.
10. Cherrung.
11. Bagh or Bijni.

It was from these Duars that the Penlops in whose jurisdiction they lay, and under the Penlops the Jongpens, and under the Jongpens the inferior frontier officers, who were sometimes Assamese and Kacharis, derived their support. When we occupied Lower Assam the British Government renewed and continued the engagements made by the Assamese with the Bhutan Government. These arrangements were complicated, and contained in themselves the elements of constant dispute. The tribute due from Bhutan was payable in kind, and as an inevitable consequence questions constantly arose as to the value of the articles given and received. But this was not the only source of complication. The five Kamrup Duars were held exclusively by the Bhutanese, and were entirely under their management, but the two Darrang Duars of Booree Goomah and Kalling were held under a very peculiar tenure, the British Government occupying them from July to November in each year, and the Bhutan Government for the remainder of the year.

Owing to the articles sent for tribute failing to realise

the value at which they were appraised by the Bhutanese, each year's tribute fell short of the fixed amount, and a constantly accruing balance was shown against them. Our demands for the liquidation of these arrears were met by evasion, aggression, and the plunder and abduction of our subjects residing on the frontier. The long series of such outrages that ensued, commencing from the attack on Chetgaree, in Darrang, on October 22, 1828, down to 1864, are given in some detail in Eden's report on his Mission. It will be sufficient to say that between 1828 and 1836 they involved five serious outrages in which British subjects were carried off and our outposts attacked, necessitating as many military expeditions by our frontier forces, the attachment of the Booree Goomah Duar from 1828 till 1834, when it was restored to the Deb Raja, the raising of the Assam Seebundy Corps (now the 2/8th Gurkha Rifles) in 1834 for the protection of the frontier, and the temporary attachment of the Banksa Duar in 1836.

The defeat of the Dewangiri Raja by Lieutenant Mathews, and the attachment of the Banksa Duar, to some extent brought the Bhutan Government to their senses. The Regent and the Tongsa Penlop addressed our Agent, declaring that none of the letters of remonstrance addressed to the Bhutan Government had ever been received, and requesting that all arrears of revenue might be taken from the Banksa Duar, and the Duar itself restored. Many of the offenders who had been engaged in outrages on our frontier were delivered up. Our Government promised to surrender the Duar on an engagement being entered into for its better management and the extradition of offenders against our Government. Unfortunately, this agreement was made with subordinate officials, as representatives of the Bhutan Government, who had, says Eden, no higher rank than that of common "chaprasis," and was never ratified by the Deb Raja, though the Duar was surrendered in anticipation of his doing so. The belief, however, that all communications from our Government were withheld from their Durbar by the Bhutanese frontier officials led to the despatch of Captain Pemberton as our envoy to the Bhutan Court in 1837. This Mission was infructuous. The draft treaty which our envoy submitted to the Durbar was agreed to by the Deb and Dharma Rajas and the rest of the council, except the Tongsa Penlop, who was then the real authority in the country, and, at his instigation, was finally rejected.

In 1839 the Bhutanese resumed their outrages on the frontier, and began by carrying off twelve British subjects, one of whom died of his wounds; another was murdered because he attempted to escape; and a third was thrown down a precipice because he refused to work. Bhutan itself was at this time in a state of anarchy and civil war. The Duars were becoming depopulated. The Governor-General's Agent proposed to remedy this state of things by our taking the Duars into farm and under our direct management. The proposal was approved of by the Government of India, and a native officer was about to be sent into Bhutan to obtain the Deb Raja's consent, when another serious aggression was committed. Five villages were seized; the Cutcherry of the Zamindar of Khoomtoghat was attacked and plundered, and one of his servants taken off. The two eastern Duars, Kalling and Booree Goomah, were then formally attached and occupied by our officers. Not long afterwards letters came from the Dharma and Deb Rajas asking that the attached Duars might be released and an envoy be sent into Bhutan. Colonel Jenkins wished to take this opportunity to push the plan of taking a farm of the Duars, but Lord Auckland was averse to sending another Mission into the country at a time of such internal disorder and when the parties contending for superiority were almost equally divided in strength, and he preferred sending a letter of remonstrance and serious warning to the Deb Raja, intimating that if Bhutan continued much longer in its present state of anarchy and inability to manage its frontier it would become necessary to annex the Duars. This was no idle threat, and not long afterwards, on September 6, 1841, on the recept of a further report from the Agent, Colonel Jenkins, depicting the miserable state of the Assam Duars, their state of increasing disorganisation, and the almost entire depopulation of the tract under the Bhutan Government, the remaining Assam Duars were permanently attached, and a sum of Rs. 10,000 paid per annum to the Bhutan Government as compensation for the loss they sustained by this resumption. No written agreement was made regarding this arrangement.

In 1842, at the request of the Bhutan Government, we took charge of the Falakata mahal, as they found themselves unable to manage the estate by their own officers, and held ourselves responsible for due payment to the Bhutanese of the net proceeds of the property. This arrangement continued till 1859, when the mahal was attached.

After this annexation of the Assam Duars comparative tranquillity reigned in this part of the frontier. Outrages, however, continued in the Bengal Duars, and Eden writes regarding them: "The aggressions committed from the Bengal Duars on our territory and on Cooch Behar, and patiently borne by us, have been unparalleled in the history of nations. For thirty years scarcely a year has passed without the occurrence of several outrages, any one of which would have fully justified the adoption of a policy of reprisal or retaliation." Dr. Campbell says on the same topic: "The whole history of our connection with Bhutan is a continuous record of injuries to our subjects all along the frontier of 250 miles, of denials of justice, and of acts of insult to our Government."

Between 1837 and 1864 thirty cases of plundering British subjects were reported, and no fewer than eighteen elephants were carried off from the immediate neighbourhood of the Jalpaiguri cantonment. As many as twenty-five British subjects were reported by the police to have been carried off into slavery. During the same period fifty outrages were committed in the Cooch Behar territory, in one of which Rs. 20,936 worth of property was said to have been plundered, and altogether sixty-nine residents of that State were kidnapped.

The Dewangiri Raja (Dungl'sang Sangsub), acting with the connivance of the Tongsa Penlop, was largely concerned in the commission of these outrages. In compliance with representations from our Government, the Deb Raja ordered the Tongsa Penlop to pay into the Treasury a sum of money equal to half the value of the property plundered by his relative and subordinate, the Dewangiri Raja. This led the Penlop to address two insolent letters to Colonel Jenkins complaining that the Agent should not have addressed the Deb Raja direct, and arrogating to himself equal powers with the Deb Raja. "I am a Raja like the Deb Raja," he wrote; "how can he possibly injure me?" There was probably a good deal of truth in this, and the inherent weakness of the central Government in Bhutan, which left the powerful officials like the Tongsa Penlop free to do entirely as they pleased, had much to do with the constant outrages on the frontier. Lord Dalhousie, in Orders No. 186, dated January 11, 1856, directed Colonel Jenkins to send strong letters of warning both to the Deb Raja and the Tongsa Penlop, requiring the latter to apologise for the disrespect he had shown to his lordship's representative, and pointing out to the Deb Raja that he must be held responsible for the malpractices of his subordinates, and that if there should be a recurrence of these predatory incursions into British territory the Agent had been authorised to take immediate measures for the permanent occupation of the Bengal Duars. The revenue of the Assam Duars was at the same time withheld. This produced an apology, and the revenue was paid, after deducting the value of the plundered property, Rs. 2868.

Even while these letters of apology were on their way another outrage was committed, and Arun Singh, an hereditary Zamindar of the Goomar Duar, was forcibly carried off into Bhutan. The Government of India advocated mild measures of remonstrance, but the Governor-General considered that, in view of past offences and warnings, the Bhutan Government should be told that if proper reparation was not made annexation of the Duars would follow. This demand was met by an impertinent letter from the Deb Raja, claiming Arun Singh as a subject of his own. Still the Government of India did not proceed to extremities, though more outrages were committed, and it was considered necessary to move a regiment up to the frontier. Sir Frederick Halliday visited the frontier, and on May 5, 1857, addressed the Governor-General, recommending that as the Bhutan Government showed indications of being about to adopt an improved foreign policy, and the rebellion which had thrown the country into confusion had ceased, an ultimatum should be addressed to the Durbar calling on it "once more, avowedly for the last time, to deliver up Arun Singh, or abide the consequences," and in the event of their failing to comply with this demand Sir Frederick Halliday proposed to annex the Ambari Falakata and Julpaish territories. The supreme Government concurred with these proposals. A cantonment was opened at Jalpaiguri, and the 73rd Regiment of Native Infantry and a detachment of the 11th Irregular Cavalry were posted there.

The mutiny, however, broke out at the time, and prevented this ultimatum from being carried into effect. Further outrages took place; further remonstrances were made. The tone of the Bhutan Government and its officials grew bolder and more insolent. The Subah of Bhulka Duar refused to investigate an outrage which had occurred in his jurisdiction until a revision was made of the frontier boundaries laid down in 1851–52. The Deb Raja, in a flippant and impertinent reply addressed to the Agent in 1859, declared that "Arun Singh had died because his days were numbered."

Even then the Lieutenant-Governor of Bengal, Sir

J. P. Grant, did not consider that the Deb's answer was such as to necessitate immediate action, and thought that "the execution of the menace of annexation should be kept back till the occurrence of some new outrage." The Governor-General, however, did not concur in this view, and directed that the Falakata estate should be annexed. This annexation was made in 1859.

Still further outrages took place, and instead of the threat of the annexation of the rest of the Duars being carried out a period of hesitation and inactivity followed, during which the best method of dealing with the question was discussed between the Agent for the North-Eastern Frontier, the Bengal Government, and the Government of India. Lord Canning inclined to the view that a Mission should be sent to Bhutan, and in Colonel Durand's letter, No. 55, dated January 23, 1862, the Agent, Captain Hopkinson, was desired to state what arrangements were necessary for the security of a Mission. While the deputation of a Mission was under consideration more aggressions occurred, and insolent demands for the payment of the Ambari Falakata revenue were made by the Dalingkote Jongpen. A considerable force of Bhutanese was marched to the Rangpur frontier, and simultaneously arrangements were made for crossing the Teesta for the purpose of attacking Darjeeling. This was met by moving up two companies of the 38th Regiment and a wing of the 10th Native Infantry to the frontier, and outposts were pushed forward from the regiment at Jalpaiguri. The result of this was that the Bhutanese immediately returned to their homes.

In July 1862 a messenger, Mokundo Singh, was despatched from Assam to the Bhutan Court announcing the intention of the Governor-General to send a Mission, and asking the Bhutan Government to name the route by which it should enter and to make arrangements for the reception of the envoy. No reply was received from Bhutan till December of the same year, and the letter that Mokundo Singh brought from the Deb Raja was evasive and contradictory. The Deb promised to send some Zinkaffs in the following spring to settle disputes. But the Zinkaffs never came, and the officers sent to receive the Assam compensation money were not even of the usual rank. The Governor-General therefore felt that the conduct of the Bhutanese Government in sending an evasive answer and in not sending the promised messengers warranted him in sending a Mission without further parley by the most convenient route. Eden was ordered to hold himself in readiness to proceed to Bhutan as the envoy of the Government, and received his instructions in Colonel Durand's letter, No. 493, dated August 11, 1863. On September 30 letters were sent to Bhutan announcing the despatch of a Mission, and on December 4 Eden, accompanied by Dr. Simpson, started from Darjeeling. The demands made on the Bhutan Government were mild in the extreme, considering the treatment we had experienced at their hands. They embraced the retention of the Ambari Falakata estate for the present, but held out hopes of its release to the Bhutan Government; arrangements for the extradition of criminals; and an explanation to the Deb Raja of the terms we stood on with reference to the Sikhim and Cooch Behar States, and that aggression on these States must be considered as an unfriendly act. Eden was also to endeavour to arrange for the appointment of an agent at the Bhutan Court at some future time, and to secure free commerce between the subjects of the two Governments. The progress of the Mission has already been noticed. The objects were defeated, principally by the Tongsa Penlop, who held a preponderating influence in the council. Our envoy was grossly insulted and his signature obtained by compulsion to a most audacious and impossible treaty, and Eden, with the members of his Mission, had practically to make their escape from Bhutan to avoid imprisonment and perhaps death.

Even after this treatment of its envoy the Government of India decided to give the Bhutan Government room for repentance. Eden made three alternative suggestions of the best measures to be adopted to punish the Bhutanese and secure the frontier from future aggressions: (1) The permanent occupation of the whole country; (2) the temporary occupation of the country, to be followed by withdrawal after destroying all the forts and impressing the people with our power; (3) the permanent annexation of the Duars, and the occupation of the hill forts commanding them.

The Government of India, however, inclined to milder measures, and determined only to annex permanently Ambari Falakata and withhold all future payment of the Assam subsidy, and to require the surrender of all British and Cooch Behar captives, failing which the whole of the Duars should be annexed. Time was given to the Bhutan Government to comply with these demands, while preparations were made for an advance on our side. The Bhutan Government, instead of taking advantage of the opportunity given of a peaceful settlement of the question, sent an impertinent letter to Chebu Lama of Sikhim, who had been attached to the Mission, accusing him of having brought about the trouble, threatening him with the consequences, and declaring their intention of abiding by the treaty that Eden had been forced to sign, and returned an evasive reply to our Government. Then at last the Government of India, in its proclamation of November 12, 1864, declared its intention of occupying and permanently annexing the Bengal Duars, and so much of the hill territory, including the forts of Dalingkote, Passaka, and Dewangiri, as might be necessary to command the passes, and the Bhutan War commenced. The command of the forces was given to Brigadier-General Malcaster, who was to operate on the right, while the two columns on the left were under the immediate command of Brigadier-General Dunsford, C.B. Operations commenced on November 28, by an advanced party, under Major Gough, V.C., crossing the Teesta near Jalpaiguri and taking, without encountering any resistance, a small Bhutan outpost at Gopalganj.

Mynaguri, Daling, Damsong, Samtsi, Dongna, and Buxa were successively occupied by the two left columns, with but little loss on our side, and the military occupation of the Bengal Duars was completed by the end of the year. On the Assam side the Bhutan hill post of Dewangiri was captured, with slight opposition, early in December. A force of some strength was then despatched to capture the fort of Bishensing, but on the arrival in its vicinity of an advanced party the supposed fort was found to consist of a single stone house, occupied by a lama or priest. The necessity for further military operations having ceased with the capture of the hill forts commanding the passes, and its annexation of the Bengal and Assam Duars being thus completed, the Government of India directed the breaking up of the Duars field forces early in February 1865, intending to leave the occupation of the country chiefly to the Bengal Police battalion of about eight hundred strong, which had accompanied the expedition, and a few cavalry posts on the frontier. But when the force was on the eve of breaking up information was received that the Bhutanese were preparing to attack the whole line of posts from Chamurchi to Dewangiri. Dewangiri was attacked by a force under the Tongsa Penlop. The first attack was repulsed. The Bhutanese, however, cut off the water supply of the fort, and succeeded in throwing up a stockade which completely commanded it; they also obtained possession of the Dorunga Pass, thus cutting off communication with the plains. Colonel Campbell was running short of ammunition, General Malcaster had refused to reinforce him, an attempt to send in ammunition failed, and under these circumstances Colonel Campbell determined to evacuate the position under cover of the night and retreat to the plains by another pass known as the Libra Pass. The evacuation commenced at one o'clock on the morning of February 5. Unfortunately, the main party lost its way in the darkness; a panic ensued, the retreat became a disorderly one, some of our wounded were left behind in the confusion, and the guns, abandoned, fell into the hands of the Tongsa Penlop.

The Bhutanese luckily stayed behind to plunder, and did not follow up their advantage, so that the force succeeded in reaching Kassurekatta with the loss of the few wounded who fell into the hands of the enemy. It is noteworthy that these prisoners were well treated by the Tongsa Penlop. The Bhutanese force on this occasion was estimated at 5000 men, but this number includes porters, coolies, musicians, and servants. Unsuccessful attempts were about the same time made to capture the posts at Bishensing and Buxa, but though these failed another reverse to our forces was sustained at Taza-jong, the stockaded post at the Bala Pass. As at Dewangiri, the Bhutanese were not discouraged by their first repulse, and threw up a stockade commanding our post. Colonel Watson arrived from the plains with reinforcements on February 4 to dislodge them, but, after engaging the enemy for two hours, was compelled to retire with the loss of Lieutenant Millett killed, Lieutenant Cameron mortally wounded, and several of the men of the 11th Native Infantry killed and wounded. The post at Chamurchi was at the same time threatened; though the Bhutanese did not succeed in driving our post out of the pass, they continued to occupy their own entrenchment. This change in the aspect of affairs necessitated the sending of reinforcements to the frontier.

Brigadier-General Tombs, C.B., V.C.. was appointed to supersede General Malcaster, and Brigadier-General Fraser Tytler, C.B., succeeded General Dunsford, who was compelled to resign from ill-health. Both these generals were given independent commands, the former of the Right, and the latter of the Left Brigade.

Bala was recaptured by General Tytler on March 15, and the Bhutanese were driven out of the stockades where they had established themselves in the vicinity of Buxa and Chamurchi by March 24; the objects of General Tytler with the Left Brigade were thus speedily effected, with but slight casualties. On the Assam side the Right Brigade recaptured Dewangiri by the end of March. As Dewangiri was considered unhealthy during the rains, it was evacuated at once after its capture, the buildings destroyed, and the troops withdrawn by April 6. The military operations in both the Assam and Bengal Duars being thus completed, so far as immediate active measures were required, General Tombs returned to his command at Gwalior, and the two brigades were placed under General Tytler, with his headquarters at Gauhati, to act, if required, on the defensive, and to be ready for a further advance if circumstances rendered this necessary. The Bhutan Government now made overtures for peace, and asked for the restoration of the Duars. Preliminary negotiations followed, during which further hostilities were suspended, and resulted in a treaty with Bhutan, which was finally concluded on November 11, 1865, at Sinchula. Under this treaty the British Government retained possession of the Assam and Bengal Duars. The Bhutan Government agreed to surrender all British subjects of Sikhim and Cooch Behar detained in Bhutan against their will; to the mutual extradition of criminals; to the maintenance of free trade; to the arbitration of the British Government in all disputes between the Bhutan Government and the Chiefs of Cooch Behar and Sikhim. This treaty is known by the Bhutanese as the Ten-Article Treaty of Rawa Pani.

The Bhutanese also agreed to deliver up the two guns which had fallen into the hands of the Tongsa Penlop, and to return the agreement which they had extorted from our envoy, Eden, with an apology for their treatment of him. On their side the British Government undertook to pay the Bhutan Government, from the revenues of the Duars, an annual sum beginning with Rs. 25,000, on fulfilment of the conditions of the treaty; on January 10 following the first payment Rs. 35,000; on January 10 following Rs. 45,000; on every succeeding January 10 Rs. 50,000. The arrangement about the surrender of the guns and delivery of the extorted treaty was recorded in a separate agreement, dated November 10, given by the two representatives of the Bhutan Government, and it was agreed that until these two conditions were fulfilled no money payment under the treaty should be due to the Bhutan Government.

The country thus ceded to the British Government comprised the Athara Duars, a narrow strip of territory averaging about twenty-two miles in width and 250 in length, lying at the foot of the hills. The eastern Duars, lying east of the Sankos River, have been incorporated with the Goalpara and Kamrup districts of Assam.

Payment of the allowance to the Bhutan Government was temporarily withheld in 1868, on account of the Bhutan Government having stopped intercommunication between Bhutan and Buxa, and on account of their disregard of Article 4 of the treaty of 1865 by sending an officer of inferior rank to receive the subsidy. In 1880 the Bhutanese were again told that the subsidy would be withheld unless certain raiders in Chunbati, near Buxa, were handed over to us. Eventually our demands were complied with, the raiders delivered up, and the captives (British subjects who had been carried off) released in July 1881.

The last civil war in Bhutan ended in 1885, when Ugyen Wang-chuk, who was then Tongsa Penlop, assisted by his relative, the Paro Penlop, defeated Aloo Dorji, the Thimboo Jongpen, and Poonakha Jongpen; the last was killed. In 1888, on the outbreak of hostilities between ourselves and the Tibetans, Shapenjoo, father of Ugyen Kazi, warned the Tibetans of the consequences of refusing to come to terms; and, on behalf of Bhutan, refused assistance to the Tibetans. During the interval between then and the Tibet Mission of 1904 the Bhutanese, under the guidance of the Tongsa Penlop, Ugyen Wang-chuk, were most friendly to us, and constant intercourse was kept up between the Tongsa Penlop and our representatives, first Mr. Paul, and later myself. During the Tibet Mission of 1904 the Bhutanese were called upon for open support, and their Government, under the guidance of Ugyen Wang-chuk, sent a Mission with General Macdonald in his advance on Lhasa. This was headed by Ugyen Wang-chuk himself, who rendered such excellent service that on the conclusion of the expedition he was honoured with a Knight Commandership of the Most Excellent Order of the Indian Empire.

Up to 1904 the political relations between Bhutan and the Indian Government had been carried on through the medium of the Government of Bengal. On hostilities breaking out in that year these political relations were transferred from Bengal to Colonel Younghusband, who corresponded direct with the Government of India. On the termination of the Mission these political relations were transferred to myself, the Political Officer of Sikhim, and at the same time I was entrusted with the political relations with Tibet. This was a change of great importance, as it brought Sikhim, Bhutan, and Tibet directly under the Government of India, and thus avoided the unnecessary and tedious delays formerly caused by corresponding through the local Government.

In 1905 I was deputed on my first Mission to Bhutan, to present to Sir Ugyen Wang-chuk the insignia of the K.C.I.E. I was accompanied by Major Rennick, of the Intelligence Branch, and by Mr. Paul, at the special invitation of Sir Ugyen; the escort was taken from the 40th Pathans. Unlike all former Missions of recent date, this Mission was received in the most friendly manner; everything was done to ensure the comfort and pleasure of its members, and most friendly relations with Sir Ugyen and all Bhutanese officials was the result.

From now onwards the Bhutanese moved steadily forward in the line of improvement. In 1906 Sir Ugyen was invited to meet H.R.H. the Prince of Wales in Calcutta, which invitation he accepted. This may be taken as one of the most important events in recent Bhutan history. This visit assured Sir Ugyen of our friendship, and brought him into contact with the outside world, of which he had previously only heard very little ; it broadened his views and showed him that there were larger and more important centres than his own small kingdom. This visit and the constant intercourse between Sir Ugyen and his officials and the British Political Officer had its effect in paving the way for the very great change which shortly took place.

In 1907 Sir Ugyen was chosen unanimously by the lamas, headmen, and people of Bhutan as their Hereditary Maharaja.

I was deputed on my second Mission to Bhutan, to be present at the installation, to represent the Government of India. I was accompanied by Major Rennick, Mr. Campbell, and Captain Hyslop, and the escort was taken from the 62nd Punjabis.

This Mission was also received in the most friendly manner, and everything possible was done to make its stay in Bhutan a pleasant one.

It will thus be seen that for the last hundred years till quite lately the governing body in India has endeavoured to keep strictly, and even contemptuously, aloof from these mountain people, and that their policy of refusing to sympathise or hold friendly intercourse with them has invariably resulted in trouble and annoyance to themselves, in return for which they have enforced full payment by depriving the weaker State of valuable territory.

It is obvious that in the case of Bhutan, Government should utilise this unique opportunity of a new *régime* in that country to enter into a new Treaty and to increase the inadequate subsidy that we now dole out as compensation for the annexation of the Duars, the most valuable tea district in India. If this is not done soon

China will acquire complete control in Bhutan, and demand from us, as she did in the parallel case of Sikhim, the retrocession of the Bhutanese plains. Further, any political disturbance on this frontier would seriously affect the supply of labour on the tea-gardens in the Duars, and so cause great loss to the tea industry. This was very ably pointed out by Edgar in 1887, when we were compelled to fight China under the guise of Tibet for supremacy in Sikhim. The neighbouring State of Nepal is in a measure subject to China under the treaty of 1780, and in all these years we have made but little progress in knowledge of that country, and have allowed our Resident to be a kind of political *détenu* in the Residency at Khatmandu. It is earnestly to be hoped that we may not drift into a similar position with Bhutan, and in order to avoid doing so constant and continued intercourse with our frontier officers should be encouraged, and a policy closely followed by which no efforts to further and advance friendly and intimate relations are spared.

CHAPTER XXII

FOREIGN RELATIONS WITH BHUTAN

China. Tibet. Nepal. Sikhim. Cooch Behar.

IT is impossible to say when the first connection with China commenced, but the right of granting a patent of investiture and seal of office to the ruler of Bhutan seems to have been claimed by China at an early date. It was revived by the Emperor Chien Lung in 1736. It is fair to assume that it was not much after Chinese power was finally established at Lhasa, and Ambans appointed there, in 1720, but it would seem to have afterwards fallen into abeyance, as Bogle tells us that one of the causes of the rebellion of Deb Jeedhur, about 1774, was that the Deb endeavoured to secure the friendship and protection of China by circulating the seal of the Emperor in Bhutan. According to Pemberton, the power of China was regarded with considerable respect by the authorities in Bhutan, and a very marked deference was shown to the supposed views and wishes of the Chinese officials at Lhasa. Once a year messengers arrived from Lhasa bearing an imperial mandate from China addressed to the Deb and Dharma Rajas, and the Penlops under their orders. It was written on fine cambric in large letters, and generally contained instructions to be careful in the government of the country, to quell promptly all internal tumult or rebellion, and to report immediately, on pain of a heavy fine, any apprehended invasion from foreign foes; and on one occasion a fine of Deba Rs. 10,000 was actually imposed for neglect of orders, which was paid in instalments spread over three years.

Twenty gold coins were always sent with the imperial mandate. The reply returned by Bhutan was always accompanied by a present of twenty-three coolie-loads of fine rice and goods, consisting mostly of silk and cotton cloths, to the value of Rs. 3000. A return present was afterwards received from China of flowered scarves and silks, coral, and moulds of silver and gold. Though the Chinese authorities at Lhasa appeared, as a rule, to exercise no direct control in the government of the country, Pemberton heard of one instance when they interfered, in the year 1830, to settle one of the frequent insurrections that had taken place against the Deb Raja of that time, by sending a body of troops into Bhutan and deciding between the claims of the rival parties. Pemberton adds that the accuracy of his information of the action of the Chinese on this occasion has been questioned, but the story is consistent with what has happened since. At his interview with the Deb Raja in 1874 Rampini was informed by him that though Bhutan was in no way tributary to China, yet an annual exchange of presents took place. Bhutan sent presents to the value of Rs. 7000 to the Chinese Ambans at Lhasa, and received presents in return to the value of Rs. 10,000.

Two instances at least have occurred in more recent years since the Bhutan War in which the Chinese authorities at Lhasa have interfered in Bhutanese politics. These were in 1876–77, when the Deb Raja reported to Lhasa the wish of the British Government that he should make a good road through Bhutan, and Chinese and Tibetan officials were sent to Bhutan to support him in refusing to do anything of the sort. In the rebellion of 1885 the defeated Deb appealed to Lhasa, and Chinese and Tibetan officials were deputed to settle the dispute. They summoned the Maharaja of Sikhim to attend the conference.

China

China

Tibet

Nepal

Tibet

IMPRESSIONS OF SEALS GIVEN TO BHUTAN
BY CHINA, NEPAL, AND TIBET

On this occasion the interference of the Chinese Ambans at Lhasa cannot be construed as an act merely of their own initiative. The Indian Government received information from her Britannic Majesty's Chargé d'Affaires at Pekin that the Chinese were disposed to take the cause of the ex-Deb in hand and support him with Chinese troops, and in consequence of the attitude taken up by China the subsidy was withheld till the dispute between the opposing Debs was finally settled.

In 1890 there occurred a further symptom of the interest taken by China in Bhutan and of the intention of the Chinese Government to revive their former suzerainty over the country. The Assistant Resident in Tibet, who was afterwards promoted to be Principal Resident, in a memorial to his Government at Pekin, suggested that the two Penlops of Tongsa and Paro should be created Chieftains, and should at the same time be invested with a title of hereditary nobility by the Emperor of China. This proposal received the imperial sanction. Subsequently the Assistant Resident modified his proposal, and, in view of the fact that the executive administration was really vested in the Tongsa Penlop, the Paro Penlop being merely nominally associated with him in the government of the country, suggested that this distinction should be recognised, and that the former should be appointed Chieftain and the latter Sub-Chieftain. This was sanctioned by the Emperor in the *Pekin Gazette* of August 22, 1890.

Her Britannic Majesty's Minister at Pekin, in his letter informing the Government of India of the step, adds :

" The action taken by the Resident in the present instance appears to be merely a continuation of the policy adopted by his predecessor in 1866, when, as reported in my Despatches Nos. 59 and 60 of the 9th and 15th November of that year, the Chinese Government asserted the right of controlling appointments to the posts of Raja or Penlop in Tibet. As explained in the second of my above-mentioned Despatches, the right of granting a patent of investiture and a seal of office to the ruler of Bhutan seems to have been claimed by China at an early date. It was revived by the Emperor Chien Lung in 1736, and when Bogle visited Bhutan forty years later he found that the introduction of the imperial seal of China was still a vexed question in the country."

In 1891 the Paro Penlop wrote to Paul to inform him that officers of the Chinese Amban had visited him at Paro on November 21, 1891, and left with him a golden letter, with the seal of the Emperor of China, for the Tongsa Penlop. It is not quite clear whether there was only the one letter, or whether the Paro Penlop received another one for himself.

The connection of Bhutan with Tibet has been much closer, although since the establishment of the Chinese power at Lhasa Tibetan control in Bhutan has been exercised in concert with or under the orders of the Chinese Ambans.

The Deb Raja, in his conversation with Rampini in 1874, repudiated the idea of his State being tributary to Tibet any more than to China, but the whole course of Bhutan history shows that though the chain which binds Bhutan to Tibet may be a loose one, it is held nevertheless by Tibet, and tightened on occasions.

Horna Della Penna, in his " Brief Account of the Kingdom of Thibet," written in 1830, says that the kingdom of Dukpa (Bhutan), along with Ladak and Nepal, were then subject to and had voluntarily made themselves tributary to Tibet, after the Emperor of China had made himself master of it.

From researches made in old Tibetan manuscripts, it is clear that the present State of Bhutan originated in a colony of Tibetans, and that the first Dharma Raja, Shabdung Nga-wang Namgyal, who introduced order and government into this colony, was a lama from Tibet, as well as the next Dharma Raja, Gyaltsap Tenzing Robgay.

The earliest connections of Bhutan with Tibet were thus evidently very close, both on the religious and secular side. Pemberton's account confirms this view. He mentions a tradition current in the country that Bhutan was once ruled by resident Tibetan officers, and that when these officers were withdrawn, and the Bhutanese allowed to govern themselves, they still consented to pay an annual tribute to Tibet, and recognised the supremacy of the Emperor of China in secular and of the Delai Lama in spiritual affairs.

Coming down to a more historical period, the time of Bogle's Mission, we find that in the letter addressed by the Regent of Tibet, the Tashi Lhunpo Lama (Penchen Rimpochi ?), to Warren Hastings, which was received on March 29, 1774, in which he mediated for peace on behalf of Deb Jeedhur, the Regent claims Bhutan as a dependency of Tibet. He says the Deb Raja "is dependent upon the Delai Lama," that if British hostilities are continued it will irritate both the Lama and all his subjects against the Indian Government, and that he has "reprimanded the Deb for his past conduct and admonished him to desist from his evil practices in future, and to be submissive to you in all matters."

Occasions on which the Tibetan authorities have interfered with Bhutan politics in concert with the Chinese have been mentioned. It may fairly be presumed that the Lhasa Government would have exercised this amount of control over Bhutan irrespective of China if Chinese supremacy had not become established at Lhasa. The Bhutanese Government at first endeavoured to hinder Bogle's progress into Tibet, and they positively refused to allow Pemberton to proceed there or to forward a letter from him to Lhasa. In both cases they were probably acting under instructions from the Lhasa Government. Bhutan does not now pay any tribute to Tibet, and it does not appear when it ceased to do so. It is probable that when China sent its Ambans to Lhasa in 1720 the tribute was transferred to China. On the other hand, Bhutan did not come to the assistance of Tibet in the Nepal War of 1792. Turner even says that the Chinese general thought of invading Bhutan after defeating the Nepalese. Tibet did not support Bhutan in the war of 1864, or oppose the annexation of the Duars, though Rennie does mention that a few soldiers who were thought to be Tibetans were seen with the Bhutanese troops; nor did Bhutan give any help to the Tibetans at the time of the British expedition against them in Sikhim in 1888–89. The Tibetans asked for assistance, but it was refused by the Tongsa Penlop.

The ordinary government of the country goes on without interference from Tibet, and Lhasa does not exercise any voice in the election of the Deb Raja. In Bogle's time Tibetans were excluded from trading in Bhutan except for the exchange of rice and salt. Disputes between the Tibetans on the Chumbi side and the Bhutanese from time to time occurred. In 1892 a Bhutanese subject, servant of the Tongsa Penlop, was murdered at Phari; and later, as the Tibetans at first neglected to make compensation, the Bhutanese threatened to invade the Chumbi Valley. The matter was eventually settled amicably in 1894. Recent frontier information shows that the Paro Penlop has levied fines from the Tomos in the Chumbi Valley in a high-handed manner, and till quite lately levied taxes upon Tibetans entering Bhutan on that side. The connection between Tibet and Bhutan is certainly an ill-defined one, and may perhaps be best expressed by saying that though Bhutan is not a dependency of Tibet, it comes within the sphere of Tibet's political influence.

The first mention of any political connection between Bhutan and Nepal is given by Bogle, who says that the ambitious Deb Raja of Bhutan, Deb Jeedhur, about 1770, with the view of making himself independent of the priestly power, strengthened his connection with the Raja of Nepal, and obtained his support so far that Nepal refused to acknowledge the Deb who was set up in Deb Jeedhur's place after the rebellion against him. Not long after this, in 1788, Bhutan sent forces to aid Sikhim in repelling the Gurkha invasion from Nepal. They were themselves in turn threatened by a Gurkha invasion after the submission of Sikhim to Nepal, but this was prevented by the defeat of the Nepalese troops by China.

This Deb, otherwise known as Migyur Tempa, was a friend of Raja Rama Sahi of Nepal, and obtained several grants of land in that country. At one time Bhutan possessed eighteen monasteries there; these were lost in 1788, on account of the Bhutanese sending help to Sikhim against the Nepalese. They now possess only two.

Bhutan has remained unmolested by the Nepalese, and this Pemberton attributes, first to the fear of China, and secondly to the bold and determined policy of Hastings, which interposed the little State of Sikhim as a barrier to the eastern progress of the Nepalese. From this period down to Pemberton's time scarcely any intercourse, either of a political or commercial nature, took place between Nepal and Bhutan. At his interview with Rampini in 1874 the Deb Raja declared that relations with Nepal were friendly, and it appears that there has always been some intercourse of a friendly character between the two countries. In recent years a large number of Nepalese have migrated to Bhutan and colonised there, along the foot hills.

Deb Jeedhur, of whom previous mention has been made, invaded Sikhim somewhere about 1770, and held possession of the country for six or seven years. The minor Raja of Sikhim fled to Lhasa, and was educated there. He ultimately obtained assistance from Lhasa and returned to his country, which the Bhutanese then promptly evacuated. During the Bhutanese occupation of Sikhim a Sikhimese chief had been confined at Poonakha. The Sikhim Raja, on his return, procured his release, and the Bhutanese, on setting him free, bribed him to remain a friend to their Government. This man's son, born in captivity, became the most powerful man in Sikhim, and kept up a continued correspondence with the Bhutanese. Some years later, when a boundary dispute arose between Sikhim and Bhutan, he treacherously gave up to Bhutan a large tract of country belonging to Sikhim, including Dalingkote, Jongsa, and Sangbay.

Bhutan, as already mentioned, came to the aid of Sikhim against the Gurkhas in 1788. Beyond this there seems to have been no political intercourse between the two States, and Sikhim sustained its share of the outrages which led to the Bhutan War of 1864. The Sinchula Treaty provided for the surrender of Sikhimese subjects carried off into Bhutan, and for the reference to the British Government for arbitration of all disputes that might arise between Bhutan and Sikhim. It was also intended by the Government of India to separate the boundary of Bhutan from Sikhim by including the tract of country west of the Jaldhaka in the annexation, in order to prevent future inroads into Sikhim by the Bhutanese. This intention was not carried out, and Bhutan continues to border on Sikhim on its western frontier. There have, however, been no aggressions on Sikhim by the Bhutanese since the Sinchula Treaty.

In earlier times the relations between Cooch Behar and Bhutan were extremely intimate, and Bhutan exercised considerable control over Cooch Behar affairs. About 1695 the Bhutanese overran Cooch Behar and usurped the government, till Santa Narayan Nazir Deo, with the assistance of the Mahomedan Viceroy, expelled them after a long struggle, and placed Rup Narayan on the throne. The Bhutanese, however, continued their control over political affairs in Cooch Behar. In 1776, when the infant Raja was murdered at the instigation of Ramanand Gosain, they, "exercising, apparently, a usual authority," put Ramanand to death, and Dhaijendra was placed on the throne. This Raja offended the Bhutan Government by depriving Ram Narayan of his office of Dewan Deo, and afterwards putting him to death; and as a punishment for this affront to their authority the Bhutanese carried him off and kept him a prisoner in Bhutan, appointing his brother, Rajendra, to rule in his place. On the death of Rajendra, Darendra, son of Dhaijendra, was set up as Raja, without the consent of Bhutan, and the Bhutanese remonstrated in vain against the election of the son of a person whom they held as prisoner. They then invaded Cooch Behar, and carried off Darendra and his brother into Bhutan. The Government of India came to the aid of the dethroned Raja, and the Bhutanese were driven out of Cooch Behar, and the first treaty made with them by Warren Hastings in 1774. The tribute of five Tangan horses, which had been paid by Bhutan to the Cooch Behar Raja for the province of Falakata, was transferred to the Company. This ended any political relations between Bhutan and Cooch Behar. As in the case of Sikhim, Cooch Behar suffered for many years from the predatory incursions of the Bhutanese, which, with the incursions into British territory, were made the *casus belli* with Bhutan by the proclamation of 1864; and in the Sinchula Treaty the same conditions were imposed upon Bhutan in respect to Cooch Behar as in respect to Sikhim.

Since the Sinchula Treaty there has been very little intercourse between Cooch Behar and Bhutan. As in our case, Bhutanese come down in small numbers to trade, but Cooch Beharis are not allowed to enter Bhutan or to trade there.

CHAPTER XXIII

ARTS AND INDUSTRIES OF SIKHIM AND BHUTAN

Chinese and Indian influence. Metal-work in Sikhim. Method of casting. Sikhim knives. Aniline dyes. Weaving school in Lachung. Carpet factory in Gangtak. Apple orchards in Lachung and Chumbi. Cheese and butter making. Bhutan metal-work. A wonderful pan-box. Beaten copper and silver work. Bells. Swords and daggers. Weaving. Needlework pictures. Basket-work. Influence of the feudal system. Inferiority of Tibetan work. Wood-carving in Sikhim, Bhutan, and Nepal.

THE arts and industries of Sikhim and Bhutan have an intimate connection with those of China, as from their earliest days these countries were in touch with China and its civilisation, long before the people had any intercourse with India. With the spread of Buddhism a certain amount of Indian influence was brought in, but it is not very apparent. It has, however, also crept in through Nepal, and wherever the Newar craftsmen have penetrated Indian designs are to be met with; and this is particularly the case in the eastern districts, in Sikhim, and along the Brahmaputra River, as far as Shigatsi and Gyantse, and to some extent also in Lhasa.

In Bhutan the effect of Indian influence is very much less marked, and that of Burmah and Siam, which has entered by way of Assam, is undoubtedly stronger.

In Sikhim the arts are now almost entirely carried on by Nepalese craftsmen, who excel in gold, silver, and brass work. Articles made in these metals are generally beaten

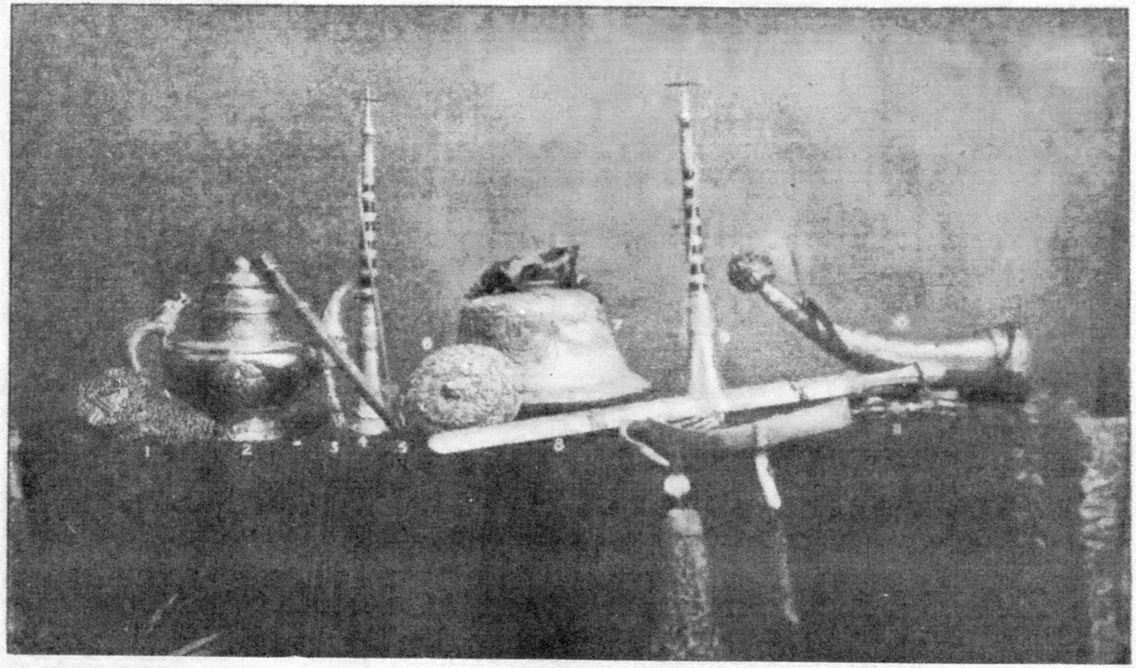

ART SPECIMENS—I

The descriptions of the articles to which reference numbers are attached will be found on page 325

into shape, backed with a lac got from the roots of the sal-tree, and the pattern hammered out with blunt tools. As the workman draws his own pattern as he works, his success depends on his ability, and he is able to express individuality in both design and execution ; and I have seen, and have in my possession, some very good specimens in gold, silver, brass, and copper work. They also cast exceedingly well in brass and bronze. The method they follow is to first model in wax the object they wish to make ; they next coat the model with successive layers of cow-dung, clay, and a little finely chopped straw ; this is allowed to dry very slowly, and when thoroughly dry the wax is melted out, leaving an excellent mould, into which the molten metal is poured. The detail obtained in this way is marvellous ; and as each model must be separately moulded it carries with it the great charm of all Oriental work—individuality.

Very good knives are manufactured in Sikhim. They used to be made from indigenous charcoal iron, but now that steel bars can be bought so cheaply the workmen—more is the pity—have entirely abandoned the old method of extracting the iron direct from the ore.

Cotton cloth is also manufactured for their own use, but the yarn is nearly all imported now, though a small portion is still made locally. The women weave at small looms set up in the different houses where the dyeing of the thread is also done ; and until lately vegetable dyes, to be found in abundance in the forests and jungles of Sikhim, were always used. Unfortunately, aniline dyes were introduced into the bazaars ; the people, finding they gave more brilliant results, were cheaper to buy and easier to use, took to them, and nearly spoilt the industry, until I was obliged to prohibit the sale of aniline dyes throughout Sikhim, and so force them to return to natural vegetable dyes, which produce such beautiful soft tints and last so much better. Carpets and woollen cloths are also made, and I started weaving schools in Lachung, and later on, under the control and supervision of the Maharani, who took great interest in the work, a carpet factory at Gangtak. The Lachung schools turned out most excellent tweeds, thanks to the assistance given by Miss Johanson, a Scandinavian missionary, under whose care the village girls came regularly to work, collected the requisite dyes from the jungle, and followed the patterns; but that supervision withdrawn, the girls would work or not as the spirit moved them, the yarn would be uneven in quality and carelessly woven, and the pattern neglected; but so long as Miss Johanson remains the output is excellent. It is the same with the carpet factory. When I was at headquarters and could occasionally look in, the carpets made were excellent—could not have been better—but if I were away for a few months on tour, and the Maharani otherwise occupied, the work immediately became careless and inferior—mistakes in the pattern, bad colouring, and inferior weaving. It shows the necessity in all these undertakings of having trained supervision at the head, if they are to be successful.

But the great difficulty was to place the output on a proper commercial footing. It is easy for a few years to sell cloth or carpets, but it does not answer in the long run unless the goods can be sold in the open market. Before I left an attempt to do this was being made, but whether it will be successful or not I cannot say.

I also tried to introduce fruit-cultivation, and planted English fruit-trees in both the Lachung and Chumbi Valleys. In the former the apple-trees have done extremely well, and a few years ago one tree alone bore 3200 apples, weighing 832 lb.; and I have gathered apples which weighed over a pound apiece. But here again the distance they had to be carried was a difficulty in placing them on the market. A very large trade is done in oranges during the winter months; but oranges are indigenous to the country, and the natives understand their cultivation; and, in addition, they grow in the hot valleys near the plains. The orchards

ART SPECIMENS—II

The descriptions of the articles to which reference numbers are attached will be found on page 325

in Chumbi had not come to maturity before the evacuation of the valley, and the trees will probably be cut down for firewood.

I also tried to introduce amongst the people butter and cheese making, which should have been profitable to the gwallahs, or cowkeepers; but without Europeans to place in charge it was difficult to achieve any success. The cheese-making was never taken up, although for a whole winter I had milk brought to the Residency, the cheese made in my own dairy, and then sold amongst my friends in India, to demonstrate to them the practicability of the scheme. They thought the trouble and care required in keeping the utensils clean was much too great for their easy-going ways. Hence that scheme was a failure, and, beyond what I myself attempted, was never tried. It seems extraordinary that the neighbouring town of Darjeeling, not to speak of Calcutta and other stations in the plains of Bengal, should get their supply of butter from Aligarh, in the United Provinces, while at Gangtak day after day throughout the year we made the finest possible butter, equal if not superior, to the best English butter, and that from the milk of cows not stall-fed or cared for in any but the ordinary way of the country, turned out each morning to graze on the hillsides. It shows what would be possible were the business taken up by any practical and energetic person.

Into Bhutan, Nepalese influence has hardly penetrated at all. The craftsmen are all Bhutanese, and the designs follow more closely the Chinese model. They excel in bronze castings and fine metal-work of all kinds. In practice they follow the same methods as in Sikhim, backing the metal on which they are employed with lac, and hammering out the patterns with blunt chisels after the manner of old alto-relievo work. One of the most exquisite specimens of workmanship in silver and silver-gilt I have ever seen was produced in Bhutan—a pan-box about 8 inches in diameter and 2½ inches deep, of a purely

Chinese dragon pattern, in relief quite a quarter of an inch or more deep.

I have also seen exceedingly fine specimens of copper and brass work, chiefly articles for the decoration of their altars, such as trumpets, candlesticks, rice-boxes, tables, &c., and they also cover many of their temple pillars with copper or silver beaten into most beautiful patterns, and the altar tables are examples of beaten work with bold designs.

The Bhutanese excel in casting bells, and I have seen some excellent specimens with very fine tones. The composition used for the best bells contains a good deal of silver, but they never make them of any great size, the largest I have seen being probably twenty-four inches in diameter and of about an equal height.

In iron-work they are also good artificers, and many of their sword-blades are of excellent manufacture and finish, and are still made from the charcoal iron. The polish they put on them is wonderful, and the blades almost look as though they had been silvered.

Their swords are very handsome weapons, with finely finished blades, elaborately wrought silver handles inlaid with turquoise and coral, and silver scabbards with gold-washed patterns, attached to handsome leather belts with brightly coloured silk cords and tassels. Their daggers are also very fine, many of them with triangular blades and fluted sides, with sheaths of exquisite open silver and gold work set with turquoise.

Every house of any importance has large workrooms attached in which weaving is carried on, and the stuffs produced, consisting of silks for the chiefs' dress, woollen and cotton goods, are excellent; and a good deal of embroidery is also done.

The monasteries possess an art which, as far as I know, is peculiar to Bhutan. They make most beautiful needlework pictures of the saints on hanging banners. Innumerable pieces of coloured silks and brocades are applied

ART SPECIMENS—III

The descriptions of the articles to which reference numbers are attached will be found on *page 326*

in a most artistic manner with elaborate stitches of all kinds. Many of them are veritable works of art.

Another industry in which the Bhutanese excel is basket-work and fine matting made from split cane. The baskets are beautifully woven of very finely split cane, and some of the lengths are coloured to form a pattern. They are made in two circular pieces, rounded top and bottom, and the two pieces fit so closely and well that they can be used to carry water. They are from six to fifteen inches in diameter, and the Bhutanese use them principally to carry cooked rice and food. They also make much larger and stronger baskets, very much in the shape of a mule-pannier, and these are used in a similar way for pack-animals.

The mats are also very finely woven of the same material, with a certain amount of the split cane dyed to form patterns. They are delightfully fine and soft, so flexible that they can be rolled up into quite a small space, and very durable, and can be got in almost any size up to about sixteen feet square, and even larger if they are required.

Possibly the excellence of the work produced in Bhutan owes much to the feudal system which still prevails there. Each Penlop and Jongpen has his own workmen amongst his retainers, men who are not paid by the piece, and are not obliged either to work up to time or to work if the spirit is not in them, and consequently they put their souls into what they do, with the result that some pieces of splendid individuality and excellent finish are still made. No two pieces are ever quite alike, and each workman leaves his impress on his work.

The same ought to apply to Tibet, but I have seen no work from Tibet which can compare in any way with that from Bhutan. Possibly the environments of Tibet are not conducive to such excellence ; the people are more servile and less independent, a condition always detrimental to good work of any kind. Metal-work in Tibet is of the same description as that in Sikhim and Bhutan, and is all made in the same way, but any specimens I have seen are inferior in workmanship. From Nepal, on the other hand, I have had some excellent work, with marked signs of individuality, especially in their brass castings. Some of the "singhis," or brass demon dogs, are very characteristic.

I have omitted to mention wood-carving, in which Nepal, Sikhim, and Bhutan all excel. In the former especially the wood-carving is of a very high order, and the houses in Khatmandu, and especially in the older city of Pathan, are exquisitely ornamented with carved doors, windows, balconies, eaves; and some of them even have carvings on the ridges of the tiled roofs.

In Sikhim and Bhutan, in nearly every monastery and Jong, and also in the better houses, many good carvings are to be found, and the work is bold and effective.

I am giving some photographs showing a few specimens of the various arts and crafts, but they hardly do justice to the best workmanship. Unfortunately, the greater part of my collection is still packed away, and I am unable to illustrate all I could wish. But I think I have said enough to show that the hill people on this frontier possess an artistic temperament, and can turn out most excellent work which compares favourably with that of other Oriental craftsmen.

ART SPECIMENS—IV

The descriptions of the articles to which reference numbers are attached will be found on page 326

APPENDIX I

THE LAWS OF BHUTAN

A Brief Outline of the Laws and Rules laid down for the Government of Bhutan

The form of government is twofold, viz., spiritual and temporal.

1. The spiritual laws are said to resemble a silken knot—*i.e.*, easy and light at first, but gradually becoming tighter and tighter.

2. The temporal or monarchical laws resemble a golden yoke—*i.e.*, growing heavier and heavier by degrees.

This twofold law was composed by a spirit of perfect disinterestedness.

This twofold system of government established in Bhutan rendered the country happy and prosperous, taking for example the system of the great Saint-King of Tibet, whose very first prohibition was against the taking of life, a crime punished by the realisation of blood-money in case of homicide, and damages or fine in case of attempted homicide. A penalty of hundredfold repayment was realisable in cases of robbery or theft of church or monastic property, eightyfold repayment in cases of stealing the king's property, eightfold repayment in cases of theft amongst subjects. Adultery was punishable by fines. Falsehood was punishable by the offender being put to oath in a temple, and the invocation of tutelar deities and gods. Over and above the prevention of the ten impious acts, all were required to regard parents with filial respect and affection, and elders with reverence, to receive with gratitude any kind action done by others to themselves, and, lastly, to avoid dishonesty and the use of false measures, which constitute the sixteen acts of social piety.

Although Bhutan had been once effectually brought under the beneficent influence of strict law and justice, it subsequently, on account of general corruption and laxity on the part of those in authority, became slack in all branches.

If this should be allowed to continue, there would be no discrimination between right and wrongdoing, no justice, and without justice human beings cannot have happiness and peace. If there were no peace or happiness for human beings, the Dukpa Hierarchy would have failed in its errand upon this earth, and it would be useless for it to exist longer. Therefore, bearing the interest of the Hierarchy at heart, every one is exhorted to leave all partiality aside and to act up to a true sense of justice, emulating the great Saint-King Srongtsan Gompo of Tibet.

For it is said that Universal Happiness depends upon the existence of the Jina's Hierarchy, and that, in its turn, depends upon the character of individual Hierarchs. But it is unfortunately the general custom now for those who are in authority to give way to their own selfish and immeasurable greed of gain, to satisfy which they resort to extortion by oppressive means—*e.g.*, binding, beating, and imprisoning—thus rendering the subjects as miserable as tantalised ghosts in this very lifetime. And the elders of the village—*i.e.*, mandals and pipons—in their turn act the part of spies and inform those above them as to who amongst the raiyats have some articles of value or riches. Thus they render the clear fountain of justice muddy and foul. Therefore it is extremely necessary that he who enjoys the privilege of being the Dharma Raja should use the utmost circumspection in finding out the real truth and facts, when it happens that cases are brought before him for trial, so that the innocent be not punished for nothing and the wrongdoer escape unpunished. To enforce temporal laws by punishing sinful and impious acts in perfect accordance with moral and religious laws is the essence of the

Commandments of the Jinas.

A Brief Outline of the Proper Course of Action for Deb Rajas

Buddha says in the Sutras, "A king, if he is fond of Dharma [Righteousness], finds the path to happiness both in this and in the future lives. The subjects will act as the ruler acts, and therefore should the ruler strive to learn Righteousness."

They should encourage religious institutions and the inculcation of knowledge, and religious sentiment therein.

They should see that the priests are properly trained in the ten pious acts; that they gain the necessary accomplishments in (*a*) dancing, (*b*) drawing, or making mandalas, and (*c*) psalm-singing; besides acquiring knowledge in the twofold method of meditation. The above should be for those who expect to spend their lives as priests. Those who are to acquire the other branches of learning, such as rhetoric, poetry, and dialectics, also must be encouraged, and their progress enforced by periodical examinations in each of these several branches.

An annual circular perwana should be issued to those in charge of the State monasteries, requiring that the monastic properties of value, whether they be ornaments for the altar, treasures, coins, plates, utensils, &c., should not be disposed of or misused in any way. To those also amongst the priesthood who are engaged in handicrafts (*e.g.*, painting, sewing, embroidery, carving, modelling, &c.), and those also who are engaged in menial service, should be taught thoroughly writing and rituals, and they should be thoroughly imbued with the ten pious sentiments. In short, the Deb should consider it a daily duty to inquire into the state of the raiyats' condition, whether they are happy or unhappy, contented or discontented, and strain his utmost power to render them happy.

They should prohibit indiscriminate life-taking, by forbidding cruel sport on the hills and fishing in the rivers. This effectually strikes at the cause of several ills in the future.

The collection of taxes, raising of labour contributions, and trial of cases constitute the administrative duties, on the proper discharge of which depends the happiness of a nation.

A constant check and inquiry as to whether, out of those who are sent on these duties, there are any who exempt certain persons, some from partiality, and tax others heavily in consequence of grudges or prejudice, should be exercised and kept up.

The officers posted on the frontiers should be constantly reminded of the fact that the peace of the central nation depends upon the conduct of the borderers. The borderers, if they commit lawless raids into others' territories in their vicinity, will give occasion for reprisals and involve the nation in the horrors of foreign warfare in an unjust cause. Therefore they should be exhorted to live peaceably.

To be brief, these are the three ends to be secured:

1. The contentment of the raiyats.
2. The proper influence of and respect for officials or authorities.
3. The support of the Sangha, or the body of the Trinity.

APPENDIX I

Therefore it is absolutely necessary that the Deb Raja, as the temporal ruler of the people, should be well versed in the method of securing these ends.

The most effectual and shortest method of securing the first end, the raiyats' happiness, is by administering strict justice. If a ruler would devote himself to administering justice impartially, he would make all his subjects happy in a single day. For it was by this means that the ancient dynasty of Tibetan kings secured happiness for their subjects and popularity for the rulers themselves, and also by which the Dharma Raja of Bhutan (Shabdung Rimpochi) succeeded in subduing the stiff-necked and lawless people of Bhutan, and rendering his reign so very glorious and popular. The main end of establishing law and justice is to give peace and security to both the ruler and his subjects, and in particular to promulgate the Dharma and to perpetuate the Hierarchy of the Buddhist Sangha, which embodies and represents the three chief principles of the Buddhist Trinity.

Of late a dangerous laxity has crept into all branches of justice.

Priests who break their vow of celibacy, and criminals who are guilty of homicide, robbery, and otherwise disturbing public peace, go unpunished. This not only sets a bad example for the future, but endangers present tranquillity, and encourages crime and breach of faith. Thus the country becomes filled with vow-breakers and knaves, and public peace is destroyed. It is said, "The violation of spiritual laws makes the Guardian Deities retreat to the Abode of Passivity, and allows the foul breath of the mischievous Fiends to pervade everywhere. The breach of Social Laws weakens the power of the Gods, and the Demons of Darkness laugh with joy." It is absolutely necessary to compel the priests who have violated their oaths to change their modes of dress and give up other priestly habits.

Moreover, at present the use of a most filthy and noxious herb, called tobacco, is spreading amongst the sepoys and raiyats, who use it incessantly. This is sure to steep the sacred images and books in pollution and filth. It has been prophesied by Ugyen Padma Jungna that it will cause wars and bring epidemics. So unless every one of the provincial Governors, Kazis, Subahs, and Headmen strives to stop the use of this poisonous and evil stuff by fining those who deal in it, and those who use it, they will be sure to feel heavily the consequences of such neglect themselves.

APPENDIX I

If those who are rulers, having the opportunity to render their subjects happy, neglect their duties, then where is the difference between them and the Prince of the Devils ? In worldly matters it is not always mild means which conquer and subdue rude and evil persons, but sometimes stern measures have to be adopted. So when there are law-breakers or evildoers the ruler's duty is to punish them sternly, putting aside all consideration of pity and sympathy. This is the path by which a king on his throne obtains salvation.

Although the rulers are responsible for the general prosperity of a nation, yet it is the local authorities on whom lie the responsibilities of a province or district. The deputies (who are sent to inquire into a case), and the headman who reports, are the chief persons on whom the real burden of a fair trial lies. The establishment of a second-grade Kuchap, as well as that of a Lama and Hyerpa combined, should consist of two orderlies or sepoys and one syce, and ordinary Kuchaps should have only one orderly and one syce. Officers' tours entail too much expense and trouble on the raiyats, so unless it be for transfers or new appointments, officers' tours should be restricted as much as possible, and they should not be allowed to travel about on any trivial pretence. The husking of paddy should not be given in dribbling quantities, but in a large quantity at one time; nor should rice be realised over the actual out-turn of the husking. The raiyats should not be dispossessed of any gold, turquoise, vessels, cattle, or ponies they may possess on frivolous pretences of extortionate rates of interest on trading capital lent by the headmen, nor should any headmen request subscriptions by means of giving charm threads or cheap clothes. All barter or trading should be carried on at fair prevailing rates, and not at extortionate and preferential ones. Forced gifts of salt or butter should not be made. No wearing wool should be given, no sheep's load should be realised. All Jongpens and Head Lamas of monasteries shall not try to realise any gifts by going round visiting raiyats.

The sale and purchase of slaves (plainsmen) must not be permitted. Any one persisting in it should be reported to the Durbar authorities. State officers will not be entitled to any coolies or rations from the State, if they are going to visit a hot spring or mineral-water spring for their own health, but they shall provide themselves with the necessary provisions and coolies on such occasions. When officers are out on their own account they shall not present themselves at the Jongs, and if they do the Jongs shall not provide them with the usual rations to which they would otherwise be entitled.

The officers in charge of the several Jongs should report to the Durbar what amount of free labour has been enforced, how many coolies supplied, or how many coolie-loads have been conveyed, and for whom, or by whose order, on what date, and so on. Should any officer at the different stages permit any load to be conveyed free of cost to the owner without reporting, he shall be liable to a heavy fine.

A Kuchap can keep one pony, and may perhaps be entrusted with the feed of a pony from the Superior Jongpen. Over and above these he may not maintain any ponies at the cost of the State. Should he do so he will forfeit the same to the Jong. He may, however, by paying a licence fee of over one hundred tankas to his Jong, be allowed to maintain one more pony. But on no account is he to be allowed to maintain more than three ponies at the cost of the State. Should he desire to give a pony in the place of the annual revenue, he may not send any raiyat to purchase it from any market. In case of complaints made to him, he may not receive anything over a measure of pachwai murwa, not so much as a square bit of silk in kind, nor a tanka in cash. A Kuchap should report all cases, be they light or important, to the Jong, and by no means decide any himself. At harvest-time a Kuchap should not take the opportunity of visiting his field border, or turn it to a means of going on a rambling visit to his raiyats. Nor should a Kuchap make slight cattle trespasses upon the border of his fields the pretence for realising heavy damages from his raiyats. The Kuchaps or other responsible officers must not be wine-bibbers, fornicators, nor adulterers. Should they be guilty of any of the above faults, they render themselves enemies to public peace, and thereby liable to dismissal from their office in disgrace.

The collection of the taxes in kind, such as meat and butter, must be considered and settled at the Kuchang's own place, with the assistance of the elders, and karbaris or mandals under him, after which he will submit the proposed demand rent-roll to the Jongpen, his immediate and chief superior, for sanction and order. Only upon obtaining such sanction can he realise the rents in kind.

Should any guests have to be provided for, it will not do for him to realise the provisions or their equivalent from the raiyats, but he should quarter them on the houses in turn. The guests should on no account expect luxuries, but bare necessaries.

The Kuchap must not grant any remission of rents of either kind, on consideration of any private gift to himself.

The Kuchap may not accept the first portion of any ceremonial feast, be it for the dead or the living. He should not accept or demand any present for marriages or separations.

When sending out for collections, he should send a pipon, who will represent an orderly, a mandal, and a karbari in one. This man shall not realise anything on his own account. He shall not accept any present from cattle-keepers. Any mandal, or lamas or shalugos who have been appointed to any posts, requiring to go to the seat of the Durbar, must not take any raiyats to accompany them, nor should they raise any tax on the pretence of nazars for the Durbar. Any officers, village headmen, who have obtained permission to retire from service on account of old age, infirmities, &c., must not linger above three days in the Jong. Any foreigners or strangers arriving in their jurisdiction must be reported and presented to their superior at the Jong. They must not harbour or receive any such. Anybody found harbouring robbers or thieves must be punished as heavily as the criminals themselves.

Any slaves attempting to escape in an unhappy mood must be detained, and should any one after having harboured one fail to detain him the same shall make good the slave. But, on the other hand, if any one succeed in handing back to the owner the escaped slave the same must be compensated, due consideration being taken regarding the distance, the time, the cost and expenses incurred in the performance of the enterprise.

Two different raiyats cannot combine into one. A holding may be enjoyed both by a son or, if there is no son, by a daughter. A raiyat who is aged, and has neither daughter nor son, may be asked only to render such labour and service for revenue as he is able to perform alone as long as he lives ; upon his or her decease the same holding shall pass to the nearest kith or kin, who will thenceforth be expected to render both labour and cash and kind revenues. No marriages or permanent connections should be allowed where the parents do not approve. And whereas, where there are two or three holdings and houses which used to pay taxes separately now combined in one, with a view of lightening the labour contribution, it must be ruled that this be not permitted or tolerated, as it is a bad precedent. If there be any, either a male or a female, heir to the property, the same should be compelled to make good the State revenue. If there are no heirs in the line, then it should be made over to the nearest kin, or to such person whom the owner wills as his assignee, who will thenceforth make good the State revenue. Those who own properties in land and houses, and yet live untaxed in towns, should be made to render proportionate labour contribution and rents in cash and kind with the value and area of their properties.

Whereas the slaughter of many animals on account of funeral ceremonies is bad, both on account of the deceased as well as the living, henceforth it is expedient to offer simple gifts on these occasions, which shall be regulated as follows :

1. For the Durbar, in lieu of a head and limb the value of half a tanka.

2. For the Lama, the price of a piece of cotton cloth.

But if the party be poor and cannot afford the gifts, but simply some offerings for the deceased, then he shall be liable to the above costs only in case of Durbar and Lama, and for the assistant priests he can give rice in lieu of meat, about four manas. But if one animal has to be slaughtered, on no account shall he exceed one life, out of which he must defray the necessary meat expenses.

A monastery Head Lama shall perform the cremation within one day in summer and two in winter ; he must not exceed this time, on his own responsibility. The number of priests to attend a funeral, and the fees to be received by them, are the same as at the capital or Durbar. But if the Head Lama is delayed in coming or prevented from coming, the layman must have the obsequies partially performed at home, and must take such stores with him with which he can have the same performed at a monastery. No freehold grants to lamas for their support shall be sold. The laymen shall not stop supporting the lamas. Should any wealthy or propertied lama die, his chief supporting layman or disciple shall utilise his property in meritorious charity. When any State-supported and retired lamas die, their effects, if they are books, images, or altar appurtenance, shall be offered to the State or Deb as obsequies offerings, and the rest shall be devoted to funeral ceremonies to the best account. When it becomes necessary to build a cell to serve as a retreat for any lama of the monastery, it shall be within the compound or in the vicinity of a monastery or other religious institution, and not in the vicinity of a village or any hill spur. Should any child be born to a couple, as the result of a connection within monastery precincts, the same couple shall be considered to have reverted to the world, and their life must be passed amongst the villages, and they shall accordingly be made to fill up any vacancy amongst the raiyats, and shall be liable to the same taxes and labour contributions as any other raiyat.

Should any member or Tape of the monastery loiter more than fifteen days amongst the villages, otherwise than on some special business of the Head Lamas, or their own, and on the usual charity begging purpose, the same shall be liable to be forced to render the usual labour contribution by the village headmen. The Head Lamas of the several monasteries, too, must, except on the occasions of the annual congregation for observing the Buddhist holidays, always pass their time in retreats. They shall use their utmost efforts to effectually put an end to any sham or charlatanism, necromancy, quackery, and false witchcraft. The licensed as well as private Manewas (those who go about singing "Om mani padmi hum") shall only enjoy such offerings as are made voluntarily; there shall be no tax for them. No one shall harbour any mischievous person who has been banished from a Jong for some roguery.

A thief or robber, killed while in the commission of theft or robbery, dies without any hope of redress. The man who kills a thief in the above manner is not liable to any punishment. But otherwise one who takes out his sword (for threatening or for striking) is liable to sword fine.

One committing homicide must be bound to the corpse of the deceased whom he has killed. If he escapes after committing homicide, he may be killed wherever and whenever he is caught. The offspring of a homicide shall be banished from their home.

Any one killing notorious highway robbers, any wild beasts which are working much havoc in a country, or who has performed heroic service amongst enemies during war should be encouraged by gifts of robes or clothes according to merit.

The headmen should inspect the products of their country industries, and see that they are honest and solid in make and texture.

The merchants who have the responsibility of the import trade at the different marts also must satisfy themselves that they get good things, and all the traders must obey the State merchant in these particulars. Any one acting in defiance of these rules, and any one found forging Government letters, or altering their meaning, or attempting detention or miscarriage of such orders issued from the seat of the Government, shall be dealt with severely, inasmuch as they shall be deprived of their sight or of life by decapitation.

From the Dharma Raja at the head of all the ruling officers, including Lamas, Jongpens, Penlops, &c., down to the Mandals and responsible village headmen, if they do not act in accordance with the above, if they do not regard public prosperity nor check their subordinates, if they suffer Karmic laws to be subverted, and tolerate the spread of evil without making an effort to remedy it, then how will the Spiritual Guardians help them! Thus, in conformity with the text "Those who offer insults to those who live in Righteousness are worthy of being exterminated," they shall surely be offered up as fitting sacrifice on the altar of the Great and Terrible Mahakal.

But, on the other hand, if all observe the above rules, which they must understand are for their general as well as individual good, they will put their faith in the threefold Rare One (Tri Ratua) as their God and witness, and regard the Chagdzöd (Deb Raja) as the human liege lord who has been entrusted with the weal of the nation and the prosperity of the Hierarchy in general, and serve him unto death most loyally and energetically, just as the great Righteous Prime Minister Garwa did formerly.

This completes the brief code of rules and regulations of the great Dharma Raja, of which this is the chapter regarding the officials and provincial governors, and their subordinate Kazis and Subahs.

APPENDIX II

THE LAWS OF SIKHIM AND MARRIAGE CUSTOMS

SIKHIM LAWS

A Brief Translation of the Sikhim Laws, taken from a Tibetan Manuscript given to me by the late Khangsa Dewan

HISTORY

The Sikhim laws are founded on those spoken by Raja Melongdong, who lived in India before the time of Buddha (914 B.C.). This Raja is mentioned in the Ka-gyur, in the thirty-first chapter.

They were again written by Kun-ga-gyal-tsan of Sa-kya-pa, who was born in 1182. He was king of thirteen provinces in Tibet, and has called the laws Tim-yik-shal-che-chu-sum, or Chu-dug, there being two sets, one containing thirteen laws and the other sixteen. These are practically the same. The laws were again written by De-si-sangye Gya-tsho, who was born in 1653 and was a Viceroy of Tibet. They were called by him Tang-shel-me-long-nyer-chik-pa.

The first set of laws deal with offences in general; the second set forth the duties of kings and Government servants, and are merely an amplification of some of the laws contained in the former.

SUMMARY OF THE SIXTEEN LAWS

No. 1. General Rules to be followed in Time of War

(*a*) It is written in the Ka-gyur that before going to war the strength of the enemy should be carefully ascertained, and whether any profit will be derived or not. It should also be seen if the dispute cannot be settled by diplomacy before going to war. Care should also be taken that by going to war no loss be sustained by your Government. Whatever the cause of dispute, letters and messengers between the contending parties should on no account be stopped, and messengers should be properly treated. Any one coming with overtures of peace should be well received.

(*b*) Should two or more enemies combine against you, no means should be left untried to separate them, and if possible to bring one over to your side, but false oaths should not be resorted to, nor the using of God's name.

(*c*) The lie of the ground should be well examined to see how the roads run, and whether your position is strong.

(*d*) If it is necessary to go to war, other methods having failed, you should all combine, and, being of one mind, should attack. See that there are no sick, lazy, or timid in the ranks, but only those who fear not death. See that your own soldiers obey the law, and all should obey the orders of the general. Experienced men only should be sent, and not those who look after their own interests.

The army should be divided into three divisions, under the command of different officers. The general and his staff should be trusted men who can guide the army; they should do their work thoroughly. Your horses, tents, and arms should be kept in good order. A doctor, a diviner, an astrologer, and a lama should be appointed.

The tents should be properly arranged the first day, and this arrangement adhered to, so as to prevent confusion. On moving, the fires should first be put out, the wounded should be cared for, and in crossing rivers order should be kept, and those behind should not push forward. Things found should be returned without asking for a reward, and should not be concealed or kept. Thieves are not to be flogged, but only to have their hands tied behind them, but they may be fined. Should one man kill another by mistake, he must pay the funeral expenses. Should several combine and kill another, they must pay twice the fine laid down by law. For any disputed loot lots must be drawn by the contending parties.

The general should appoint sentries, who must look to the water-supply and see they do not easily become alarmed. They should allow no armed stranger to enter the camp, and should be careful not to kill any messenger. If a sentry kills a messenger coming with terms of peace, he shall be sent to his home in disgrace on some old, useless horse with broken harness.

APPENDIX II

No. 2. For those who are being defeated and cannot fight

When a fort is surrounded those in the fort should remain quiet and should show no fear. They should not fire off their arms uselessly, with no hope of hitting the enemy. The well within the fort should be most carefully guarded. Those within the fort should not be allowed to communicate with the enemy for fear of treachery. They must not be lazy. Until peace is declared the messenger should receive no reward.

Should you be defeated, you must give up your arms, and those who give them up must not be killed. Should any one kill a man who has given up his arms he must be derided and scoffed at as a coward.

If during a conflict you capture a general or officer of rank, you should bind his hands in front with a silk scarf; he should be allowed to ride his own horse or another good horse, and should be treated well, so that in the event of your ever falling into his hands he may treat you well also. Any other prisoners should have their hands tied behind them, and they should be made to walk. Officers should be placed on old, worn-out horses, with broken harness and rope stirrups. Should an army be defeated and obliged to fly, they should not be reprimanded, but they should not be rewarded or receive any presents, even though the leader be a great man. The prisoners should receive what is necessary for subsistence, and also expenses for religious ceremonies, and men of rank should be treated well and with consideration.

A man can only make a treaty for himself and his own descendants.

No. 3. For Officers and Government Servants

These officers should abandon their own work and apply themselves entirely to Government work; they should obey the orders of the Viceroy, and head of the Church, should not change the Shari (hat sects) and Tub-tha (religious sects).

In the fifth month they should kill no animals, and the Raja's store should be well kept, so that there be no deficiency. They should repair the images, temples, and books, and all passes and roads. Also on the 10th of this month the "dadok"* ceremony must be performed.

If a man be sent on private business, the name of Government should not be used. Debts may be recovered through officers, who should patiently hear the case, and not give arbitrary orders. They

* This puja is performed in order to remove our enemies.

should give just judgments, and not favour those who can reward them. They should inquire diligently into all cases, and leave no case undecided, so that all men can say their work has been well done.

No. 4. Law of Evidence

You should listen carefully to what is said by both parties. Equals by birth should be heard at the same time and place. Those that are not equals should be heard separately. Should any one not obey your decision, he can be fined.

If evidence be false both parties are fined, according to which has given the most false evidence.

If after a decision has been given the parties wish to compound between themselves, one-half of the fine only is imposed.

No. 5. Grave Offences.

There are five sins: (1) The murder of a mother; (2) the murder of holy men; (3) the murder of a father; (4) making mischief amongst lamas; and (5) causing hurt to good men. There are also the sins of taking things from Rajas and lamas for our own use; causing a good man to fall through no fault of his own; administering poison; killing any one for gain; causing strife in a peaceful country; and making mischief.

For the above offences punishments are inflicted, such as putting the eyes out, cutting the throat, having the tongue cut out, having the hands cut off, being thrown from cliffs, and being thrown into deep water.

No. 6. Fines inflicted for Offences in order to make People remember

Certain crimes may be punished by money fines, varying in accordance with the gravity of the offence.

When a number of men have committed dacoity, they may be fined from 25 to 80 gold srang.* For small offences smaller fines are imposed, and can be paid either in money or in kind, the amount to be settled by the officer trying the case.

No. 7. Law of Imprisonment

Any one rioting, using arms, and disputing near the court can be imprisoned. Thieves, and those who destroy property, and

* 1 srang = 1 oz.

those who do not obey the village headman, those who give bad advice, those who abuse their betters, can be bound and put in the stocks and fined according to the law, and only released if some one in authority makes himself responsible for the fine and petitions for their release.

No. 8. In the Case of Offenders who refuse to appear an Orderly must be sent expressly to inquire into the Case

A messenger who is sent off at a moment's notice should receive three patties* of barley per diem for food and a small sum in money, according to the importance of the case in which he is employed, but the messenger's servants should not be fed. The messenger is allowed one-fourth of the fine for his expenses.

Should an agent not settle a case properly, he must return to the villagers what he took, otherwise the villagers will have much trouble given them.

The agent should report having received the fine, on penalty of forfeiting one-fourth what he has taken. When a fine is imposed, it should be at once collected, no excuse being taken. If an agent is sent to collect rent he should be fed twice by the headman.

Of stolen property recovered by an agent the Government receives one-tenth value.

No. 9. Murder

For killing a man the fine is heavy—even up to many thousands of gold pieces. In the Tsalpa law-book it is written that if a child, a madman, or animal kills any one no fine is taken, but that money must be given by the relations of the first two for funeral expenses, and one-fourth of that amount must be given by the owner of the animal towards these expenses.

Should one man kill another and plead for mercy, he must, besides the fine, give compensation and food to the relatives of the deceased.

Should a man kill his equal and the relatives come to demand compensation, he must give them 18 oz. of gold in order to pacify them. The price of blood should never be too much reduced, or a man may say, " If this is all I have to give, I will kill another."

An arbitrator must take the seal of each party, saying they will abide by his decision, and they must each deposit 3 oz. of gold as security.

* 17 patties = 1 maund, or 82 lb.

APPENDIX II

Fines can be paid in cash, animals, and articles of different kinds.

The price for killing a gentleman who has 300 servants, or a superintendent of a district, or a lama professor, is 300 to 400 gold srang. For full lamas, Government officers, and gentlemen with 100 servants the fine is 200 oz. of gold.

For killing gentlemen who possess a horse and five or six servants, or working lamas, the fine is 145 to 150 oz. of gold.

For killing men with no rank, old lamas, or personal servants the fine is 80 oz. of gold.

For killing a man who has done good work for Government the fine is 50 to 70 oz. of gold.

For killing common people and for villagers the price is 30 to 40 oz. of gold.

For killing unmarried men, servants, and butchers the price is 30 gold srang; and for killing blacksmiths and beggars, 10 to 20 oz. of gold.

These prices can also be paid in grain. The prices for funeral expenses must be paid within forty-nine days.

On the fines being paid, a letter must be written, and a copy given to each party, saying that everything has been settled. If a case is reopened a fine must be paid by him who opens the case. The murderer must write to the effect he will not commit such a crime again. Part of the fines can be given towards the funeral expenses of the deceased.

No. 10. Bloodshed

In the old law it is written that for any drop of blood shed the price varies from one to one-quarter zho.* A man may even be beheaded for wounding a superior. For wounding his own servant a man is not fined, but he must tend the wounded man. Should two men fight and one wound the other, he who first drew his knife is fined, and he who is wounded must be tended by the other till his wounds be well. The fines are payable in money or kind. Should one man wound another without any fight, he is fined according to the law of murder.

If in a fight a limb or an eye is injured the compensation to be given is fixed by Government.

* The word "zho" means a drachm, or is a coin two-thirds of a rupee.

APPENDIX II

No. II. For those who are False and Avaricious the following Oaths are required

If it is thought a man is not telling the truth an oath should be administered. At the time of taking the oath powerful gods should be invoked, and those who are to administer the oath must be present. It is written in ancient law that the bird of Paradise should not be killed, the poisonous snake should not be thrown down, the raven should not be stoned, and the small turquoise should not be defiled. Thus pure lamas and monks should not be sworn.

Magicians, shameless persons, women, fools, the dumb, and children should not be sworn.

Men should be employed who know both parties and are intelligent and truthful. Those willing to take an oath should be of equal rank. When all are present the case should first be settled, if possible, by arbitration. If this fails the ordeal either by hot stone or boiling oil is resorted to.

Ordeal by Oil.—The oil must be supplied by Government, and must be pure. It is boiled in a pan at least three inches deep. In the oil a black stone and a white stone are placed, of equal size and weight. He who has to take the oath must first wash his hands in water, in milk, and in widow's urine. His hand is then bound in a cloth and sealed. This is done a day or two before the ordeal, in order to give him a chance of confessing. The vessel with the boiling oil is then placed so that the stones cannot be seen, and he has to take one out. If he takes out the white one without any burn he wins his case. He who gets the black stone is sure to be burnt, and loses his case. Should he who gets the white stone be slightly burnt, it means he has partially spoken the truth, and wins half his case.

Ordeal by Hot Stone.—The stone is made hot by the blacksmith, taken out of the fire with tongs, and placed on a brass dish. The man's hands are washed as before, examined to see what marks there are produced by labour, and the hot stone placed in the palm. With the stone he must walk four to seven paces. His hand is then bound up, and left for three to seven days. On examination, if there are no marks, or if there is a long mark called rdo-lam, he wins his case. He also wins his case if the stone bursts three times in being heated. It depends on the number of marks how much of his case he wins.

A cloth and a rug have to be paid as expenses, and the brass vessels go to the blacksmith. In order to test the oil for boiling, a grain of barley is thrown in; if it flies into the air the oil is ready.

Whilst placing his hand in the oil or holding the hot stone a statement in writing of the case is placed on the person's head.

The ordeal by oil may be gone through without using the stone.

Mud and water can be used in place of oil. Hot iron used to be employed in place of the stone, but is now discontinued.

No. 12. Theft

For taking a Jongpen's or other great man's property 10,000 times their value has to be given in return. For taking a lama's property eighty times their value has to be given, a neighbour's property nine times, and a villager's seven times; for taking a stranger's property four times.

Beggars who steal from hunger have only to give back what they took.

Should one man accuse another falsely of stealing, he must give him as compensation what he accused him of stealing.

Should a man find anything on the road, and without telling take it for himself, he must be fined double its value; but should he tell, he receives one-third the value. Should any one recover stolen property, but not be able to catch the thief, he receives half the property recovered.

Should any one find a horse, any cattle, yaks, or sheep, and keep them for a year without discovering the owner, he receives one-fourth the value, provided he has not in the meantime used the animals for his own benefit.

Should any one wound a thief he is not fined.

If a thief whilst running away be killed by an arrow or stone, a small fine only is taken.

Should any one, having caught a thief, kill him, he is fined according to the law of murder. The reward for catching a thief is from 1 to 5 oz. of gold, according to the amount of the property stolen.

No. 13. Disputes between near Relatives, between Man and Wife, and between Neighbours who have Things in Common

If a husband wishes to be separated from his wife, he must pay her from 18 zho, the amount varying in accordance with the length of time they have been married.

If the wife wishes to leave her husband, she must pay him 12 zho and one suit of clothes. The wife, on separation, also receives the clothes given to her at her marriage, a list of which is always taken, or its equivalent in money.

Should there be children, the father takes the boys and the mother the girls, the father paying from 5 to 15 zho for each son, called the price of milk. If the woman has committed no fault she receives her ornaments.

Should a family wish to separate, a list of the whole property should be taken and it should be divided according to circumstances. The father and mother are asked with whom they would like to live, and if there is any dispute lots are drawn. The married children's property is first separated from the rest, and if any children are going to school their expenses must be taken from the whole before decision.

No. 14. Adultery or taking another's Wife

The old law runs that if any one takes a Raja's or lama's wife he may be banished or have his hands cut off. For violating a woman of different position 3 oz. of gold have to be paid to the woman's relations, and 4 gold srang to Government, besides many things in kind.

For violation of a woman of the same position 2 or 3 gold srang and several kinds of articles have to be paid.

If the woman goes of her own accord to the man he has only to pay 1 gold srang and three kinds of articles.

Should one man's wife entice another married man to go with her, she has to pay seven things in kind.

Should a man and a woman cohabit on a journey there is no fine.

No. 15. Law of Contract

Should any one take a loan of cattle, yaks, sheep, &c., and they die in his charge, he must pay for them. Should they die one night after being returned, it is the owner's loss. If they die before midnight of the night they are returned the borrower has to pay.

Should a horse die from a wound whilst on loan, one-fourth to one-third its value will have to be paid.

Should any one, having made an agreement to take anything, refuse to take it, the articles being good, he must pay one-fourth of the value. If there be any mistake in an account, it can be rectified up to one year.

No. 16. For Uncivilised People

These laws apply only to such uncivilised people as Bhuteas, Lepchas, Mongolians, who know no law; therefore what is written below is not required in Tibet. The Mongolians also have their law, written by Raja Kesar, of which we know little.

Any Government messenger must be supplied with what he wants (such as horses, food, &c.), and if not provided he can take them. Also whilst halting he must be supplied with food and fire. But the messenger must not draw his sword or use his bow, or he will be liable to a fine, and he must only take what is necessary to the performance of the Government work.

MARRIAGE CUSTOMS AMONGST THE SIKHIMESE, TIBETANS, AND BHUTANESE

These customs have been gathered from actual observation, and are those now observed by the people.

If the eldest brother takes a wife she is common to all his brothers.

If the second brother takes a wife she is common to all the brothers younger than himself.

The eldest brother is not allowed to cohabit with the wives of the younger brothers.

Should there be children in the first case, the children are named after the eldest brother, whom they call father; in the second case, after the second brother, and so on.

Three brothers can marry three sisters, and all the wives be in common, but this is not very often met with. In such a case the children of the eldest girl belong to the eldest brother, of the second to the second, and of the third to the third, if they each bear children. Should one or more not bear children, then the children are apportioned by arrangement. Two men not related can have one wife in common, but this arrangement is unusual.

The marriage ceremony consists almost entirely in feasting, which takes place after the usual presents have been given to the girl's relations. These presents constitute the woman's price, and vary in accordance with the circumstances of both parties.

APPENDIX II

The only religious ceremony is performed by the village headman, who offers up a bowl of murwa to the gods, and, presenting a cup of the same murwa to the bride and bridegroom, blesses them, and hopes the union may be a fruitful one. Lamas take no part in the ceremony.

The marriage tie is very light, and can be dissolved at any time by either the man or the woman.

A man may marry his mother's brother's daughter, but he can marry none of his other first cousins till the second generation.

The law of succession seems to be generally, though not always as follows:

1. Son.
2. Grandson, through the male line.
3. Brother by same mother.
4. Father's brother's son
Father's sister's son
Mother's brother's son
Mother's sister's son
} by choice.
5. If a man leaves only distant relatives, they receive a portion, a portion also going to the lamas, and the remainder to Government.
6. If a man dies without relatives, a sufficient amount for funeral expenses goes to the lamas, and the remainder to Government.

APPENDIX III

A LIST OF SOME OF THE PRINCIPAL ANIMALS AND BIRDS TO BE FOUND IN THESE COUNTRIES, AND THEIR HABITAT

Elephants.—Along the lower hills and in the Duars, penetrating in the rainy season into the hills to an elevation of 11,000 feet.

Rhino.—In a few of the lower valleys of Bhutan, but not common.

Bison.—In the lower valleys and outer hills of Bhutan.

Mythun.—Do. do.

Tiger.—In all the outer hills and valleys, and occasionally in the lower valleys up to 9000 feet.

Common Leopard.—Throughout the hills up to an elevation of 8000 feet.

Clouded Leopard.—At elevations from 4000 feet to 6000 feet.

Snow Leopard.—Rare, and only met with at high elevations above 11,000 feet.

Black Leopard.—Rare, but met with in the dense jungles at elevations of 3000 feet to 4000 feet.

Lynx.—Rare; only at high elevations bordering on Tibet over 16,000 feet.

Wolf.—Do. do.

Jackal.—Has been imported from the plains of India, and is occasionally seen as high as 6000 feet.

Wild Dog.—Not very common, but is met with in packs between the plains and a height of 6000 feet. There is said to be a second species, but I have never met with it.

Shau (*Cervus affines*).—Inhabits a tract to the north-east of the Chumbi Valley.

Sambur.—In all the lower hills.

Cheetah.—Do. do.

Hog-deer.—Do. do.

APPENDIX III

Barking Deer.—Throughout the hills up to an elevation of 9000 feet.

Musk Deer.—In the higher valleys at an elevation of 11,000 feet.

Goral.—Throughout the hills at an elevation of 4000 feet to 8000 feet.

Serow.—Throughout the hills at elevations from 4000 feet to 9000 feet.

Thar.—Somewhat rare; at elevations from 6000 feet to 14,000 feet.

Takin (*Budorcas taxicolor Whitei*).—Very rare; only occasionally in Bhutan, at elevations from 12,000 feet upwards.

Tibetan Gazelle.—At elevations of from 17,000 feet to 19,000 feet in a few of the higher valleys opening into Tibet.

Nyen (*Ovis ammon*).—Only found on very high ground on the borders of Tibet, from 17,000 feet upwards.

Nao, or *Burhel* (*Ovis nahura*).—Throughout the hills at high elevations from 16,000 feet upwards.

Kyang.—Very rare; at high elevations on the borders of Tibet.

Bear.—Three species, one inhabiting high altitudes from 11,000 feet to 12,000 feet; the common black bear, found everywhere, from 6000 feet downwards; and a third species, also said to be common, inhabiting the lower valleys.

Monkeys.—Three species, one inhabiting the slopes near the plains, one at an elevation from 3000 feet to 6000 feet, and the langur, found from 7000 feet to 12,000 feet.

Cat-bear.—Not uncommon at elevations from 7000 feet to 12,000 feet.

Cats.—Many species, which inhabit the dense jungle all along the hills.

GAME-BIRDS

Jungle Fowl.—Throughout the hills, up to 4000 feet.

Kelij Pheasant.—Throughout the hills at elevations of 2000 feet to 4000 feet.

Tragopan, or *Argus Pheasant.*—Throughout the hills at elevations of 7000 feet to 9000 feet.

Blood Pheasant.—In the Sikhim hills and in Western Bhutan at 9000 feet to 13,000 feet.

Monal.—Throughout the hills at elevations of 9000 feet to 15,000 feet.

Wood Partridge.—There are two species, distinguished only by a white marking on the neck and a slight difference in size. Found throughout the hills in dense bamboo jungle at 5000 feet to 8000 feet.

Snow Partridge.—Throughout the hills above 15,000 feet.

Snow Cock.—Do. do.

Woodcock.—In the cold season in the middle valleys and in summer in the higher valleys, but not above 13,000 feet.

Solitary Snipe.—In wet, marshy ground above 11,000 feet.

Ram Chicoor.—Throughout the hills at elevations above 14,000 feet.

Tibetan Sand Grouse.—Along the Tibetan boundary above 17,000 feet.

Quail.—Found in cornfields in Bhutan at 9000 feet in May and June.

Partridge.—Only a few at high elevations.

Duck.—Cold-weather visitors. Only a very few breed on the higher lakes.

Geese.—Do. do.

Snipe.—Do. do.

Pigeons.—Imperial, snow, blue rock, and many species of wood pigeons are found throughout both countries.

APPENDIX IV

DESCRIPTIONS OF THE ART SPECIMENS ILLUSTRATED IN CHAPTER XXIII

Plate I

1. Pierced copper-gilt ornaments used with a rice puja (Bhutan).
2. Copper teapot, with silver mounts (Bhutan).
3. Brass purpa or demon dagger used at services in Northern Buddhist monasteries (Bhutan).

4 and 9. Wood, silver, and silver-gilt gyeling (trumpets) used in temples (Bhutan).

5. Dagger with open-work, pierced, and embossed silver and silver-gilt sheath, set with turquoise (Bhutan).
6. Embossed silver and silver-gilt pan-box, set with coral and turquoise (Bhutan).
7. Temple bell, cast in Bhutan.
8. Sword with silver and silver-gilt scabbard, and silver-mounted leather belt with silk tassels (Bhutan).
10. Wine-flask made from a mythun horn mounted in copper (Bhutan).
11. Brass dorji, or thunderbolt, used by lamas at services (Tibet).

Plate II

1, 3, 5, 13. Ginger-jars, plate, and bottle brought from Lhasa (China).

2 and 4. Brass cymbals (Tibet).

6. Steel helmet (Bhutan).

7 and 11. Copper embossed ladles used to pour oil on bodies during cremation (Tibet).

8. Small skull drum (Tibet).
9. Silver-gilt hat ornament, set with turquoise and carbuncle (Shigatse, Tibet).

10. Lacquer cymbal-box, with copper binding, and copper and iron fittings (China).
12 and 15. Old cloisonné bowls (China).
14. Carved wooden frame for a small Buddha (Tibet).

Plate III

1 and 7. Pair of iron water-bottles, inlaid with silver (Tibet).
2. Small brass teapot (Tibet).
3. Copper-gilt Urn of Life used for puja (Tibet).
4. Teapot (Sikhim).
5 and 15. Copper-gilt images of Buddha (Tibet).
6. Brass box for jade teacup (Tibet).
8. Hand-bell (Tibet).
9. Copper dorji, or thunderbolt (Tibet).
10 and 21. Bell-metal cymbals (Tibet).
11. Carved, gilt, and coloured book-back (Tibet).
12 and 22. Silver altar butter-lamps (Tibet).
13. Enamel box (China).
14, 16, 18, and 20. Part of a set of Tashi Tagye, in copper-gilt, used at puja (Tibet).
17. Temple bell (Tibet).
19. Brass spectacle-case (Tibet).
23. Jade teacup with silver cover and stand (Tibet).

Plate IV

1. Copper-gilt Urn of Life (Bhutan).
2. Long-stemed porcelain teacup in copper-gilt stand (Tibet).
4. Teapot in copper-gilt, with silver mounts set with small turquoise (Tibet).
10. Copper-gilt rice offering-box (Tibet).
(*Nos.* 2, 4, *and* 10 *belonged to the late Regent of Tibet, and were sold on his downfall.*)
3. Silver amulet-case (Bhutan).
5. Silver prayer-wheel (Sikhim).
6. Silver bowl used to receive grease off buttered tea (Tibet).
7. Glass bowl (Tibet).
8. Skull rice-bowl, with silver stand and cover (Sikhim).
9. Copper-gilt amulet-case (Tibet).
11. Silver amulet-case (Tibet).
12. Carved and painted wooden table (Sikhim).

INDEX

INDEX

INDEX

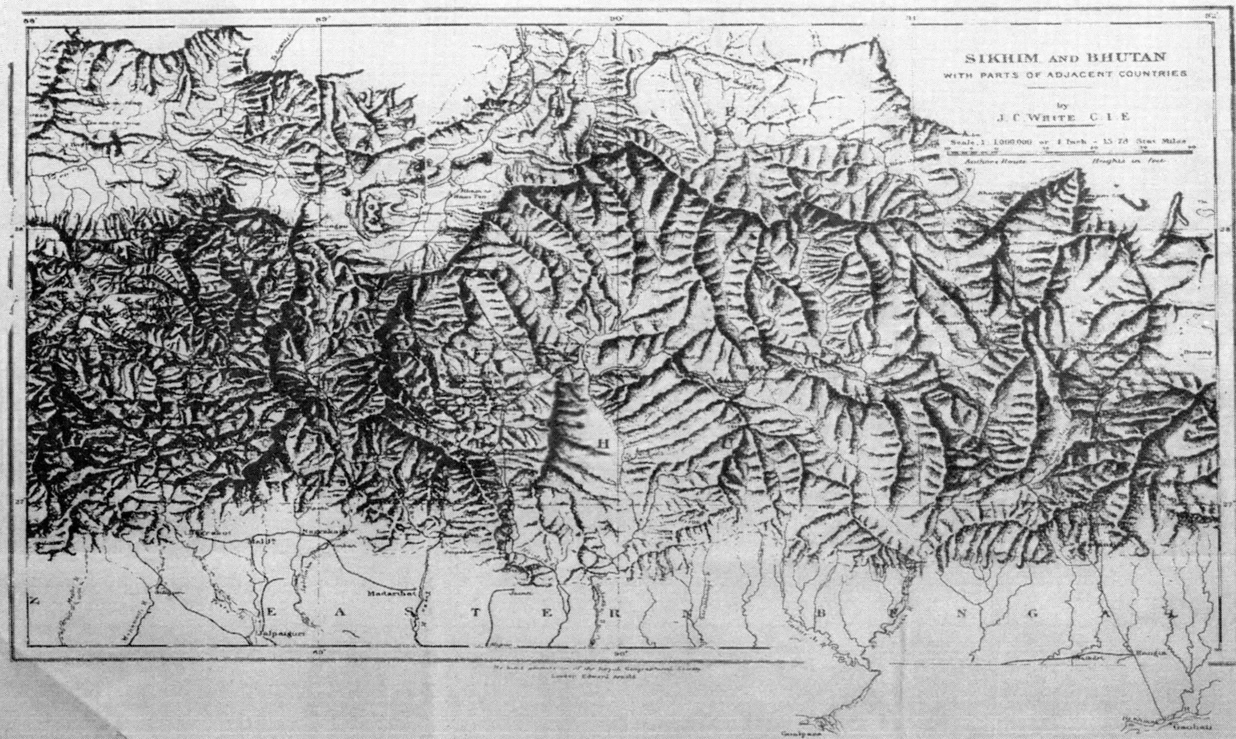
SIKHIM AND BHUTAN
WITH PARTS OF ADJACENT COUNTRIES
by
J. C. WHITE C.I.E.
E A S T E R N B E N G A L
Jalpaiguri
Madarihat